THE INDUSTRIAL REVOLUTION

THE
INDUSTRIAL
REVOLUTION

Edited by C. STEWART DOTY

University of Maine

THE DRYDEN PRESS
HINSDALE, ILLINOIS

Cover illustration: First industrial use of a railroad, near a coal mine, Newcastle, England. Color print by George Walker. (*The Bettmann Archive*)

CONTENTS

Introduction   1

THE PROCESS OF INDUSTRIALIZATION

ARNOLD TOYNBEE—The Classic Statement of the Industrial
Revolution   11

J. H. CLAPHAM—The Statement Challenged: The Industrial
Revolution Incomplete in 1851   15

JOHN U. NEF—Another Challenge: Two Industrial Revolutions   22

W. W. ROSTOW—The Industrial Revolution as Take-off   29

E. J. HOBSBAWM—The Take-off Supported   32

PHYLLIS DEANE—The Take-off Challenged   43

THE STANDARD OF LIVING: PROGRESS OR POVERTY?

A Contemporary Pessimist and Optimist

FRIEDRICH ENGELS—Deterioration of Living and Working
Conditions Under Industrialization   53

G. R. PORTER—Progress Shown by Population, Wage, and
Consumption Statistics   59

Pessimism and Optimism Reworked

J. L. and BARBARA HAMMOND—Nineteenth-century Capitalist
Attitudes at Fault   66

T. S. ASHTON—Economics Responsible for Living Conditions   75

A Debate on the Quantitative Approach

E. J. HOBSBAWM—Inadequacy of Quantitative Evidence in
Support of the Optimists' Case   84

R. M. HARTWELL—The Standard of Living Quantitatively
Higher   96

Reappraisal of Methods

A. J. TAYLOR—An Attempt at Quantitative Synthesis   107

E. P. THOMPSON—The Qualitative Method Continued   119

Suggested Additional Readings   131

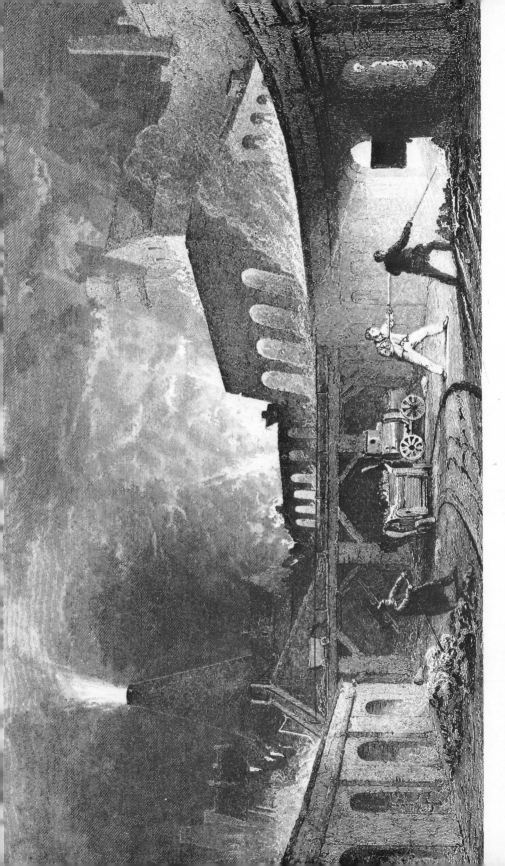

Lymington Iron Works on the Tyne River. (*New York Public Library*)

INTRODUCTION

Historians are fascinated with the word revolution. In addition to essentially political ones like the Puritan, French, 1848, and Russian revolutions, historians have conjured up all kinds of nonpolitical revolutions all the way from the Urban Revolution of ancient Egypt and Mesopotamia to the Commercial Revolution, the Scientific Revolution, the Agricultural Revolution, and the Intellectual Revolution, to mention only a few. According to popular writers it seems that some kind of revolution is always taking place, with the more recent additions being the Sexual Revolution, the Computer Revolution, and the Student Revolution.

Of all of these nonpolitical revolutions the one with the longest and widest currency is doubtless the Industrial Revolution. The term had some circulation among French writers by the 1820s, was in fairly wide use on the European continent when Friedrich Engels used it in his *Conditions of the Working Class in England* (1845), and passed permanently into the English language with the reception gained by Arnold Toynbee's *Lectures on the Industrial Revolution* (1884).[1] Today, even those who do not believe the changes came quickly enough to be called revolutionary apply the term Industrial Revolution to those changes of the late eighteenth and nineteenth centuries which transformed Great Britain and other nations from agricultural and commercial economies to industrial ones, brought a high degree of urbanization and population growth with all their problems and prospects, introduced wide adoption of machine power and the factory system with the enormous amounts of goods resulting from them, created a rapid rate of economic growth and capital accumulation, and greatly expanded the middle and working classes. It was logical for French writers to be the first to label these changes an industrial revolution. In their minds and in the minds of many moderns, the economic and social changes of the Industrial Revolution complemented the monumental political and social transformation wrought by their own French Revolution.

No matter how much historians may disagree in handling those changes, the discussion of the Industrial Revolution has revolved around two issues. First, there was the economic process of industrialization, taking into account what it was and why, when, and how it occurred. Secondly, there was the social effect, whether this industrialization raised or lowered the workers' standard of living. The selections in this book are representative views on each of these two issues. Moreover, the selec-

---

[1] G. N. Clark, *The Idea of the Industrial Revolution* (Glasgow, 1953).

tions on each issue are arranged chronologically to show how historical knowledge has unfolded, how new evidence has been discovered, and how each new group of historians has reinterpreted the Industrial Revolution in the light of the new evidence. The selections on the process of industrialization were written from the 1880s to the 1960s. Those on the standard of living, from the 1840s to the 1960s.

The process of industrialization raises a number of questions. If there was something that can be called an industrial revolution, what exactly were its characteristics? How did it begin? When did it begin and why then? When can it be called complete and why then? Where did it begin and why there, and why begin at all? Did it involve a general economic growth or growth only in some industries and, if so, why these? Was it limited to economic change, or did it involve political, social, and cultural change as well? Answers to these questions may not be found in any one of the selections in this book, but answers to all of them are necessary for an understanding of the nature of the Industrial Revolution.

The classic statement of the process of industrialization was formulated by Arnold Toynbee in a series of lectures given in 1880–1881. According to Toynbee the Industrial Revolution "at the end of the eighteenth and beginning of the nineteenth centuries" had as its "essence" the "substitution of competition for the medieval regulation."[2] This was made possible by a number of developments:

1. The rapid increase in population, generally with a decline of agricultural population
2. Greatly increased agricultural production by fewer farmers because of the end of the common-field system, selective breeding, crop rotation, and improved implements
3. The substitution of the factory system for the domestic system (cottage industry), especially in the cotton textile and iron industries, thanks to machines
4. The expansion of trade due to improved communications
5. The redistribution of wealth into the hands of capitalists and farmers at the expense of the workers.

Toynbee did not live long enough to amplify and qualify his suggestive lectures, but in 1906 a French follower of his, Paul Mantoux, did so in a classic work entitled *La révolution industrielle au XVIIIe siècle* (translated in 1928 as *The Industrial Revolution in the Eighteenth Century*). Through Mantoux and others the essentials of Toynbee's criteria became incorporated into the popular view of the Industrial Revolution, and as a result provided a starting point for any re-evaluation of the event.

Nor was such a re-evaluation long in coming. Toynbee had suggested that around 1750 there was a sharp break with an earlier economic pattern and that this break was followed by a rapid and general industrialization which was complete by around 1850. In the twentieth century, historians came to question both

---

[2]Arnold Toynbee, *The Industrial Revolution* (Boston: Beacon Press, 1958), pp. 1 and 58.

these tenets. J. H. Clapham, for example, points out that by 1850 the Industrial Revolution had witnessed anything but a general industrialization. Quite the contrary, it had been limited mainly to cotton textiles and iron. While these industries had been revolutionized through machinery and the factory system by 1850, industrialization had not reached other textile industries such as wool. Even in cotton textiles the application of machine power had not been as rapid as Toynbee had suggested. Just as Clapham criticizes Toynbee for ending the Industrial Revolution too early, John U. Nef faults him for starting it too late. Nef argues that the sixteenth and seventeenth centuries saw economic changes fully as remarkable as those of the late eighteenth and early nineteenth centuries in the introduction of new industries or new technology in old industries. He even casts doubt on Toynbee's notion of the Industrial Revolution as being historical discontinuity, a break with the past. Nef writes, "The rise of industrialization in Great Britain can be more properly regarded as a long process stretching back to the middle of the sixteenth century and coming down to the final triumph of the industrial state toward the end of the nineteenth, than as a sudden phenomenon associated with the late eighteenth and early nineteenth centuries."[3] In short, either there was no Industrial Revolution, in the sense of a rapid and general industrialization, or there were two.

By mid-twentieth century the Clapham and Nef qualifications of the Toynbean view had become so widely accepted and had stretched out the rise of capitalism over such a long period of time that it was even difficult to speak any longer of an industrial revolution. "The system of human relationships that is sometimes called capitalism had its origins long before 1760," wrote T. S. Ashton in 1948, "and attained its full development long after 1830: there is a danger of overlooking the essential fact of continuity. But the phrase 'Industrial Revolution' has been used by a long line of historians and has become so firmly embedded in common speech that it would be pedantic to offer a substitute."[4] The Industrial Revolution now seemed to be such a long process that it was hard to call it "revolutionary," and it was so difficult to date that textbook writers, for example, could not agree on whether to put the Industrial Revolution chapter ahead of or behind that of the French Revolution.

In the late 1950s, however, the Toynbean view of the Industrial Revolution as historical discontinuity was resurrected in a new form thanks to the increased concern of economic historians with theories of economic growth. The next selection is from *The Stages of Economic Growth: A Non-Communist Manifesto* (1960) by W. W. Rostow, óne of the more influential of the economic historians. As both economic theorist and economic historian, Rostow is not only concerned with understanding and explaining industrial revolutions of the past in Great Britain and other economically developed nations. He is equally interested in the lessons of

---

[3] John U. Nef, "Progress of Technology and the Growth of Large-scale Industry in Great Britain, 1540–1640," *Economic History Review*, V (October, 1934), p. 22.

[4] T. S. Ashton, *The Industrial Revolution* (London: Oxford University Press, 1948), p. 2.

history and in using the experience of the developed nations to formulate a theory of economic development capable of aiding today's economically underdeveloped nations reach industrialization. He argues that all of today's economically developed nations went through five stages of economic growth: those of a traditional society, the preconditions for take-off, the take-off, the drive to maturity, and the age of mass consumption. The last stage in which the society produces a wide range of abundant consumer goods, especially automobiles, does not concern us here, because it is a twentieth-century development. What does concern us is that Rostow sees the take-off period as a Toynbean Industrial Revolution but one that lasted only a generation rather than two or three. By his use of the graphic term take-off, Rostow means that the decisive stage is the one which gets the industrial economy airborne. Once airborne, it can more easily climb to higher altitudes. The climb, the drive to maturity, can provide an explanation for Clapham's objection to the Toynbean view. In the take-off the Industrial Revolution is limited to one or two sectors of the economy (in the case of Great Britain, cotton textiles and iron), but by triggering the economic potential the take-off extends the industrialization to other sectors or industries during the drive to maturity. At the same time the take-off is possible only after certain preconditions have broken down the landlord-dominated, feudal, pre-Newtonian traditional society of the middle ages. In Britain, those preconditions were established in the period Nef describes with its creation of a capitalistic class with broad horizons and some political power, banks and stock companies for mobilizing an increasing amount of capital, and a more effective state.

It should be easy to imagine the impact of Rostow's thought because of its ability seemingly to reconcile Toynbee, Clapham, and Nef. Almost every book on the Industrial Revolution since Rostow's somehow uses the term take-off. His theory even inspired an international conference at Konstanz, Germany, in 1962 to discuss the merits of his theory and its application to nations as varied as Great Britain, France, Germany, Russia, Japan, and the United States.[5] The last two selections in the first half of the book are representative reactions to the Rostow theory and indicate the present state of the debate on the Industrial Revolution. E. J. Hobsbawm basically accepts it. Phyllis Deane, who co-authored the Konstanz paper on Great Britain, objects to it. To understand the Industrial Revolution, then, and to formulate answers to the questions raised earlier about the process of industrialization, one must hold up Rostow and Hobsbawm to the criticism of Deane. In particular, when was the period of crucial change and why? Was it before 1750 as Nef suggests? Or was it between 1783 and 1802 as Rostow contends? Or the second quarter of the nineteenth century as Clapham holds? Were the decisive industries cotton and iron after all, or were they railroads and some other industry? Or is it more fruitful to follow Phyllis Deane's line of argument and look

---

[5]Both the scholarly papers and the sometimes heated discussion of them were subsequently published: W. W. Rostow (ed.), *The Economics of Take-Off into Sustained Growth* (London and New York, 1963).

for a "cluster of innovations," as Joseph A. Schumpeter did,[6] than to seek a trigger-ing industry or two in Rostow's fashion?

The remaining selections deal with the second principal issue in understand-ing the Industrial Revolution: the effect of industrialization on the standard of living of the workers. Born with the Industrial Revolution, this subject has been debated, sometimes hotly, by every generation since. The course of this century-old debate has been interesting for two reasons. For one thing, while everyone agrees that in the long run the living standard did improve, not everyone agrees that it improved throughout the Industrial Revolution's entire initial period of, say, 1790 to 1850. Some historians, dubbed "pessimists," have always insisted that most of this period saw a deterioration in the standard of living; others, the "optimists," have argued the contrary. The debate has also been interesting because optimists and pessimists have used different kinds of historical evidence most of the time, and over the years their use of this evidence has become more sophisticated. Optimists have found their case best supported by the *quantitative* evidence of wage, consump-tion, population, and mortality statistics, and by the twentieth century they were able to construct this data into cost-of-living and real-wage indices. The argument of the pessimists has been best served most of the time by the *qualitative* and "liter-ary" testimony of the Blue Books, the early nineteenth-century reports of numerous royal commissions and parliamentary committees investigating conditions in Brit-ish mines and factories, and the books, pamphlets, and articles by contemporary observers and witnesses. Increasingly, they have come to use this evidence with more care.

To point out how the increasingly sophisticated methodology and the persis-tence of the debate have yielded new evidence for our understanding of the stan-dard-of-living problem, the rest of the book pairs optimists and pessimists of three successive periods and concludes with one selection seeking to summarize and reconcile the current state of the debate within the quantitative school and another selection trying to update the qualitative arguments of the pessimists. Yet to get any satisfactory solution to the standard-of-living problem from these selections, we must keep one central question in mind: How do we determine what a "standard of living" is? Does it consist merely of material conditions such as wages, purchas-ing power, food and diet, housing, health and length of life, population growth, and clothing? Is it, in short, the quantitative measurement the optimists have tended o prefer? Or, as the pessimists have always contended, does it also embrace qualitative factors, perhaps incapable of being measured, such as home and family life, education, play and leisure, the conditions of work, the psychological adapta-tion from handwork to the time clock and machine discipline of the factory system, and the oppressiveness of child and woman labor?

The first pair of optimists and pessimists comes from the 1840s, the period of the Industrial Revolution itself, and even this early established the arguments and

---

[6]Joseph A. Schumpeter, *Business Cycles* (New York, 1939), Vol. I, pp. 87–102 and Chaps. 6 and 7.

methodology of the two sides. The selection by Friedrich Engels, the pessimist, describes one of the many slums he portrays in his book, the working man's clothes and the low quality and adulteration of his food, and the deleterious effect of this food, housing, and clothing on the health of the working class. Engels insists that these conditions were new to the Industrial Revolution. He also holds that the very establishment of the factory system injured health while its discipline destroyed the worker's freedom and independence. For evidence Engels, like later pessimists, relies chiefly on the qualitative testimony, such as is found in the Blue Books, newspaper exposés, and accounts of observers. In contrast to his view G. R. Porter, an optimist, argues that the lot of the worker improved throughout the early nineteenth century. Porter, with his quantitative data, showers the reader with figures and tables showing the rising population, the lowering mortality rate, the relation of wages to prices (an admittedly crude effort), and the rising consumption figures on items as varied as housing, wheat, sugar, tea, beer, meat, and tobacco. Certainly, his quantitative method is primitive by modern standards for he seldom does more than tabulate raw data. But it is enough to show that even at the beginning of the dispute optimists and pessimists, by using different methodology and sources, could arrive at different conclusions. Only once, in these selections, do Engels and Porter draw upon the same source, the population report of the Registrar General for 1841, but both are greatly indebted to the numerous public and private investigations of the time into the conditions of the laboring poor. Indeed, the very volume of such investigations shows that early nineteenth-century Britain was concerned with those conditions. Yet, at this stage of the debate the pessimists, be they socialists like Engels or conservatives like Benjamin Disraeli, Charles Dickens, and Thomas Carlyle, clearly led the field.

Although they would soon be challenged, the pessimists still had the upper hand as the twentieth century opened. Even Arnold Toynbee had written that by the end of the eighteenth century "we now approach a darker period—a period as disastrous and as terrible as any through which a nation has passed."[7] No one set forth this judgment more forcefully in the early twentieth century than J. L. and Barbara Hammond, authors of the next selection. In a series of books[8] on various kinds of workers and their movements as well as a biography of Lord Shaftesbury, the chief author of the hours-limiting Factory Acts of the 1830s, the Hammonds established the popular view on the standard of living just as Toynbee had on the process of industrialization. The tenor of their examination can be gauged by the titles of the two chapters that have been excerpted: "In the Shadow of the Slave Trade" points out the similarity between the nineteenth-century arguments in favor of child labor and those that upheld the trade in black slavery; "The Curse of Midas" insists that the drive for profits cast aside every obstacle in its way—beauty,

---

[7] Toynbee, *The Industrial Revolution*, p. 57.

[8] *The Village Labourer, 1760–1832* (1911), *The Town Labourer, 1760–1832* (1920), *The Skilled Labourer, 1760–1832* (1919), *The Age of the Chartists, 1832–1854* (1930), and *Lord Shaftesbury* (1936).

culture, leisure, and humanity. The method is qualitative; the argument impassioned.

It was not long before the widely held view of the pessimists, under the spell of the Hammonds, was seriously challenged. Even as the Hammonds wrote, the quantitative school constructed its data, most of which had been available to Porter, into an impressive array of statistical studies far more sophisticated than his. At the turn of the century A. L. Bowley and G. H. Wood put together a wage index, and later N. J. Silberling, E. W. Gilboy, and R. T. Tucker established cost-of-living indices. The coupling of the price and wage indices demonstrated to J. H. Clapham "The fact that, after the price fall of 1820–21, the purchasing power of wages in general—not, of course, everyone's wages—was definitely greater than it had been just before the revolutionary and Napoleonic Wars." For him these wage and cost-of-living indices made the pessimists' case a "legend."[9] "In 1831 the cost of living was 11 per cent higher than in 1790," wrote T. S. Ashton of these indices, "but over this span of time urban wages had increased, it appears, by no less than 43 per cent."[10] In 1929 even J. L. Hammond admitted, "Let us take it that so far as statistics can measure improvement, there was improvement." Yet, he added, "On what men enjoy and what they suffer through their imagination statistics do not throw a great deal of light. If you think that enjoyment and suffering unimportant, you can measure progress by the statistics of material prosperity: if you think them important, you give such statistics only a subordinate part of your estimate."[11]

In the next selection, T. S. Ashton introduces these wage and cost-of-living indices and attacks what even Hammond admitted was the last redoubt of the pessimists—the nonstatistical qualitative evidence. To both points Ashton applies the quantitative method to see what really happened to the economy in the early Industrial Revolution. Certainly there had been bad times, but such troubles were not due to the callousness of capitalists and politicians as the Hammonds had charged. Rather, they were due, for one thing, to the great demands placed on the economy by the Napoleonic Wars and postwar readjustment: wartime shortages caused prices to rise faster than the slower rising wages; government demands for money drove up interest rates for all investors and made money unstable; and wartime shortage of building materials and capital, coupled with skyrocketing demand for housing, created abominable housing conditions. These bad housing conditions were made even more unavoidable by the hidebound nature of the building trades, the high taxes on building materials and real estate, and the low return on decent working-class rental housing. Moreover, argues Ashton, the qualitative pessimists romanticized the eighteenth-century conditions of rural industry, uncritically applied Blue Book evidence for miserable conditions in underindustrialized

---

[9] J. H. Clapham, *An Economic History of Modern Britain* (London: Cambridge University Press, 1964), Vol. 1, p. vii.

[10] Ashton, *The Industrial Revolution,* pp. 108–109.

[11] J. L. Hammond, "The Industrial Revolution and Discontent," *The Economic History Review,* II (1930), 210–220.

manufacturing sectors to industrialized ones (indeed, the Blue Books themselves were evidence of a rising humanitarianism), and blamed abuses in housing on capitalism rather than on the unavoidable process of economic development. In short, capitalism was innocent, and industrialization improved both the quantity and quality of life.

By mid-twentieth century, thanks to their amassing of wage and price data and logical economic explanations for the pessimists' "quality of life" argument, the optimists had seemingly won the field at last. Indeed, so compelling had the quantitative approach become that the next pair of pessimists and optimists, E. J. Hobsbawm and R. M. Hartwell, both use it. Hobsbawm's purpose is not to prove that the standard of living declined during the Industrial Revolution, but rather to demonstrate that the quantitative evidence of the optimists does not prove their case. Hartwell, on the other hand, seeks to buttress the sketchy quantitative data with arguments based on recent theories of economic growth and new data. Both agree that in the long run growth in national income, savings, productivity, and capital formation outran population to make the standard of living higher in 1850 than it had been in 1800. The quantitative studies from Bowley-Wood on had accomplished at least that much. Hobsbawm and Hartwell also agree that the living standard rose throughout the eighteenth century. What they disagree on is whether or not this rise occurred for all classes of workers in all times during the period from 1800 to 1850.

In dealing with this broad question they disagree on specific points. First, they evaluate the wage indices differently. Hobsbawm insists that these tell us very little because they do not take into account the wages of unskilled workers or the wide unemployment during the periodic depressions. Since there are no wage indices for the mass of unskilled workers and since these doubtless suffered most in the periodic unemployment, Hobsbawm contends, the optimists' case is not proved. Hartwell, on the other hand, notes that per capita income (total income divided by the number of people) rose and that this rise would be shared by the workers since modern analyses of economic growth show an increasing per capita income accompanied by more equal income distribution, since fairly complete post-1860 data indicate that the wage share of national income stayed fairly constant, and since taxes became increasingly less regressive and social services more abundant after 1820. Secondly, each interprets mortality figures differently, Hobsbawm to show a worsening mortality rate after an initial improvement and Hartwell to see it improving throughout. Thirdly, they disagree on the use of the consumption indices. Hobsbawm argues that while the use of tea, sugar, and tobacco show no marked increase, they show no fall either. The use of meat and white bread, however, did drop considerably. While meat could be offset with the rise of fish consumption and bread with that of potatoes, the change itself most likely indicated a lowering standard of living. Hartwell, for his part, disputes Hobsbawm's evidence and insists that consumption of all these foods increased. As to potatoes and fish, their increased use meant a more varied and hence better diet and standard of living. One final problem that divides the two writers is the choice of dates. For Hobsbawm the early 1840s were the turning point, since conditions improved significantly after that time. If Hobsbawm's dating is correct, Hartwell's conclusions based in part on social reforms, tariff and tax reductions, and savings deposits are weakened, because those did not become really effective until the 1840s. The contrary would be true, of course, if we accept Hartwell's date of 1850 or that of the Great Exhibition of 1851.

With such disparate views as these, the student of history can but wonder where the quantitative approach to the standard of living question has left us. The next selection provides direction signs, if not a road map. Its author, A. J. Taylor, not only reviews the literature of the quantitative as well as qualitative schools; he also seeks to sum up and discover some common ground on the quantitative questions of wages, mortality, population growth, and consumption which were raised by Hobsbawm, Hartwell, Ashton, and even Porter. Phyllis Deane has erected sign posts similar to those of Taylor. After pointing out how sketchy and circumstantial the evidence is (Hobsbawm and Hartwell both admit this and Hobsbawm uses that fact to buttress his case), she suggests that the available evidence indicates that the standard of living tended to fall between 1780 and 1820, *probably* rose slightly or *possibly* fell slightly from 1820 to 1840, and rose significantly after that.[12]

The extended discussions by Ashton, Hobsbawm, Hartwell, and Taylor should not lead us to conclude that the qualitative approach has in any sense been superceded by the quantitative one. Had the latter been able to demonstrate with certainty that the material standard of living had improved significantly and regularly throughout the Industrial Revolution, the discontent of the poor over the quality of life could have been dismissed. It would have meant, in Hobsbawm's paraphrase of the optimists' argument, that the poor "merely wept all the way to their increasingly substantial Sunday dinners."[13] But when qualified optimists like Taylor and Deane can no longer say that, perhaps the quantitative school, in Hobsbawm's words again, "has risked diverting us from the real historical problem," from seeing that "the effects of the Industrial Revolution on the labouring poor are both economic (in the narrowly quantitative sense) and social," and that "the two cannot be isolated from each other."[14] In short, the quantitative school, in its concern for material conditions, tended to ignore the social ones and the discontent that sprang from them, but social analysis was always the core of the qualitative school. For this reason, the selection by E. P. Thompson is a recent example of the school that includes Engels and the Hammonds.

Indeed, the selection by Thompson, following as it does those of quantitative

---

[12]Phyllis Deane, *The First Industrial Revolution* (London: Cambridge University Press, 1965), pp. 237–253 and especially pp. 250–251.
[13]E. J. Hobsbawm, *Labouring Men* (New York: Basic Books, 1964), p. 122.
[14]*Ibid.*

historians, brings us back to the central question of this half of the book: What really is a standard of living and how can we decide whether it rose or fell during the Industrial Revolution? As Thompson argues, is the qualitative "way of life," or what might be called a "standard of happiness," as important or more important than the quantitative "standard of life"? Put this way, what kind of evidence for an improving or deteriorating standard of living is likely to be less biased and more compelling: wage rates, mortality figures, and the amounts of food and clothing sold, or eyewitness accounts of housing, living, and working conditions? In this regard quantitative evidence is quite impressive because it is measurable and statistics are "neutral," *but* have the figures of any of these authors been complete enough to demand acceptance of their conclusions, or are they too sketchy to warrant any judgment? Even complete statistical evidence has many pitfalls, not the least being one warned of in an old adage: "Figures don't lie but liars figure." Incomplete statistical data is even more vulnerable to charges of inaccuracy. But is the qualitative evidence of Engels, the Hammonds, and Thompson any better? The eyesight or memory of the witness might have been defective, his examples too selective or unrepresentative to round out the picture or too biased in favor of either reform or the *status quo,* and besides such personal accounts might be so impressionistic as to render measurement impossible. It may be that the regional and class studies which are now underway will reveal a fuller picture. In the meantime, such quantitative and qualitative data are all that the historian has to go on, but while the evidence may have limitations, it is still sufficient to evaluate what there is and make tentative judgments.

To do so, perhaps it would be well to consider one further set of questions in these selections. Writers like Rostow are interested in the lessons of history for the industrialization of today's underdeveloped nations. Does the history of the Industrial Revolution's living standard have any lessons also for those underdeveloped nations? Everyone recognizes that whether or not the standard of living improved, it was still bad. Why was this so? Were low wages, child labor, and poor unsanitary housing inevitable and unavoidable in the initial stages of the Industrial Revolution, because of such varied factors as the inflation during the Napoleonic Wars, periodic depressions, technological unemployment, the need to plow back profits into economic growth rather than sharing them with the workers, and the demand for housing outrunning the ability to provide decent housing, water, and sewerage? Or were these conditions due to the failure of the collective human will, reason, and humanity: to the callousness of the affluent businessmen and politicians, the very nature of industrializing under laissez-faire capitalism, or the apathy, prodigality, and inadaptability of the workers themselves? In short, what explains the condition of the laboring poor in the years 1790 to 1850?

In the reprinted selections, footnotes appearing in the original sources have in general been omitted unless they contribute to the argument or better understanding of the selection.

ARNOLD TOYNBEE (1852–1883) taught economics and economic history at Bailliol College, Oxford University, from his graduation in 1878 until his death a little over four years later at the age of thirty-one. His powerful and popular *Lectures on the Industrial Revolution* (1884) is his only published work, but it had an enormous impact in establishing the classic and long-accepted statement on the Industrial Revolution. The twentieth-century historian of the same name is his nephew.*

Arnold Toynbee

The Classic Statement of the Industrial Revolution

The essence of the Industrial Revolution is the substitution of competition for the mediaeval regulations which had previously controlled the production and distribution of wealth. . . .

Coming to the facts of the Industrial Revolution, the first thing that strikes us is the far greater rapidity which marks the growth of population. Before 1751 the largest decennial increase, so far as we can calculate from our imperfect materials, was 3 per cent. For each of the next three decennial periods the increase was 6 per cent; then between 1781 and 1791 it was 9 per cent; between 1791 and 1801, 11 per cent; between 1801 and 1811, 14 per cent; between 1811 and 1821, 18 per cent. This is the highest figure ever reached in England, for since 1815 a vast emigration has been always tending to moderate it; between 1815 and 1880 over eight millions (including Irish) have left our shores. But for this our normal rate of increase would be 16 or 18 instead of 12 per cent in every decade.

Next we notice the relative and positive decline in the agricultural population. In 1811 it constituted 35 per cent of the whole population of Great Britain; in 1821, 33 per cent; in 1831, 28 per cent. And at the same time its actual numbers have decreased. In 1831 there were 1,243,057 adult males employed in agriculture in Great Britain; in 1841 there were 1,207,989. In 1851 the whole number of persons engaged in agriculture in England was 2,084,153; in 1861 it was 2,010,454, and in 1871 it was 1,657,138.

*From Lecture VIII of Arnold Toynbee, *Lectures on the Industrial Revolution* (Rivington, 1884). Footnotes omitted.

Contemporaneously with this change, the centre of density of population has shifted from the Midlands to the North; there are at the present day 458 persons to the square mile in the counties north of the Trent, as against 312 south of the Trent. And we have lastly to remark the change in the relative population of England and Ireland. Of the total population of the three kingdoms, Ireland had in 1821 32 per cent, in 1881 only 14.6 per cent.

An agrarian revolution plays as large part in the great industrial change of the end of the eighteenth century as does the revolution in manufacturing industries, to which attention is more usually directed. Our next inquiry must therefore be: What were the agricultural changes which led to this noticeable decrease in the rural population? The three most effective causes were: the destruction of the common-field system of cultivation; the enclosure, on a large scale, of common and waste lands; and the consolidation of small farms into large. We have already seen that while between 1710 and 1760 some 300,000 acres were enclosed, between 1760 and 1843 nearly 7,000,000 underwent the same process. Closely connected with the enclosure system was the substitution of large for small farms. In the first half of the century Laurence, though approving of consolidation from an economic point of view, had thought that the odium attaching to an evicting landlord would operate as a strong check upon it. But these scruples had now disappeared. Eden in 1795 notices how constantly the change was effected, often accompanied by the conversion of arable to pasture; and relates how in a certain Dorsetshire village he found two farms where twenty years ago there had been thirty. The process went on uninterruptedly into the present century. Cobbett, writing in 1826, says: "In the parish of Burghclere one single farmer holds, under Lord Carnarvon, as one farm, the lands that those now living remember to have formed fourteen farms, bringing up in a respectable way fourteen families." The consolidation of farms reduced the number of farmers, while the enclosures drove the labourers off the land, as it became impossible for them to exist without their rights of pasturage for sheep and geese on common lands.

Severely, however, as these changes bore upon the rural population, they wrought, without doubt, distinct improvement from an agricultural point of view. They meant the substitution of scientific for unscientific culture. "It has been found," says Laurence, "by long experience, that common or open fields are great hindrances to the public good, and to the honest improvement which every one might make of his own." Enclosures brought an extension of arable cultivation and the tillage of inferior soils; and in small farms of 40 to 100 acres, where the land was exhausted by repeated corn crops, the farm buildings of clay and mud walls and three-fourths of the estate often saturated with water, consolidation into farms of 100 to 500 acres meant rotation of crops, leases of nineteen years, and good farm buildings. The period was one of great agricultural advance; the breed of cattle was improved, rotation of crops was generally introduced, the steam-plough was invented, agricultural societies were instituted. In one respect alone the change was injurious. In consequence of the high prices of corn which prevailed during the French war, some of the finest permanent pastures were broken up. Still, in spite of this, it was said in 1813 that during the previous ten years agricultural produce had increased by one-fourth, and this was an increase upon a great increase in the preceding generation.

Passing to manufactures, we find here the all-prominent fact to be the substitution of the factory for the domestic system, the consequence of the mechanical discoveries of the time. Four great inventions altered the character of the cotton manufacture; the spinning-jenny, patented by Hargreaves in 1770; the waterframe, invented by Arkwright the year before; Crompton's mule introduced in 1779, and the self-acting mule, first invented by Kelly in 1792, but not brought into use till Roberts improved it in 1825. None of these by themselves would have revolutionised the industry. But in 1769—the year in which Napoleon and Wellington were born—James Watt took out his patent for the steam-engine. Sixteen years later it was applied to the cotton manufacture. In 1785 Boulton and Watt made an engine for a cotton-mill at Papplewick in Notts, and in the same year Arkwright's patent expired. These two facts taken together mark the introduction of the factory system. But the most famous invention of all, and the most fatal to domestic industry, the power-loom, though also patented by Cartwright in 1785, did not come into use for several years, and till the power-loom was introduced the workman was hardly injured. At first, in fact, machinery raised the wages of spinners and weavers owing to the great prosperity it brought to the trade. In fifteen years the cotton trade trebled itself; from 1788 to 1803 has been called its "golden age"; for, before the power-loom but after the introduction of the mule and other mechanical improvements by which for the first time yarn sufficiently fine for muslin and a variety of other fabrics was spun, the demand became such that "old barns, cart-houses, out-buildings of all descriptions were repaired, windows broke through the old blank walls, and all fitted up for loom-shops; new weavers' cottages with loom-shops arose in every direction, every family bringing home weekly from 40 to 120 shil-

lings per week." At a later date, the condition of the workman was very different. Meanwhile, the iron industry had been equally revolutionised by the invention of smelting by pit-coal brought into use between 1740 and 1750, and by the application in 1788 of the steam-engine to blast furnaces. In the eight years which followed this later date, the amount of iron manufactured nearly doubled itself.

A further growth of the factory system took place independent of machinery, and owed its origin to the expansion of trade, an expansion which was itself due to the great advance made at this time in the means of communication. The canal system was being rapidly developed throughout the country. In 1777 the Grand Trunk canal, 96 miles in length, connecting the Trent and Mersey, was finished; Hull and Liverpool were connected by one canal while another connected them both with Bristol; and in 1792, the Grand Junction canal, 90 miles in length, made a water-way from London through Oxford to the chief midland towns. Some years afterwards, the roads were greatly improved under Telford and Macadam; between 1818 and 1829 more than a thousand additional miles of turnpike road were constructed; and the next year, 1830, saw the opening of the first railroad. These improved means of communication caused an extraordinary increase in commerce, and to secure a sufficient supply of goods it became the interest of the merchants to collect weavers around them in great numbers, to get looms together in a workshop, and to give out the warp themselves to the work-people. To these latter this system meant a change from independence to dependence; at the beginning of the century the report of a committee asserts that the essential difference between the domestic and the factory system is, that in the latter the work is done "by persons who have no

property in the goods they manufacture."
Another direct consequence of this expansion of trade was the regular recurrence of
periods of over-production and of depression, a phenomenon quite unknown under
the old system, and due to this new form of
production on a large scale for a distant
market.

These altered conditions in the production of wealth necessarily involved an
equal revolution in its distribution. In agriculture the prominent fact is an enormous
rise in rents. Up to 1795, though they had
risen in some places, in others they had
been stationary since the Revolution. But
between 1790 and 1833, according to Porter, they at least doubled. In Scotland, the
rental of land, which in 1795 had
amounted to £2,000,000, had risen in 1815
to £5,278,685. A farm in Essex, which before 1793 had been rented at 10s. an acre,
was let in 1812 at 50s., though, six years
after, this had fallen again to 35s. In Berks
and Wilts, farms which in 1790 were let at
14s., were let in 1810 at 70s., and 1820 at
50s. Much of this rise, doubtless, was due
to money invested in improvements—the
first Lord Leicester is said to have expend-
ed £400,000 on his property—but it
was far more largely the effect of the enclosure system, of the consolidation of farms,
and of the high price of corn during the
French war. Whatever may have been its
causes, however, it represented a great
social revolution, a change in the balance
of political power and in the relative position of classes. The farmers [i.e. tenant
farmers] shared in the prosperity of the
landlords; for many of them held their
farms under beneficial leases, and made
large profits by them. In consequence,
their character completely changed; they
ceased to work and live with their labourers, and became a distinct class. The high
prices of the war time thoroughly demora-
lised them, for their wealth then increased
so fast, that they were at a loss what to do

with it. Cobbett has described the change
in their habits, the new food and furniture,
the luxury and drinking, which were the
consequences of more money coming into
their hands than they knew how to spend.
Meanwhile, the effect of all these agrarian
changes upon the condition of the labourer
was an exactly opposite and most disastrous one. He felt all the burden of high
prices, while his wages were steadily falling, and he had lost his common-rights. It
is from this period, viz., the beginning of
the present century, that the alienation
between farmer and labourer may be
dated.

Exactly analogous phenomena appeared
in the manufacturing world. The new class
of great capitalist employers made enormous fortunes, they took little or no part
personally in the work of their factories,
their hundreds of workmen were individ-
ually unknown to them; and as a consequence, the old relations between masters
and men disappeared, and a "cash nexus"
was substituted for the human tie. The
workmen on their side resorted to combination, and Trades-Unions began a fight
which looked as if it were between mortal
enemies rather than joint producers.

The misery which came upon large sections of the working people at this epoch
was often, though not always, due to a fall
in wages, for, as I said above, in some industries they rose. But they suffered likewise from the conditions of labour under
the factory system, from the rise of prices,
especially from the high price of bread before the repeal of the corn-laws, and from
those sudden fluctuations of trade, which,
ever since production has been on a large
scale, have exposed them to recurrent periods of bitter distress. The effects of the Industrial Revolution prove that free competition may produce wealth without producing well-being. We all know the horrors that ensued in England before it was
restrained by legislation and combination.

As much as any man J. H. CLAPHAM (1873–1946) founded the modern writing of economic history. During practically all of his long teaching career he was associated with Cambridge University, where he was professor of economic history and vice-provost of King's College. In addition to a biography of Abbé Siéyès of the French Revolution (1912), he wrote widely on the economic history of Britain, France, and Germany. The following selection from his greatest book, *An Economic History of Modern Britain,* first published in 1926 and reprinted as recently as 1964, carefully traces the development of the textile and to lesser extent iron industries, the two industries Toynbee called the most crucial to the making of the Industrial Revolution. Clapham's research was so careful and exhaustive that he could but conclude that even as late as 1851 the cotton industry was not completely transformed and the woolen industry hardly at all. With this conclusion, he became the first major critic of Toynbee's interpretation.*

J. H. Clapham

The Statement Challenged: The Industrial Revolution Incomplete in 1851

Because no single British industry had passed through a complete technical revolution before 1830, the country abounded in ancient types of industrial organisation and in transitional types of every variety. Even in cotton spinning the early wooden machinery with metal fittings was in common use; the "self-acting" mule, built of metal, was but newly invented and only used in the more progressive mills. There were still plenty of wooden spinning-jennies, turned by hand, in the Lancashire mills in 1824, though the drawing process, preparatory to spinning, was always done by power. But nine years later "those that are now jenny-spinners are getting I think, into the decline of life," so quickly was the industry moving. Weaving by the new method was just entering on the stage of rapid development, after twenty years of experiment and hostility. The first Manchester steam-loom factory had been set up in 1806. Guest's estimate for 1818 was that fourteen such factories existed in Manchester, Salford, Middleton, Hyde, Stayley Bridge and elsewhere: he thought they

*From J. H. Clapham, *An Economic History of Modern Britain* (London: Cambridge University Press, 1930), second edition, vol. 1, pp. 143–145, 147–150, 155–156, 184–189; vol. 2, pp. 26–29. Footnotes omitted.

contained about 2000 looms. Writing in 1823 he reckoned that "at present not less than 10,000" power looms were at work in Great Britain. They made chiefly common print cloth and shirtings, but were rapidly conquering new lines of work. He supposed that there were 360,000 cotton weavers in the country, but probably his guess was high. An estimate made in 1830 put the figures for England and Scotland at 55,000–60,000 power looms and 240,000 hand looms. Baines, writing in 1835, did not anticipate the rapid disappearance of the older instrument, and his anticipation proved right.

The wool industries, because of their antiquity, their long regulation by the state—which cotton had entirely escaped—their wide distribution, and the extreme diversity of their products, had as yet been very incompletely transformed. Even the flying-shuttle was not in "very general use" in the West Riding until round about 1800. Carpet weavers still threw the shuttle across the loom by hand in the old ancient way, down to 1840 and later. The worsted, that is to say, the combed wool, yarn was now almost entirely mill spun on the frame, though even the distaff was not quite extinct in England in 1820; but the essential preliminary process of combing was a handicraft in spite of various experiments in machine combing. There was an analogous gap in the process of woollen spinning. Here the preliminary business of carding had been among the first to be taken over by power in the chief manufacturing areas, carding "engines"—cylinders set with wire teeth and revolving against one another to open out the wool—being often installed in the old water-driven fulling mills. But, in between carding and spinning there came in 1835, when Ure published his *Philosophy of Manufacture*, what he called a "handicraft operation," that of "slubbing" or preparing the rough rope of

wool, which was to be spun on the mule, on a wooden, hand-worked, machine called a "billy." "The slubbers," Ure writes, "though inmates of factories, are not, properly speaking, factory workers, being independent of the moving power." He noted that a patent had just been announced in December 1834, by which a second carding engine could prepare and deliver, by the process now known as condensing, the loose rope for the mule. The general adoption of this critical invention only took place in the second half of the century.

In a backward district such as Gloucestershire, even the mule only began to come into use about 1828, the hand-worked "billy" leading to the spinning "jenny," also worked by hand; though carding and some other processes were done by power. . . .

Of the weaving of wool and other textiles, it need only be said here that power was first tried experimentally, with the usual result—a riot, for the relatively light fabrics of the worsted industry in the early twenties, and that power weaving remained experimental down to 1830. For the heavier woollen broadcloths, pilot-cloths, uniform-cloths, blankets and the like, the power-loom had not yet been tried. Nor had it, as may be supposed, in carpet-weaving, and only tentatively in the roughest linen-weaving and for some kinds of silks. A Committee reporting in 1830 discussed, as a speculative question, what might happen "should it ever be found practicable to make use of it extensively in the fabric of woollens or silks." Next year Lardner expressed himself as "very doubtful whether" its use was "susceptible of much extension in any save the commonest branches of the silk manufacture.". . .

Machinery had already gripped a number of the final textile processes. The grip was not always a new thing. For centuries, in the "fulling stocks," the big water-driven wooden hammers had thudded down on the wet cloth, beating and thickening it; though in eighteenth-century London the motive power was a horse. Shearing the nap of the cloth mechanically instead of with monstrous scissors, had prevailed against the bitter opposition of the shearmen, and was in general use. So was the printing of calico by rollers, an invention comparatively recent but quickly adopted because the rollers were easily driven even by ordinary "milling" machinery. Metal rolling by water power was an old story and the mere mechanism was similar. It was easy also to use power, instead of the "horses or men," which no doubt had sufficed John Gilpin's good friend, to drive the heavy "calendars or mangles" used to glaze cloth, silk, linen and calico. Pressing and packing by hydraulic power followed rather rapidly on Bramah's invention of the hydraulic press in 1795; for they had penetrated to Dundee by the twenties. The revolution in dyeing, by chemistry not by the machine, was as yet far in the future. . . .

The primary metallurgical industries had nearly completed the first of their revolutions by 1825–30; although Neilson's application of a hot-air blast to the furnaces, which trebled the ratio between iron produced and fuel consumed in Scotland, came only in 1828–9. So recently as 1788 there had been still twenty-six of the old charcoal furnaces in Great Britain, producing about a fifth of the British pig iron. The total output was 68,000 tons. Then came steam for the blast, followed by a long-sustained munitions demand after 1793. This was of the utmost importance for "during the eighteenth century iron foundery became almost identified with the casting of cannon," as Dionysius Lardner wrote in 1831. By 1806, 162 coke and 11 charcoal furnaces in blast were turning out nearly 260,000 tons—the proportion of charcoal iron being now almost negligible—and new uses were being found for cast iron daily. By 1830, between 250 and 300 furnaces in blast had an output of from 650,000 to 700,000 tons, more than two-fifths of which came from South Wales and about a third from Staffordshire. "Happily," said Lardner, "the business of cannon casting on the large scale appears to be at an end"; but by this time the new civil uses of iron, especially for gas and water mains, pillars, railings, cables and bridging material, kept up the stimulus. . . .

Meanwhile, methods of producing wrought iron quickly and economically had been perfected and widely adopted. The puddling furnace, in which the pig was melted and stirred to get rid of its impurities, and the application of grooved rollers to draw the iron rods were patented by Henry Cort of Gosport in 1783. Puddling and rolling, while the puddled iron was yet soft, were to replace the slow and laborious refining of pig iron under the hammer, and to provide abundance of tough metal for rails, plates, chains and the like, without which the new metallic age could not have entered in. Cort's process, itself not entirely original, was no great success until the Homfrays of Penydaren improved it by adopting, among other things, a coke refining furnace which preceded the puddling furnace proper, in which originally raw coal was used. For a time the process was so much confined to Wales that it was commonly known as "the Welsh method." It was well established in Staffordshire and other English iron districts by the twenties; but the first puddlers were only brought into Scotland about 1830. When Lardner wrote, both furnaces were coke-fired: in the second the lumps, now nearly free of carbon, were heated for half an hour, then puddled; and as they "came into nature," that is, began to show the mysterious ropy, almost muscular, structure of the wrought iron, they were taken out, hammered and rolled; again heated; and finished under "a ponderous hammer moved by water power." Water-power was no longer indispensable, for steam had been applied to the hammers since 1782, but it was still widely used. . . .

The steam-engine itself, the prime mover, was still small and, outside a limited group of leading industries, comparatively little used: the group includes mining, where the use of steam for winding as well as for pumping became general from about 1790–1800; blast furnace work; cotton and, to a less extent, the other textiles; lastly, after 1820, coastal and river navigation. There are no comprehensive statistics for the country; but those which fortunately exist for Glasgow, at once a representative port and a representative manufacturing town of the newest type, are complete. In 1831, Glasgow and its suburbs contained upwards of 200,000 people and 328 steam-engines. Of these more than sixty were on steamboats. The largest steamboat was of 387 tons and it had two engines, each of 110 horse-power. The remaining engines were nearly all in the hundred and seven power-driven cotton mills, many of which contained several. The average engine, land or marine, was of 25.6 horse-power, and the total horse-power of the city and the Clyde would have driven one modern cruiser. . . .

When factory legislation began, cotton-spinners constantly protested against the singling out of their industry for control and the censure which control implies. Their arguments were often sound; but the action of the reformers and of parliament is easily comprehensible. Long hours and overworked children were certainly not confined to cotton-spinning; but there was

a wholesaleness, a monstrosity, about the great cotton mills which marked them down for public notice; although the less observant and less sensitive public of the eighteenth century had paid little attention to the perhaps greater evils of silk-throwing mills, some few of which were almost equally monstrous. Small concerns there were of course in quantity, in the early days of cotton-spinning machinery, and in them some of the worst abuses. Dan Kenworthy told a committee in 1832 how when he was a lad they constantly worked "day and night the back end of the week and all Sunday." Who? said the committee. "Only my sister and her husband and me; sometimes another boy." "Do you mean . . . these were all the workpeople employed. Yes; belonging to that business." But the size of the average steam spinning mill in the chief manufacturing centres, even in 1815–16, was something unprecedented in British industry. Forty-one Glasgow mills averaged 244 workpeople each. Three mills in the neighbouring country, all owned by one firm—Jas. Finlay and Co.—averaged over 500; and, at New Lanark, Dale and Owen employed over 1600. In England, the Strutts, at Belper and Millford, had 1494 workpeople. A list of forty-three important mills, in and about Manchester, gave an average employment figure of exactly 300: two firms out of the forty-three, McConnel and Kennedy, and George and Adam Murray, each employed more than 1000. In the year of the Reform Bill, a similar list of about the same number of Manchester mills gives a figure of nearly 401.

When the spinner also controlled the organisation of weaving, an arrangement rare in 1816 but become common before 1830, the aggregate figures of mill workers and outworking weavers were, in extreme cases, gigantic. Monteith, Bogle and Co., of Glasgow, in 1816, had 4000 workers on their books—spinners, some power-loom weavers, 300 dyers in two distinct dye-works, and an army of outworking muslin weavers. At the same date Horrocks, Miller and Co., of Preston, employed 700 spinners, in four separate mills, and a whole country-side of hand-loom weavers, nearly 7000 people all told.

These all are the great concerns. Average figures would be immensely reduced were it possible to include the mills of the type in which Dan Kenworthy worked down to 1814. But when, in the course of the next twenty years, the smallest type had been almost squeezed out and the combination of spinning and power-loom weaving had become rather more common, the average cotton mill visited by the newly appointed inspectors, in the early thirties, employed on the premises certainly under 200, but probably upwards of 150, people. . . .

So late as 1850 it was not claimed, even by an admiring statistician, that the average British coal mine employed more than about eighty "men, women and boys under ground and above." Twenty years earlier, in view of the great number of pits which were mere delvings on the outcrop—especially in Yorkshire—the figure must have been very much smaller; although on Tyneside and along the Wear pits were great and deep, with large average outputs and large working staffs. In 1800 the old Wallsend colliery had been reckoned capable of turning out over 160,000 tons a year. In 1830, forty-one working collieries on Tyneside had an output somewhere between 2,250,000 and 3,000,000 tons a year and a working force, above and below ground, of about 12,000—say 300 workers, of whom 200 were underground, turning out 60,000 to 70,000 tons at the average colliery. The Wear figures were even higher. But, for coal mining as a whole, such figures were exceptional. There was, however, certainly one most ancient industry of the first rank and possibly a second, whose average figures were comparable with those of the parvenu cotton. The first is tin and copper mining, which was at the height of its strength and output in the thirty years from 1826 to 1856, together with certain sections of the copper and brass industries that were based on it. . . .

The second industry whose scale of operations was possibly comparable with cotton is iron-working. There had been iron masters with great businesses long before the first cotton mill was built. Just when the textile inventions were being made, some of these businesses were already gigantic. Antony Bacon, iron merchant from Whitehaven, who began the creation of Merthyr "Tudful" in 1765, eventually became an M.P. and "considering himself as moving in a superior orbit . . . transferred, in the year 1783 . . . his lease and ironworks at Cyfarthfa to . . . Rd. Crawshay Esq., reserving to himself and assigns a clear annuity of £10,000." . . .

Bacon's ordnance contract, which had served him well in the Seven Years' War, had already been transferred to Carron—the works which Roebuck developed and in which James Watt was for a time interested. By 1814, having made "carronades" during many years · of war and taken advantage of the power which Watt had harnessed, the Carron works were claimed, by a Scotsman, as "the most, extensive manufactory in Europe": they employed 2000 men. The average Scottish iron-foundry, however, at that date employed only about twenty.

In the same group as Carron were the greater English and Welsh iron works of the years after Waterloo. Crawshay also has been credited with a working staff of more than 2000 men during the wars; and

Cyfarthfa remained active. There were said to be ten iron works in the Black Country in 1812, each of which had cost over £50,000 at the start. A traveller credits the Low Moor and Bowling company, near Bradford, with 1500 men, in the twenties, including the colliers. In 1824 Samuel Walker and William Yates employed 700 men in their works at Gospel Oak, Staffordshire, and perhaps 1300 "colliers and ironstone getters." But they only had use for seven steam-engines of 350 horsepower all told. . . .

No figures are available for an exact comparison of the average firm in the primary iron industries with the average cotton firm or Cornish mine. If there were only a few small iron works about Merthyr, there were many elsewhere in South Wales, Monmouthshire, and the Black Country—the districts which together contained more than three-quarters of the British blast furnaces in 1830. The combination of smelting with puddling and the subsequent processes was not by any means universal. Yet it seems probable that the average ironmaster, the primary producer, would rank, as capitalist and entrepreneur, on equal terms with the cotton spinner; though, as the Scottish figures of 1814 show, there were very many small foundries all over the country for utilising the now abundant and fashionable cast iron. . . .

Nothing is more remarkable than the complete localisation of some textile industries and the attainment by others of a localisation which, although not complete, was not to be altered appreciably during the next half-century. Under pressure of bad times in the forties, cotton had fallen back on South Lancashire and the adjacent parts of Cheshire and the West Riding, leaving a strong detached force in Clydesdale and various weak ones in other districts. From nearly a dozen English and

Scottish counties came complaints of local falls in population resulting from the closing down of cotton mills. The area with the better competitive facilities had come best through a spell of bad trade. Of approximately 527,000 cotton workers in the country, some 312,000 were in Lancashire, 55,000 in Cheshire and the West Riding, and 58,000 in Lanarkshire.

The most complete concentration was that of the worsted industry into the West Riding. Its oldest home, Norwich, had been losing ground ever since the eighteenth century, but was still a fairly active manufacturing centre in 1831, though it had adopted little modern machinery, if any. By 1841 the trade was nearly dead: during that decade the population of Norwich had stood still. About 1840 a belated attempt to recover the old industry was made by the establishment of spinning mills. Norwich had been buying yarn from Yorkshire and she wished to end this dependence. It was much too late; for in the next few years Yorkshire perfected combing machinery and went ahead again. In 1850 the factory inspectors reported nearly 865,000 worsted spindles and 32,617 power-looms for worsted in England: there were hardly any in Scotland or Wales. Of the spindles 746,000, and of the looms 30,850, were in Yorkshire. Norfolk had 19,216 spindles and 428 looms. The thing was done, a clean decisive defeat. Worsted had become the Yorkshire industry which it would remain.

The woollen manufacture had almost reached the pitch of concentration which it showed in the twentieth century. It was, and is, less concentrated than cotton and much less concentrated than worsted. Of 138,000 people who described themselves as engaged in it in 1851 only 56,000 were in the West Riding; 15,000 in Scotland; 11,000 in Lancashire; 9000 in Gloucestershire; 7000 in Wiltshire—and the rest scattered over the remaining counties of England and Wales as the industries map suggests, Devon being the county next to Wiltshire in order of importance. Fifty years later the West Riding had still only half the woollen spindles in the kingdom, which implies only a slight increase of concentration during that long and economically decisive age. . . .

It is not easy to exaggerate the importance of the textile manufactures in the industrial life of the country. Although not even that of cotton was completely mechanised—there may have been still 40,000 to 50,000 cotton hand-looms at work—they stood as the representative industries of the age of machinery and power, even though coal-mining and metallurgy had more final significance. Because they were so much mechanised their output was prodigious. Because they were not completely mechanised they carried with them in their march, and often left to fall by the wayside, a host of those who had now become handworking camp-followers. Not counting hosiery and lace, they found employment for—or should we say gave a trade name to?—nearly eleven hundred thousand people.

Their social importance can perhaps be best brought out by a comparison of 1851 with 1901. . . . The trades, or their nearest equivalents, which at the opening of the twentieth century employed 1 in 37 of the population had employed 1 in 19 in the year of the Great Exhibition. The handworking camp-followers outside the mills, and the relative imperfection of machinery inside, account for the astonishing figures of 1851. It is to be remembered that, although there were nearly 250,000 power-looms in the cotton industry in 1850, there were less than 33,000 in worsted, less than 10,000 in woollen, barely 6000 in flax and not 1200 in silk.

While Clapham criticizes the Toynbean view by questioning how revolutionary the Industrial Revolution was, JOHN U. NEF (b. 1899) goes on to suggest that if there was an Industrial Revolution, there were two of them. Associated with the University of Chicago and its Center for Human Understanding during almost all of his career, Nef has been most interested recently in the relationship between culture and industrialization and not merely in that relationship's pre-eighteenth-century origins. The article, excerpted below, was originally published in *The Economic History Review* (1934) and revised for republication in 1964. In it Nef argues that the period from 1540 to 1640 saw economic changes every bit as revolutionary as the ones Toynbee describes for a later period.*

John U. Nef

Another Challenge:
Two Industrial Revolutions

Since Arnold Toynbee, the elder, gave his famous lectures at Oxford, eighty years ago, closer study has taken from the concept of the "industrial revolution" much of its revolutionary character. Nowhere, perhaps, has the revision of earlier notions concerning the period from 1760 to 1832 been more drastic than with respect to the nature and magnitude of the changes in industrial technique and organization. The industrial plant staffed by dozens and sometimes scores or even hundreds of workmen was not the novelty it was once believed to be. Large-scale industry, in this sense, had developed extensively in Europe during the later Middle Ages and particularly at the time of the Renaissance. Evidence has been piling up to prove that in Great Britain similarly large enterprises, controlled to a much greater degree than those of the Continent by private capitalists, became common in mining and many branches of manufacture long before the middle of the eighteenth century. At the same time, more detailed studies of nineteenth-century economic history, especially the quantitative survey of Professor Clapham, have shown that earlier writers, with their eyes focused upon cotton and iron and upon the most advanced industrial areas, have exaggerated the place of the steam engine and of large-scale industry in the economy of the 1830's.

But it is still common to regard the 1760's and 1770's as an important historical boundary, in the sense that there began

*Reprinted from *The Conquest of the Material World* by John U. Nef by permission of The University of Chicago Press. Copyright ©1964 by The University of Chicago. Pp. 121–129, 135–136, 140–141. Footnotes omitted.

at this time the first great speeding up of industrial development. If Toynbee had lived to reply to some of the criticisms of the phrase "industrial revolution," he might have defended his position by referring to the passage in Macaulay's celebrated third chapter—which may possibly have influenced him during his short life—where Macaulay says that about the middle of the eighteenth century economic progress became for the first time "portentously rapid."

Was this the first period of English history during which a remarkable speeding up of industrial development occurred? The opinion is gaining strength that there was at least one earlier period during which the rate of change was scarcely less striking. This period begins at about the time of the dissolution of the monasteries, and the industrial development becomes most rapid during Shakespeare's lifetime, during the latter half of Elizabeth's reign and the reign of James I. The forces of rapid change then set in motion continued throughout the seventeenth and early eighteenth centuries, but it was not until the 1780's, on the eve of the French Revolution and at the time when the Constitution of the United States was drafted, that an even greater speeding up in the rate of economic growth announced itself in Great Britain, preparing the way directly for the atomic age.

Support for this view is to be found in the excellent book of Mr. Wadsworth and Miss Mann on the cotton textile industry. It is there suggested that the growth of an elaborate network of middlemen, who supplied the materials upon which thousands of domestic workpeople labored at their spinning wheels and looms, was so remarkable in the late sixteenth and early seventeenth centuries that the changes in the face of industrial Lancashire were scarcely less important than between 1760 and 1832, when the county was the classic home of the "revolution" in cotton manufacture. Evidence of an equally remarkable expansion, beginning about the middle of the sixteenth century and becoming decisive in the 1580's, the decade of the Armada, in the output of coal, salt, glass, and ships, and in the production of many other industrial commodities, such as alum, soap, gunpowder, metal goods and accessories, will be found in my book on the coal industry. . . . The rate of growth per decade in the production of mines and manufactures was, it seems probable, no less from about 1540 to 1640 than from about 1735 to 1785, the period when, according to Macaulay, economic progress first became "portentously rapid." Recent research seems to indicate that the rapid growth of industry and the striking increase in the importance and complexity of the domestic system, which began in the Elizabethan Age, were accompanied in England by a remarkable expansion in the use of machinery driven by water and horse power and by a concentration (unprecedented in previous history) on inventive objectives primarily aimed at the reduction of labor *costs* in the interest of quantitative production.

Three kinds of technical development helped the growth of large-scale, privately controlled enterprise between 1540 and 1640. The first was the introduction of a series of industries which had appeared somewhat earlier on the Continent, but which hardly gained a foothold in Great Britain until after the Reformation. The second was the application to old industries of various technical processes known before, especially in some districts on the Continent, but hitherto very little used in Great Britain. The third was the discovery and application of new technical methods, little known in Europe at the Reformation.

The Introduction of "New" Industries

During the last sixty years of the sixteenth century the first paper and gunpowder mills, the first cannon foundries, the first alum and copperas factories, the first sugar refineries, and the first considerable saltpeter works were all introduced into the country from abroad. The discovery of calamine, the ore of zinc, in Somerset and elsewhere, together with the first really effective attempts to mine copper ore, made possible the establishment of brassmaking and battery works for hammering brass and copper ingots into plates.

Not all the commodities turned out by these manufactures were being produced in England for the first time. If English-made sugar and brass were new, some paper and alum, probably some saltpeter and gunpowder, and perhaps some copperas had been obtained from native workshops before the sixteenth century. But the quantities had been insignificant. The important thing about the "new" Elizabethan industries, for the spread of capitalistic ventures, was that in all of them plant was set up involving investments far beyond the sums which groups of master craftsmen could muster, even if these artisans were men of some small substance. While in London, Sheffield, or any provincial town, the typical workshop of the smith, the cutler, or the weaver could be equipped with its forge or grinding wheel or loom and other necessary tools for a few pounds, the establishments erected in these new industries cost hundreds, and in many cases thousands, of pounds, at a time when a wage earner did well if he earned more than five pounds a year. A further heavy outlay had to be made on materials and labor, because the process of production freqently required a long time, and it was many months before any return could be expected from sales.

In the reign of James I, the alum houses erected near Whitby, on the Yorkshire coast, were great wooden structures. Each contained large brick furnaces and cisterns, piles of alumstone, coal, and wood fuel and about ten metal pans for heating the ingredients. Many thousands of pounds were spent on each of these houses, and the annual expense of the materials consumed in the manufacture exceeded £1,000 . . . .

In the reign of Charles I, the copperas house at Queenborough in Kent, with its great wooden troughs, leaden pipes, and cisterns, was built on a similar scale to an alum house. In 1613 John Browne, later crown commissioner for making ordnance and shot and official gunmaker to the Parliament in the Civil War, employed some 200 men in his cannon foundry at Brenchley in Kent. At Dartford, in the same county, a paper mill had been set up by John Spilman, a naturalized German, about the middle of Elizabeth's reign . . . .

One of the two great waterwheels which drive the hammers for beating the cloth and the stamping machinery had formerly been used to drive the bellows of a blast furnace on the same site, and the cost of converting it to its new purpose is said to have been between £1,400 and £1,500 in money of that time, which should be multiplied by more than twenty to get its equivalent in terms of today. Powder mills, introduced into Surrey just after the middle of the sixteenth century, were also driven by water power, and the machinery was perhaps no less costly than at the paper mills . . . . The battery works introduced from Germany in Elizabeth's reign, with their furnaces and numerous great hammers, some of which weighed five hundred pounds, probably cost as much to build as the larger powder and paper mills. The hammers were driven by water power at a heavy cost. As in all the rising English industries the overshot wheel was generally used rather than the less expensive under-shot wheel. To turn the former a stream had to be diverted from its course, and a dam built to store up the water against a drought.

There was nothing new about the use of the overshot wheel in industry, but its adoption during the late sixteenth and early seventeenth centuries in England appears to have been unprecedentedly rapid, and large water-driven wheels had probably come into more widespread use by 1640, on the eve of the Civil War, than in other countries.

Among other industries introduced into England during the last sixty years of the sixteenth century, sugar-refining and brassmaking by the process of cementation also required an extensive outlay in buildings, furnaces, boilers, machinery, tools, and materials. Sugarmakers had to invest scores and sometimes hundreds of pounds in lead pipes, cisterns, copper kettles, and iron rollers for grinding the cane. Brass-makers had to provide expensive metal pots, in which the copper was mixed with prepared calamine, and one or more large ovens in which eight or more of the pots were placed for heating. . . .

It is probable, nevertheless, that the number of considerable establishments at work in all these "new" manufactures, taken together, had reached several scores before the Civil War. And the introduction of such establishments, with their elaborate water-driven machinery, their large furnaces and accessories, must have had an influence upon the growth of industrial capitalism in England beyond that which can be measured in terms of the output or the number of workpeople engaged in them. Mechanics and inventors could study the new machinery, furnaces, and boilers with a view to adapting them to suit other processes of manufacture. Land-lords and merchants, with capital to invest

in other industries, were stimulated by example to set up works on a larger scale than they might otherwise have done. For a variety of reasons, they were able as time went on to develop their enterprises free from government participation and even government regulation to a degree that had not been common hitherto in Europe, if indeed anywhere in the world. While the period preceding the Reformation had been, on the Continent especially, a time of increasing political control over industry, the late sixteenth and seventeenth centuries were in Great Britain a time when private enterprise increasingly escaped effective government interference.

The Progress of Advanced Technical Methods in Old Industries

A larger number of workpeople and a greater amount of capital were drawn into such capitalistic enterprises by the extensive changes in old industries than by the introduction of these "new" manufactures. The very rapid growth of markets for coal and ore was making it imperative to adopt less primitive methods in mining and the production of metals. As a result of the application of improved methods known before the middle of the sixteenth century, at least on the Continent, conditions in these industries were largely transformed during the century following the dissolution of the monasteries.

Before the sixteenth century, in Great Britain, the expensive adit or long tunnel for draining mines was rare, machinery driven by water or horse power for pumping out water or raising minerals was perhaps still rarer. The problems of prospecting for coal and ore, of sinking through rocky strata, and of ventilating the pits to force out noxious gases, hardly tried the ingenuity of the miner, for the depths of the workings seldom exceeded a few fathoms. Except at silver mines, which were scarce in Great Britain, and at a very few tin and coal mines, mining seldom required the investment of much capital. Ore and coal were normally dug by independent partnerships of working miners.

Great changes occurred in the importance of mining and metallurgy as a result of the very rapid expansion in the demand for copper, lead, iron, and above all coal. Seams of that base mineral abounded, and the rate of growth in the output of coal was more rapid than the rate of growth in the output of silver had been during the previous hundred years in Central Europe. Production of coal in Great Britain increased some seven- or eightfold or even more between the 1530's and the 1630's. In order to meet the demand it became necessary to sink to depths of twenty, thirty, and even forty or fifty fathoms. In many parts of England, Scotland, and Wales miners were threatened by water which drowned out their workings and by gas explosions which killed scores. Never before in any country had mining and the transport of coal engaged as workers so large a proportion of the population as in Great Britain on the eve of the Civil War, which is to say in the 1630's.

During the reigns of Elizabeth and her two Stuart successors, money was poured out lavishly in the construction of hundreds of adits, ventilation shafts, and drainage engines, driven by water or more often by horse power, at tin, copper, and lead mines and, above all, at collieries. As the digging and lining of an adit often cost thousands of pounds (the equivalent of hundreds of thousands of dollars in today's money), and as the expense of operating a horse-driven pump sometimes amounted to about £2,000 a year, the new mining enterprises had to be conducted on a scale which would have seemed almost incredible to an untraveled Englishman of the time of Henry VIII and Sir Thomas More. What he would have considered large-scale industry was becoming, except in backward shires, the normal form of enterprise both in mining and metallurgy.

While the annual output of a coal mine before the middle of the sixteenth century had rarely exceeded a few hundred tons, and much of the mining had been done casually by manorial tenants who worked part of the year as husbandmen, collieries producing from ten to twenty-five thousand tons of coal, representing an investment of many thousands of pounds in money of that time, and employing scores and sometimes hundreds of miners, became common before 1640. They were to be found not only in the north of England but also in Scotland, and even in the Midlands which had no direct access to the mounting trade in seaborne coal. Large enterprises were the rule in the mining of copper, as well as in the much less extensive mining of silver; considerable investments of capital were common in the mining of tin and were not unknown in the mining of lead.

In the conversion of metallic ores into metals, and the preparation of these metals for the smiths, nailers, and other craftsmen who fashioned them into finished articles, the scale of enterprise grew also strikingly. The blast furnace for producing cast iron was probably introduced from the Continent toward the end of the fifteenth century. But it was little used at that time even in Sussex, the center of the English iron industry, and apparently not at all elsewhere, until after 1540. . . . Between 1540 and 1640, the process of ironmaking assumed a more capitalistic form, and the changes were second in importance only to those which revolutionized the industry during and after the eighties of the eighteenth century. . . .

[The Discovery and Application of New Technical Methods]

In an age that Jevons and other nineteenth-century writers believed to be virtually barren of practical inventive achievement, England was actually becoming a busy hive of experiments designed to reduce labor. Shortly before the end of Elizabeth's reign, boring rods for finding out the nature of underground strata and railed ways with large horse-drawn wagons for carrying coal were devised by the ingenuity of some inventors who remain anonymous. In southern Nottinghamshire, at about the same time, in 1589, William Lee gave the world his stocking-knitting frame.

It is impossible to determine to what extent workmen were drawn into capitalistic plants before 1640 as a result of such English inventions. In some cases, the technical discoveries had little, if any, effect upon the form of industrial enterprise. In most of the metallurgical finishing trades and in many branches of the textile industry, small domestic enterprises were still the rule even after the widespread adoption of coal in place of wood fuel. Framework knitting remained domestic until the nineteenth century, for Lee's invention did not cause a sufficiently great increase in the capital required to draw the industry into the factory. Boring rods added something, but not much, to the costs of mining. Railed ways involved a far heavier outlay, especially where collieries were worked at some distance from navigable water and where the terrain between was full of hills and ravines. Their installation eliminated the independent local carter, who plied his horse and cart for hire, and changed the transportation of coal into a capitalistic industry. But neither railed ways nor boring rods made much headway in connection with mining until the end of the seventeenth century . . . .

Wherever coal was substituted for wood in manufactures, it tended not only to increase the costs of the installation, but also to cheapen the quality of the product and reduce the prestige attaching to manual work. By cheapening the quality of the product it widened the market for it, and thus increased the potential advantages of large-scale production. Quite apart from the direct influence of the substitution of coal for wood in encouraging large-scale manufacture, it is clear that the inventions making this substitution possible enabled several capitalistic industries, which would otherwise have withered, to flourish as they could not in foreign countries lacking cheap and easily accessible coal supplies. . . .

Conclusion

Without a thorough investigation of many industries hitherto neglected by economic historians, no quantitative estimate can be made of the total number of laborers employed in capitalistically owned mines and manufacturing establishments in the 1630's, on the eve of the Civil War. No doubt the great majority of all the workpeople engaged in industry labored in their homes, in town cellars or garrets or in village cottages. But that majority was by no means so overwhelming as was supposed in Toynbee the elder's time. During the hundred years from 1540 to 1640 the proportion so employed had been notably reduced. Tens of thousands of workpeople had been swept from the country dwellings and town shops of their forefathers or from a ragged existence of vagabondage into hundreds of new, capitalistically owned enterprises. The introduction of new industries and of new machinery, tools, and furnaces in old industries, had brought about technical changes in the methods of mining and manufacturing only less momentous than those associated with the great inventions of the late eighteenth and early nineteenth centuries. The expansion of mining and metallurgy after about 1580 also raised in more acute forms than ever before three technical problems which remained partly unsolved in 1640, in spite of all the busy work that had been done on them during the previous sixty years: the substitution of steam for water, wind, and horse power for driving machinery; the laying of railed ways for the transport of bulky goods; the substitution of coal for wood fuel in the production of metals, particularly iron. It was further work which led to the solution of all these problems in Great Britain at the juncture of the eighteenth and nineteenth centuries. These discoveries precipitated the still greater speeding up in the rate of industrial development which began in the 1780's and led to the conquest of the material world. The concentration of inventive skill on these three problems at the juncture of the sixteenth and seventeenth centuries was novel. It is another aspect of the "early English industrial revolution."

It must not be supposed that the developments we have attempted to sketch came to an end in the mid-seventeenth century. While workpeople were perhaps drawn into large-scale industry at a somewhat less rapid *rate* in the hundred years following than in those preceding 1640, the striking changes in technique and the greatly increasing concentration of capital which began in the Elizabethan Age led directly to the rapid industrial progress which we associate with the nine-teenth and twentieth centuries. It follows that if we are concerned with the relations of other historical developments to the *origins* of industrial civilization, these must perhaps be sought more in the late sixteenth and seventeenth centuries than at the time of the "industrial revolution" as described by Toynbee the elder and his followers.

The rise of industrialism in Great Britain can be more properly regarded as a long process stretching back to the middle of the sixteenth century and coming down to the final triumph of the industrial state toward the end of the nineteenth, than as a sudden phenomenon associated with the late eighteenth and early nineteenth centuries. It is no longer possible to find a full explanation of "the great inventions" and the new factories of the late eighteenth century in a preceding commercial revolution which increased the size of markets. The commercial revolution, if that is the proper term to apply to a rapid growth in foreign and domestic trade during a period of two centuries, had a continuous influence reaching back beyond the Reformation upon industrial technology and the scale of mining and manufacturing. But the progress of industry, in turn, had continually stimulated in a variety of ways the progress of commerce. The former progress was quite as "revolutionary" as the latter, and quite as directly responsible for the speeding up of industrial growth in Great Britain at the juncture of the eighteenth and nineteenth centuries which led to the triumph of industrialism.

W. W. ROSTOW (b. 1916) has had a most varied career, as economic historian at the Massachusetts Institute of Technology, as theorist of economic growth, and as government official. This experience has caused him to write widely on economic history, economics, and foreign and defense policies. With A. D. Gayer and A. J. Schwartz he wrote *The Growth and Fluctuation of the British Economy, 1790–1850,* perhaps the most detailed quantitative study of the British Industrial Revolution since Clapham's. In recent years he has served in the U.S. Department of State and as a special assistant to both Presidents Kennedy and Johnson. More famous for his controversial "take-off" theory, the following passage summarizes it.*

W. W. Rostow

The Industrial Revolution as Take-off

We come now to the great watershed in the life of modern societies: the third stage in this sequence, the take-off. The take-off is the interval when the old blocks and resistances to steady growth are finally overcome. The forces making for economic progress, which yielded limited bursts and enclaves of modern activity, expand and come to dominate the society. Growth becomes its normal condition. Compound interest becomes built, as it were, into its habits and institutional structure. . . .

There are several problems of choice involved in defining the take-off with precision. We might begin with one arbitrary definition and consider briefly the two major alternatives.

For the present purposes the take-off is defined as requiring all three of the following related conditions:

(1) a rise in the rate of productive investment from, say, 5% or less to over 10% of national income (or net national product (NNP));

(2) the development of one or more substantial manufacturing sectors, with a high rate of growth;

(3) the existence or quick emergence of a political, social and institutional framework which exploits the impulses to expansion in the modern sector and the potential external economy effects of the take-off and gives to growth an on-going character. . . .

This definition is designed to isolate the early stage when industrialization takes

*From W. W. Rostow, *The Stages of Economic Growth: A Non-Communist Manifesto* (London: Cambridge University Press, 1960), pp. 7, 39–40, and 54–56. Some footnotes omitted.

hold rather than the later stage when in-dustrialization becomes a more massive and statistically more impressive phenom-enon.[1] In Britain, for example, there is no doubt that it was between 1815 and 1850 that industrialization fully took hold. If the criterion chosen for take-off was the period of most rapid overall industrial growth, or the period when large-scale industry ma-tured, all our take-off dates would have to be set later; Britain, for example, to 1819–48; the United States, to 1868–93; Sweden, to 1890–1920; Japan, to 1900–20; Russia, to 1928–40. The earlier dating is chosen here because it is believed that the decisive transformations (including a de-cisive shift in the investment-rate) occur in the first industrial phases; and later indus-trial maturity can be directly traced back to foundations laid in these first phases.

This definition is also designed to rule out from the take-off the quite substantial economic progress which can occur in an economy before a truly self-reinforcing growth process gets under way. Consider, for example, British economic expansion between, say, 1750 and 1783; Russian eco-nomic expansion between, say, 1861 and 1890, Canadian economic expansion be-tween 1867 and the mid-1890's. Such peri-ods—for which there is an equivalent in the economic history of almost every grow-ing economy—were marked by extremely important, even decisive, developments. The transport network expanded, and with it both internal and external com-merce; a revolution in agricultural produc-tivity was, at least, begun; new institutions for mobilizing savings were developed; a class of commercial and even industrial

entrepreneurs began to emerge; industrial enterprise on a limited scale (or in limited sectors) grew. And yet, however essential these pre-take-off periods were for later de-velopment, their scale and momentum were insufficient to transform the economy radically or, in some cases, to outstrip popu-lation growth and to yield an increase in *per capita* output.

With a sense of the considerable vio-lence done to economic history, we are here seeking to isolate a period when the scale of productive economic activity reaches a critical level and produces changes which lead to a massive and pro-gressive structural transformation in econo-mies and the societies of which they are a part, better viewed as changes in kind than merely in degree. . . .

Why did the development of a modern factory system in cotton textiles lead on in Britain to a self-sustaining growth process, whereas it failed to do so in other cases? Part of the answer lies in the fact that by the late eighteenth century the precondi-tions for take-off in Britain were very fully developed. Progress in textiles, coal, iron and even steam power had been consid-erable throughout the eighteenth century; and the social and institutional environ-ment was propitious. But two further tech-nical elements helped determine the upshot. First, the British cotton-textile in-dustry was large in relation to the total size of the economy. From its modern begin-nings, but notably from the 1780's forward, a very high proportion of total cotton-tex-tile output was directed abroad, reaching 60% by the 1820's.[2] The evolution of this industry was a more massive fact, with wider secondary repercussions, than if it were simply supplying the domestic mar-ket. Industrial enterprise on this scale had

---

[1]Rostow's tentative and approximate dates for "take-off" in the major nations:
Great Britain (1783–1802), France (1830–1860), Belgium (1833–1860), United States (1843–1860), Germany (1850–1873), Sweden (1868–1890), Japan (1878–1900), Russia (1890–1914), Canada (1896–1914).—Ed.

[2]The volume (official value) of British cotton-goods exports rose from £355,060 in 1780 to £7,624,505 in 1802. . . .

secondary reactions on the development of urban areas, the demand for coal, iron and machinery, the demand for working capital and ultimately the demand for cheap transport, which powerfully stimulated industrial development in other directions.

Second, a source of effective demand for rapid expansion in British cotton textiles was supplied, in the first instance, by the sharp reduction in real costs and prices which accompanied the technological developments in manufacture and the cheapening real cost of raw cotton induced by the cotton-gin. In this Britain had an advantage not enjoyed by those who came later; for they merely substituted domestic for foreign-manufactured cotton textiles. The substitution undoubtedly had important secondary effects by introducing a modern industrial sector and releasing, on balance, a pool of foreign exchange for other purposes; but there was no sharp fall in the real cost of acquiring cotton textiles and no equivalent rise in real income.

The introduction of the railroad has been historically the most powerful single initiator of take-offs. It was decisive in the United States, France, Germany, Canada, and Russia; it has played an extremely important part in the Swedish, Japanese and other cases.

The railroad has had three major kinds of impact on economic growth during the take-off period. First, it has lowered internal transport costs, brought new areas and products into commercial markets and, in general, performed the Smithian function of widening the market. Second, it has been a prerequisite in many cases to the development of a major new and rapidly enlarging export sector which, in turn, has served to generate capital for internal development, as, for example, the American railroads before 1914. Third, and perhaps most important for the take-off itself, the development of railways has led on to the development of modern coal, iron and engineering industries. In many countries the growth of modern basic industrial sectors can be traced in the most direct way to the requirements for building and, especially, for maintaining substantial railway systems. When a society has developed deeper institutional, social and political prerequisites for take-off, the rapid growth of a railway system, with these powerful triple effects, has often served to lift it into self-sustained growth. Where the prerequisites have not existed, however, very substantial railway building has failed to initiate a take-off, as for example in India, China, pre-1895 Canada, pre-1914 Argentina, etc. . . .

American professional historians have more trouble writing good history for the general but educated reader than do their British or French counterparts, such as E. J. HOBSBAWM (b. 1917), who wrote the following passage in his *Age of Revolution* (1962) on the "dual revolution" of the French and Industrial Revolutions. Reader in history at Birkbeck College and lecturer at the University of London, Hobsbawm has written on economic and social history, especially that of working-class movements, for both the general and specialized reader. In the following selection he follows Rostow's initiatives, but casts them in a broader framework.*

E. J. Hobsbawm

The Take-off Supported

What does the phrase "the Industrial Revolution broke out" mean? It means that some time in the 1780s, and for the first time in human history, the shackles were taken off the productive power of human societies, which henceforth became capable of the constant, rapid and up to the present limitless multiplication of men, goods and services. This is now technically known to the economists as the "take-off into self-sustained growth." No previous society had been able to break through the ceiling which a pre-industrial social structure, defective science and technology, and consequently periodic breakdown, famine and death, imposed on production. The "take-off" was not, of course, one of those phenomena which, like earthquakes and large meteors, take the non-technical world by surprise. Its pre-history in Europe can be traced back, depending on the taste of the historian and his particular range of interest, to about AD 1000, if not before, and earlier attempts to leap into the air, clumsy as the experiments of young ducklings, have been flattered with the name of "industrial revolution"—in the thirteenth century, in the sixteenth, in the last decades of the seventeenth. From the middle of the eighteenth century the process of gathering speed for the take-off is so clearly observable that older historians have tended to date the Industrial Revolution back to 1760. But careful enquiry has tended to lead most experts to pick on the 1780s rather than the 1760s as the decisive

*Reproduced by permission of Weidenfeld & Nicolson, Ltd., and The World Publishing Company from *The Age of Revolution 1789–1848* by E. J. Hobsbawm. Copyright ©1962 by E. J. Hobsbawm. Pp. 28–38, 42–47, 51–52. Footnotes omitted.

decade, for it was then that, so far as we can tell, all the revelant statistical indices took that sudden, sharp, almost vertical turn upwards which marks the "take-off." The economy became, as it were, airborne.

To call this process the Industrial Revolution is both logical and in line with a well-established tradition, though there was at one time a fashion among conservative historians—perhaps due to certain shyness in the presence of incendiary concepts—to deny its existence, and substitute instead platitudinous terms like "accelerated evolution." If the sudden, qualitative and fundamental transformation, which happened in or about the 1780s, was not a revolution then the word has no commonsense meaning. The Industrial Revolution was not indeed an episode with a beginning and an end. To ask when it was "complete" is senseless, for its essence was that henceforth revolutionary change became the norm. It is still going on; at most we can ask when the economic transformations had gone far enough to establish a substantially industrialized economy, capable of producing, broadly speaking, anything it wanted within the range of the available techniques, a "mature industrial economy" to use the technical term. In Britain, and therefore in the world, this period of initial industrialization probably coincides almost exactly with the period with which this book deals, for if it began with the "take-off" in the 1780s, it may plausibly be said to be concluded with the building of the railways and the construction of a massive heavy industry in Britain in the 1840s. But the Revolution itself, the "take-off period," can probably be dated with as much precision as is possible in such matters, to some time within the twenty years from 1780 to 1800: contemporary with, but slightly prior to, the French Revolution.

By any reckoning this was probably the most important event in world history, at any rate since the invention of agriculture and cities. And it was initiated by Britain. That this was not fortuitous, is evident. If there was to be a race for pioneering the Industrial Revolution in the eighteenth century, there was really only one starter. There was plenty of industrial and commercial advance, fostered by the intelligent and economically far from naïve ministers and civil servants of every enlightened monarchy in Europe, from Portugal to Russia, all of whom were at least as much concerned with "economic growth" as present-day administrators. Some small states and regions did indeed industrialize quite impressively for example, Saxony and the bishopric of Liège, though their industrial complexes were too small and localized to exert the world-revolutionary influence of the British ones. But it seems clear that even before the revolution Britain was already a long way ahead of her chief potential competitor in *per capita* output and trade, even if still comparable to her in total output and trade. . . .

Fortunately few intellectual refinements were necessary to make the Industrial Revolution. Its technical inventions were exceedingly modest, and in no way beyond the scope of intelligent artisans experimenting in their workshops, or of the constructive capacities of carpenters, millwrights and locksmiths: the flying shuttle, the spinning jenny, the mule. Even its scientifically most sophisticated machine, James Watt's rotary steam-engine (1784), required no more physics than had been available for the best part of a century. . . . Given the right conditions, the technical innovations of the Industrial Revolution practically made themselves, except perhaps in the chemical industry. This does not mean that early industrialists were not often interested in science and on the look-out for its practical benefits.

But the right conditions were visibly present in Britain, where more than a century had passed since the first king had been formally tried and executed by his people, and since private profit and economic development had become accepted as the supreme objects of government policy. For practical purposes the uniquely revolutionary British solution of the agrarian problem had already been found. A relative handful of commercially-minded landlords already almost monopolized the land, which was cultivated by tenant-farmers employing landless or smallholders. A good many relics of the ancient collective economy of the village still remained to be swept away by Enclosure Acts (1760–1830) and private transactions, but we can hardly any longer speak of a "British peasantry" in the same sense that we can speak of a French, German or Russian peasantry. Farming was already predominantly for the market; manufacture had long been diffused throughout an unfeudal countryside. Agriculture was already prepared to carry out its three fundamental functions in an era of industrialization: to increase production and productivity, so as to feed a rapidly rising non-agricultural population; to provide a large and rising surplus of potential recruits for the towns and industries; and to provide a mechanism for the accumulation of capital to be used in the more modern sectors of the economy. (Two other functions were probably less important in Britain: that of creating a sufficiently large market among the agricultural population—normally the great mass of the people—and of providing an export surplus which helps to secure capital imports.) A considerable volume of social overhead capital—the expensive general equipment necessary for the entire

economy to move smoothly ahead—was already being created, notably in shipping, port facilities, and the improvement of roads and waterways. Politics were already geared to profit. The businessman's specific demands might encounter resistance from other vested interests; and as we shall see, the agrarians were to erect one last barrier to hold up the advance of the industrialists between 1795 and 1846. On the whole, however, it was accepted that money not only talked, but governed. All the industrialist had to get to be accepted among the governors of society was enough money.

The businessman was undoubtedly in the process of getting more money, for the greater part of the eighteenth century was for most of Europe a period of prosperity and comfortable economic expansion; the real background to the happy optimism of Voltaire's Dr. Pangloss. It may well be argued that sooner or later this expansion, assisted by a gentle inflation, would have pushed some country across the threshold which separates the pre-industrial from the industrial economy. But the problem is not so simple. Much of eighteenth-century industrial expansion did not in fact lead immediately, or within the foreseeable future, to industrial *revolution*, i.e. to the creation of a mechanized "factory system" which in turn produces in such vast quantities and at such rapidly diminishing cost, as to be no longer dependent on existing demand, but to create its own market. For instance the building trade, or the numerous small scale industries producing domestic metal goods —nails, pots, knives, scissors, etc.—in the British Midlands and Yorkshire, expanded very greatly in this period, but always as a function of the existing market. In 1850 while producing far more than in 1750, they produced in substantially the old manner. What was needed was not any kind of expansion, but the special kind of expansion which produced Manchester rather than Birmingham.

Moreover, the pioneer industrial revolutions occurred in a special historical situation, in which economic growth emerges from the crisscrossing decisions of countless private entrepreneurs and inventors, each governed by the first commandment of the age, to buy in the cheapest market and to sell in the dearest. How were they to discover that maximum profit was to be got out of organizing industrial revolution rather than out of more familiar (and in the past more profitable) business activities? How were they to learn, what nobody could as yet know, that industrial revolution would produce an unexampled acceleration in the expansion of their markets? Given that the main social foundations of an industrial society had already been laid, as they almost certainly had in the England of the later eighteenth century, they required two things: first, an industry which already offered exceptional rewards for the manufacturer who could expand his output quickly, if need be by reasonably cheap and simple innovations, and second, a *world* market largely monopolized by a single producing nation.

These considerations apply in some ways to all countries in our period. For instance, in all of them the lead in industrial growth was taken by the manufacturers of goods of mass consumption—mainly, but not exclusively, textiles—because the mass market for such goods already existed, and businessmen could clearly see its possibilities of expansion. In other ways, however, they apply to Britain alone. For the pioneer industrialists have the most difficult problems. Once Britain had begun to industrialize, other countries could begin to enjoy the benefits of the rapid economic expansion which the pioneer industrial evolution stimulated. Moreover, British

success proved what could be achieved by it, British technique could be imitated, British skill and capital imported. . . .

Between 1789 and 1848 Europe and America were flooded with British experts, steam engines, cotton machinery and investments.

Britain enjoyed no such advantages. On the other hand it possessed an economy strong enough and a state aggressive enough to capture the markets of its competitors. In effect the wars of 1793–1815, the last and decisive phase of a century's Anglo-French duel, virtually eliminated all rivals from the non-European world, except to some extent the young USA. Moreover, Britain possessed an industry admirably suited to pioneering industrial revolution under capitalist conditions, and an economic conjuncture which allowed it to: the cotton industry, and colonial expansion.

I I

The British, like all other cotton industries, had originally grown up as a by-product of overseas trade, which produced its raw material (or rather one of its raw materials, for the original product was *fustian*, a mixture of cotton and linen), and the Indian cotton goods or *calicoes* which won the markets that the European manufacturers were to attempt to capture with their own imitations. To begin with they were not very sucessful, though better able to reproduce the cheap and coarse goods competitively than the fine and elaborate ones. Fortunately, however, the old-established and powerful vested interest of the woollen trade periodically secured import prohibitions of Indian calicoes (which the purely mercantile interest of the East India Company sought to export from India in the largest possible quantities), and thus gave the native cotton industry's substitutes a chance. Cheaper than wool, cotton and cotton mixtures won themselves a modest but useful market at home. But their major chances of rapid expansion were to lie overseas.

Colonial trade had created the cotton industry, and continued to nourish it. In the eighteenth century it developed in the hinterland of the major colonial ports, Bristol, Glasgow but especially Liverpool, the great centre of the slave trades. Each phase of this inhuman but rapidly expanding commerce stimulated it. In fact, during the entire period with which this book is concerned slavery and cotton marched together. The African slaves were bought, in part at least, with Indian cotton goods; but when the supply of these was interrupted by war or revolt in and about India, Lancashire was able to leap in. The plantations of the West Indies, where the slaves were taken, provided the bulk of the raw cotton for the British industry, and in return the planters bought Manchester cotton checks in appreciable quantities. Until shortly before the "take-off" the overwhelming bulk of Lancashire cotton exports went to the combined African and American markets. Lancashire was later to repay its debt to slavery by preserving it; for after the 1790s the slave plantations of the Southern United States were extended and maintained by the insatiable and rocketing demands of the Lancashire mills, to which they supplied the bulk of their raw cotton.

The cotton industry was thus launched, like a glider, by the pull of the colonial trade to which it was attached; a trade which promised not only great, but rapid and above all unpredictable expansion, which encouraged the entrepreneur to adopt the revolutionary techniques required to meet it. Between 1750 and 1769 the export of British cottons increased more than ten times over. In such situations

the rewards for the man who came into the market first with the most cotton checks were astronomical and well worth the risks of leaps into technological adventure. But the overseas market, and especially within it the poor and backward "under-developed areas," not only expanded dramatically from time to time, but expanded constantly without apparent limit. Doubtless any given section of it, considered in isolation, was small by industrial standards, and the competition of the different "advanced economies" made it even smaller for each. But, as we have seen, supposing any one of the advanced economies managed, for a sufficiently long time, to monopolize *all* or almost all of it, then its prospects really were limitless. This is precisely what the British cotton industry succeeded in doing, aided by the aggressive support of the British Government. In terms of sales, the Industrial Revolution can be described except for a few initial years in the 1780s as the triumph of the export market over the home: by 1814 Britain exported about four yards of cotton cloth for every three used at home, by 1850 thirteen for every eight. And within this expanding export market, in turn, the semi-colonial and colonial markets, long the main outlets for British goods abroad, triumphed. During the Napoleonic Wars, when the European markets were largely cut off by wars and blockades, this was natural enough. But even after the wars they continued to assert themselves. In 1820 Europe, once again open to free British imports, took 128 million yards of British cottons; America outside the USA, Africa and Asia took 80 millions; but by 1840 Europe took 200 million yards, while the "under-developed" areas took 529 millions....

Cotton therefore provided prospects sufficiently astronomical to tempt private entrepreneurs into the adventure of industrial revolution, and an expansion suffi-

iently sudden to require it. Fortunately it
lso provided the other conditions which
lade it possible. The new inventions
hich revolutionized it—the spinning-
nny, the water-frame, the mule in spin-
ing, a little later the power-loom in weav-
ig—were sufficiently simple and cheap,
nd paid for themselves almost immediate-
· in terms of higher output. They could
e installed, if need be piecemeal, by small
en who started off with a few borrowed
ounds, for the men who controlled the
eat accumulations of eighteenth-century
ealth were not greatly inclined to invest
rge amounts in industry. The expansion
· the industry could be financed easily out
· current profits, for the combination of its
st market conquests and a steady price-
flation produced fantastic rates of profit.
t was not five per cent or ten per cent," a
ter English politician was to say, with
stice, "but hundreds per cent and thou-
nds per cent that made the fortunes of
ancashire." In 1789 an ex-draper's assis-
nt like Robert Owen could start with a
orrowed £100 in Manchester; by 1809 he
ought out his partners in the New Lanark
ills for £84,000 *in cash*. And his was a
latively modest story of business suc-
ss. . . .

But the cotton manufacture had other
lvantages. All its raw material came from
road, and its supply could therefore be
panded by the drastic procedures open
white men in the colonies—slavery and
e opening of new areas of cultivation—
ther than by the slower procedures of
uropean agriculture; nor was it hampered
the vested interests of European
riculturalists. From the 1790s on British
tton found its supply, to which its for-
nes remained linked until the 1860s, in
: newly-opened Southern States of the
SA. Again, at crucial points of manufac-
·e (notably spinning) cotton suffered
m a shortage of cheap and efficient la-

bour, and was therefore pushed into
mechanization. An industry like *linen,*
which had initially rather better chances of
colonial expansion than cotton, suffered in
the long run from the very ease with which
cheap, non-mechanized production could
be expanded in the impoverished peasant
regions (mainly in Central Europe, but
also in Ireland) in which it mainly
flourished. For the *obvious* way of industrial
expansion in the eighteenth century, in
Saxony and Normandy as in England, was
not to construct factories, but to extend the
so-called "domestic" or "putting-out" system, in which workers—sometimes former
independent craftsmen, sometimes former
peasants with time on their hands in the
dead season—worked up the raw material
in their own homes, with their own or
rented tools, receiving it from and deliver-
ing it back to merchants who were in the
process of becoming employers. Indeed,
both in Britain and in the rest of the economically progressive world, the bulk of
expansion in the initial period of industrialization continued to be of this kind. Even
in the cotton industry such processes as
weaving were expanded by creating hosts
of domestic handloom weavers to serve the
nuclei of mechanized spinneries, the primitive handloom being a rather more efficient device than the spinning-wheel.
Everywhere weaving was mechanized a
generation after spinning, and everywhere,
incidentally, the handloom weavers died a
lingering death, occasionally revolting
against their awful fate, when industry no
longer had any need of them.

I I I

The traditional view which has seen the
history of the British Industrial Revolution
primarily in terms of cotton is thus correct.
Cotton was the first industry to be revolutionized, and it is difficult to see what
other could have pushed a host of private

entrepreneurs into revolution. As late as the 1830s cotton was the only British industry in which the factory or "mill" (the name was derived from the most widespread pre-industrial establishment employing heavy power-operated machinery) predominated; at first (1780–1815) mainly in spinning, carding and a few ancillary operations, after 1815 increasingly also in weaving. The "factories" with which the new Factory Acts dealt were, until the 1860s, assumed to be exclusively textile factories and predominantly cotton mills. Factory production in other textile branches was slow to develop before the 1840s and in other manufactures was negligible. Even the steam engine, though applied to numerous other industries by 1815, was not used in any quantity outside mining, which had pioneered it. In 1830 "industry" and "factory" in anything like the modern sense still meant almost exclusively the cotton areas of the United Kingdom.

This is not to underestimate the forces which made for industrial innovation in other consumer goods, notably in other textiles, in food and drink, in pottery and other household goods, greatly stimulated by the rapid growth of cities. But in the first place these employed far fewer people: no industry remotely approached the million-and-a-half people directly employed by or dependent on employment in cotton in 1833. In the second place their power to transform was much smaller: *brewing*, which was in most respects a technically and scientifically much more advanced and mechanized business, and one revolutionized well before cotton, hardly affected the economy around it, as may be proved by the great Guinness brewery in Dublin, which left the rest of the Dublin and Irish economy (though not local tastes) much as it was before its construction. The demand derived from cotton—

for more building and all activities in the new industrial areas, for machines, for chemical improvements, for industrial lighting, for shipping and a number of other activities—is itself enough to account for a large proportion of the economic growth in Britain up to the 1830s. In the third place, the expansion of the cotton industry was so vast and its weight in the foreign trade of Britain so great, that it dominated the movements of the entire economy. The quantity of raw cotton imported into Britain rose from 11 million lb. in 1785 to 588 million lb. in 1850; the output of cloth from 40 million to 2,025 million yards. Cotton manufactures formed between 40 and 50 per cent of the annual declared value of *all* British exports between 1816 and 1848. If cotton flourished, the economy flourished, if it slumped, so did the economy. Its price movements determined the balance of the nation's trade. Only agriculture had a comparable power and that was visibly declining.

Nevertheless, though the expansion of the cotton industry and the cotton-dominated industrial economy "mocks all that the most romantic imagination could have previously conceived possible under any circumstances," its progress was far from smooth, and by the 1830s and early 1840s produced major problems of growth, not to mention revolutionary unrest unparalleled in any other period of recent British history. This first general stumbling of the industrial capitalist economy is reflected in a marked slowing down in the growth, perhaps even in a decline, in the British national income at this period. Nor was this first general capitalist crisis a purely British phenomenon. . . .

The industry was thus under immense pressure to mechanize (i.e. to lower costs by labour-saving) to rationalize and to expand its production and sales, thus making up by the mass of small profits per unit he fall in the margins. Its success was vari-ble. As we have seen the actual rise in roduction and exports was gigantic; so, fter 1815, was the mechanization of itherto manual or partly-mechanized oc-upations, notably weaving. This took the orm chiefly of the general adoption of ex-ting or slightly improved machinery rath-r than of further technological revolu-on. Though the pressure for technical in-ovation increased significantly—there ere thirty-nine new patents in cotton inning, etc., in 1800–20, fifty-one in the 320s, eighty-six in the 1830s and a hun-red and fifty-six in the 1840s—the British otton industry was technologically sta-lized by the 1830s. On the other hand, ough the production per operative in-eased in the post-Napoleonic period, it d not do so to any revolutionary extent. he really substantial speed-up of opera-ons was to occur in the second half of the ntury.

There was comparable pressure on the te of interest on capital, which contem-rary theory tended to assimilate to prof-But consideration of this takes us to the xt phase of industrial development—the nstruction of a basic capital-goods in-stry.

I V

It is evident that no industrial economy n develop beyond a certain point until it ssesses adequate capital-goods capacity. is is why even today the most reliable gle index of any country's industrial po-tial is the quantity of its iron and steel oduction. But it is also evident that un-r conditions of private enterprise the ex-mely costly capital investment necessary much of this development is not likely be undertaken for the same reasons as industrialization of cotton or other con-ner goods. For these a mass market al-dy exists, at least potentially: even very

primitive men wear shirts or use household equipment and foodstuffs. The problem is merely how to put a sufficiently vast mar-ket sufficiently quickly within the purview of businessmen. But no such market exists, e.g., for heavy iron equipment such as gird-ers. It only comes into existence in the course of an industrial revolution (and not always then), and those who lock up their money in the very heavy investments re-quired even by quite modest iron-works (compared to quite large cotton-mills) be-fore it is visibly there, are more likely to be speculators, adventurers and dreamers than sound businessmen. . . .

These disadvantages applied particu-larly to metallurgy, especially of iron. Its capacity increased, thanks to a few simple innovations such as that of puddling and rolling in the 1780s, but the non-military demand for it remained relatively modest, and the military, though gratifyingly large thanks to a succession of wars between 1756 and 1815, slackened off sharply after Waterloo. It was certainly not large enough to make Britain into an outstand-ingly large producer of iron. In 1790 she out-produced France by only forty per cent or so, and even in 1800 her output was considerably less than half of the com-bined continental one, and amounted to the, by later standards, tiny figure of a quarter of a million tons. If anything the British share of world iron output tended to sink in the next decades.

Fortunately they applied less to mining, which was chiefly the mining of *coal*. For coal had the advantage of being not merely the major source of industrial pow-er in the nineteenth century, but also a major form of domestic fuel, thanks largely to the relative shortage of forests in Britain. The growth of cities, and especially of Lon-don, had caused coal mining to expand rap-idly since the late sixteenth century. By the early eighteenth it was substantially a primitive modern industry, even employing the earliest steam engines (devised for similar purposes in non-ferrous metal mining, mainly in Cornwall) for pumping. Hence coal mining hardly needed or underwent major technological revolution in our period. Its innovations were improvements rather than transformations of production. But its capacity was already immense and, by world standards, astronomic. In 1800 Britain may have produced something like ten million tons of coal, or about 90 per cent of the world output. Its nearest competitor, France, produced less than a million.

This immense industry, though probably not expanding fast enough for really massive industrialization on the modern scale, was sufficiently large to stimulate the basic invention which was to transform the capital goods industries: the railway. For the mines not only required steam engines in large quantities and of great power, but also required efficient means of transporting the great quantities of coal from coalface to shaft and especially from pithead to the point of shipment. The "tramway" or "railway" along which trucks ran was an obvious answer; to pull these trucks by stationary engines was tempting; to pull them by moving engines would not seem too impractical. Finally, the costs of overland transport of bulk goods were so high that it was likely to strike coal-owners in inland fields that the use of these short-term means of transport could be profitably extended for long-term haulage. The line from the inland coalfield of Durham to the coast (Stockton–Darlington 1825) was the first of the modern railways. Technologically the railway is the child of the mine, and especially the northern English coalmine. George Stephenson began life as a Tyneside "engineman," and for years virtually all locomotive drivers were recruited from his native coalfield.

No innovation of the Industrial Revolution has fired the imagination as much as the railway, as witness the fact that it is the only product of nineteenth century industrialization which has been fully absorbed into the imagery of popular and literate poetry. Hardly had they been proved technically feasible and profitable in England (c. 1825–30), before plans to build them were made over most of the Western world, though their execution was generally delayed. The first short lines were opened in the USA in 1827, in France in 1828 and 1835, in Germany and Belgium in 1835 and even in Russia by 1837. The reason was doubtless that no other invention revealed the power and speed of the new age to the layman as dramatically; a revelation made all the more striking by the remarkable technical maturity of even the very earliest railways. (Speeds of up to sixty miles per hour, for instance, were perfectly practicable in the 1830s, and were not substantially improved by later steam-railways.) The iron road, pushing its huge smoke-plumed snakes at the speed of wind across countries and continents, whose embankments and cuttings, bridges and stations, formed a body of public build-ing beside which the pyramids and the Roman aqueducts and even the Great Wall of China paled into provincialism, was the very symbol of man's triumph through technology.

In fact, from an economic point of view its vast expense was its chief advantage. No doubt in the long run its capacity to open up countries hitherto cut off by high transport costs from the world market, the vast increase in the speed and bulk of over-land communication it brought for men and goods, were to be of major importance. Before 1848 they were economically less important: outside Britain because railways were few, in Britain because for geographical reasons transport problems were much less intractable then in large landlocked countries. But from the perspective of the student of economic development the immense appetite of the railways for iron and steel, for coal, for heavy machinery, for labour, for capital investment, was at this stage more important. For it provided just that massive demand which was needed if the capital goods industries were to be transformed as profoundly as the cotton industry had been. In the first two decades of the railways (1830–50) the output of iron in Britain rose from 680,000 to 2,250,000, in other words it trebled. The output of coal between 1830 and 1850 also trebled from 15 million tons to 49 million tons. That dramatic rise was due primarily to the railway, for on average each mile of line required 300 tons of iron merely for track. The industrial advances which for the first time made the mass production of steel possible followed naturally in the next decades.

The reason for this sudden, immense, and quite essential expansion lay in the apparently irrational passion with which businessmen and investors threw themselves into the construction of railways. In 1830 there were a few dozen miles of railways in all the world—chiefly consisting of the line from Liverpool to Manchester. By 1840 there were over 4,500 miles, by 1850 over 23,500. Most of them were projected in a few bursts of speculative frenzy known as the "railway manias" of 1835–7 and especially in 1844–7; most of them were built in large part with British capital, British iron, machines and know-how. These investment booms appear irrational, because in fact few railways were much more profitable to the investor than other forms of enterprise, most yielded quite modest profits and many none at all; in 1855 the average interest on capital sunk in the British railways was a mere 3.7 per cent. No

doubt promoters, speculators and others did exceedingly well out of them, but the ordinary investor clearly did not. And yet by 1840 £28 millions, by 1850 £240 millions had been hopefully invested in them.

Why? The fundamental fact about Britain in the first two generations of the Industrial Revolution was, that the comfortable and rich classes accumulated income so fast and in such vast quantities as to exceed all available possibilities of spending and investment. (The annual investible surplus in the 1840s was reckoned at about £60 millions.) No doubt feudal and aristocratic societies would have succeeded in throwing a great deal of this away in riotous living, luxury building and other uneconomic activities. . . . But the bulk of the middle classes, who formed the main investing public, were still savers rather than spenders. . . .

Again, a modern socialist or welfare society would no doubt have distributed some of these vast accumulations for social purposes. In our period nothing was less likely. Virtually untaxed, the middle class therefore continued to accumulate among the hungry populace, whose hunger was the counterpart of their accumulation. And as they were not peasants, content to hoard their savings in woollen stockings or as golden bangles, they had to find profitable investment for them. But where? Existing industries, for instance, had become far too cheap to absorb more than a fraction of the available surplus for investment: even supposing the size of the cotton industry to be doubled, the capital cost would absorb only a part of it. What was needed was a sponge large enough to hold all of it. . . .

Whether it could have found other forms of home investment—for instance in building—is an academic question to which the answer is still in doubt. In fact it found the railways, which could not conceivably have been built as rapidly and on as large a scale without this torrent of capital flooding into them, especially in the middle 1840s. It was a lucky conjuncture, for the railways happened to solve virtually all the problems of the economy's growth at once. . . .

[V]

In this rather haphazard, unplanned and empirical way the first major industrial economy was built. By modern standards it was small and archaic, and its archaism still marks Britain today. By the standards of 1848 it was monumental, though also rather shocking, for its new cities were uglier, its proletariat worse off, than elsewhere, and the fog-bound, smoke-laden atmosphere in which pale masses hurried to and fro troubled the foreign visitor. But it harnessed the power of a million horses in its steam-engines, turned out two million yards of cotton cloth per year on over seventeen million mechanical spindles, dug almost fifty million tons of coal, imported and exported £170 millions worth of goods in a single year. Its trade was twice that of its nearest competitor, France: in 1780 it had only just exceeded it. Its cotton consumption was twice that of the USA, four times the French. It produced more than half the total pig-iron of the economically developed world, and used twice as much per inhabitant as the next-most industrialized country (Belgium), three times as much as the USA, more than four times as much as France. Between £200 and £300 million of British capital investment—a quarter in the USA, almost a fifth in Latin America—brought back dividends and orders from all parts of the world. It was, in fact, the "workshop of the world."

And both Britain and the world knew that the Industrial Revolution launched in these islands by and through the traders and entrepreneurs, whose only law was to buy in the cheapest market and sell without restriction in the dearest, was transforming the world. Nothing could stand in its way. The gods and kings of the past were powerless before the businessmen and steam-engines of the present.

Fellow of Newnham College and university lecturer at
Cambridge University, PHYLLIS DEANE co-authored
with W. A. Cole *British Economic Growth, 1688–1959* (1962
and 1967). The following passage from her book on the
Industrial Revolution is less technical than much of her
other writing. Like the other writers in this section, she
pays a great deal of attention to the cotton and iron
industries. Does she seem more in agreement with
Toynbee or Clapham? Why does she disagree with
Rostow? What theory would she substitute for that of his
take-off?*

Phyllis Deane

The Take-off Challenged

The Cotton Industry

Now it is time to come to grips with the
process that is generally assumed to be at
the heart of the first industrial revolution,
that is the growth of modern manufacturing industry and all that this implies—
large-scale units of operation, labour-saving machinery, and regimentation of labour, for example. There were two industries which more than any other first experienced the early revolutionary changes
in technology and economic organization
that made Britain the "workshop of the
world." They were cotton and iron. It
seems to be generally agreed that the
prime mover was the cotton industry. This
is the industry which Professor Rostow, for
example, has described as the "original

sector in the first take-off" and to which
Schumpeter referred when he asserted
that "English industrial history can
(1787–1842) ... be almost resolved into
the history of a single industry." There
seems to be no doubt of the tremendous
importance of the cotton industry in the
British industrial revolution. The interesting question is why cotton rather than any
other industry should have led the way
and how a single industry came to play
such an important part in reshaping the
economy of a nation. . . .

In retrospect, the progress of the cotton
industry looks spectacularly rapid: and so
it did to contemporaries. By the end of the
eighteenth century an industry which
contributed less than half a million pounds
to national income in the early 1760's and

*From Phyllis Deane, *The First Industrial Revolution* (London: Cambridge University Press, 1965),
pp. 84–85, 92–103, 114–118. Footnotes omitted.

exported goods worth probably no more than a quarter of a million pounds overall was adding over £5 millions to national income and a similar amount to the declared value of exports. The speed with which the imports of raw material multiplied is staggering—from under 10 million pounds per annum in the early 1780's to ten times as much in the period of Waterloo and fifty times as much in the early 1840's.

Yet in some ways the transformation of the industry was quite gradual, and it was partly this that permitted the expansion in output to be strongly sustained through wars and depressions. To begin with, expansion was achieved by taking up the slack in existing under-employed resources rather than by diverting resources from other uses. The jenny multiplied the productivity of labour in the spinning branch and enabled weavers to work regularly at their looms. The water-frame and the mule were more than mere labour-saving devices; they were substitutes for human skill, for they permitted the production of stronger, finer yarn by relatively unskilled labour. They were the beginning of a new era in economic organization, for they required a docile labour force working in the disciplined atmosphere of the factory.

The factories, however, provided only part of the immense increase in output that put cotton at the head of the British manufacturing industry. Most of it was produced by a multitude of outworkers—the domestic spinners to whom the capitalist mill-owner served out raw cotton, and the hand-loom weaver whom he supplied with the appropriate yarn. When trade was bad it could be largely concentrated in the factories and it was the domestic spinners and weavers who took the full brunt of depression. When trade was good it was generally possible to attract new spinners and hand-loom weavers without having to raise the level of wages, for there

remained a dearth of alternative avenues of employment; so that the capitalist employer reaped the main benefit of the boom, and escaped the worst effects of the slump. Having a minimum of overheads to carry on his own costs he still had a virtually inexhaustible reservoir of surplus labour and machine capacity to draw upon at will.

The persistence of the domestic cotton industry is thus not altogether surprising. On the one hand there was the natural and dogged resistance of the independent head of household to being dragooned into factory employment. The hand-loom weavers paid heavily for their independence, but they held out in force until the 1830's. On the other hand, there was the capitalist employer's reluctance to sink his capital into buildings and plant that might reduce his profits in depression when he could meet the boom demand by turning to outworkers. These two factors delayed the general adoption of the power-looms for three to four decades after it was effectively available.... It was not until the early 1840's that the number of power-loom weavers exceeded the number of handloom weavers and not until the 1850's that the latter were effectively extinguished.

Throughout the period of mechanization of the cotton industry, which could be said to have been virtually complete by 1850, the capitalist manufacturer was in a very strong position. He could shift the main burden of adjustment to technical change to the domestic producers who owned the hand-looms which were being rendered obsolete. He could readily contract or expand the working time of a large unorganized labour force composed mainly of women and children or young persons, for it was not until the 1850's that maximum-hours legislation became effective. In 1835 not many more than a quarter of the operators in cotton factories were men over the age of eighteen; 48 per cent were women and girls and 13 per cent were children under fourteen. There was not much competition for this unskilled semi-dependent labour force until the industrial revolution gathered momentum in other industries and provided additional openings for women and children in light industry. At the same time the cotton manufacturer was producing a commodity with a mass market at a price which sheltered it from competition until technical change had had time to spread to other textile industries and other counties.

There is no doubt that the sustained progress of the cotton industry in the period 1780–1850 and its leading role in the industrial revolution owed much to the favoured position in which its capitalist manufacturers found themselves. For the British industrial revolution was a spontaneous industrial revolution, not a forced industrialization as some of its successors have been. Its development depended on the unfettered response of private enterprise to economic opportunity.

A great deal of stress has been put on the role of the textile inventions in stimulating the industrial revolution and hence, understandably, on the leading role of the cotton industry. It is important, however, not to overstate their importance. For it is arguable that the fact that the cotton industry led the way at this period was due more to the drive of its entrepreneurs than to the skill of its inventors.

In examining the process of economic growth through technological change it is convenient to distinguish, as Schumpeter has done, between invention and innovation, for it is the latter which is revolutionary in its economic effects, not the former. Invention is the basic original discovery, the crucial breakthrough in the realm of either theoretical or practical knowledge which makes a change in productive methods possible. Innovation is the application of this new knowledge or the use of the new machine in practical economic activity. Thus invention can be and often is a purely external factor to the economic situation: of itself it has no economically relevant effects and it does not necessarily induce innovation. A new machine or a new technique may be known to its original inventor and accessible to producers for years or decades before it is put into practice.

Innovation, on the other hand, is the heart and core of technological progress. It is this that enlarges the possibilities of production, requires new combinations of factors and production, and creates new cost structures. Not all innovations are the product of what we should classify as invention, traceable to some identifiable conquest in the realm of theoretical or practical knowledge made in the immediate or remote past. On the other hand an invention—the steam-engine, for example—may give rise to a variety of innovations. Indeed the essence of Schumpeter's theory of innovation is that innovations tend to occur not in a steady stream, but in a series of bunches emanating from some specially fruitful invention, and hence that growth tends to take place not steadily but in waves. In any case, whether we subscribe to the theory of "bunched innovations" or not, it is evident that what we want to focus on in tracing the course of economic change is not the initial inventions or new knowledge which made it possible, but on the response of businessmen which made it real, that is, on what is sometimes called the "technological dynamism" of the economy's entrepreneurs.

The reward for innovation in a private enterprise economy is profit. The first entrepreneur to carry an innovation into effect sells a commodity at the old price but at a lower cost and takes the whole of the difference as profit. He becomes that much richer than his rivals. His example, or rather the size of his profit, encourages imitation and, as the number of his imitators increases, two factors tend to narrow the gap between price and cost: (1) competition between producers to invade existing markets, which tends to diminish price, and (2) competition for existing factors of production which are in inelastic supply. If the gap narrows too quickly the rate of innovation falls off smartly both because entrepreneurs have less incentive to change their methods and because they have smaller profits with which to finance new kinds of capital equipment.

The interesting thing about the cotton industry at this period is that although prices fell steeply—between 1815 and 1845 for example, the prices of cotton cloth exports fell by about three-quarters—profits were well maintained. In part of course this was because producers continued to innovate, though perhaps not as fast as they could have done. . . .

But possibly the most important reason for the cotton industry's ability to maintain its profits and hence its rate of investment was the fact that it enjoyed an almost inexhaustible low-priced labour supply. While women and girls and pauper children could be put to work for 12 to 16 hours a day in cotton-mills at bare subsistence wages and while the sons of hand-loom weavers were prepared to adopt their fathers' trade and to work longer and longer hours for a smaller and smaller return, the cotton industry could nearly always command more labour than it needed and wages stayed pitifully low. Between about 1820 and about 1845 the industry's total output quadrupled and total incomes generated in Britain increased by 50 per cent, but the workers' wages barely rose at all.

In this surely lies one of the most important reasons for the powerfully sustained growth of the cotton industry over the period 1780–1850. An increasing proportion of the incomes that it generated went to the entrepreneurs, and they in their turn were ready to plough back a substantial proportion of earnings into more plant and machinery. This high rate of ploughback meant two things: (1) that the industry went on expanding its capacity to produce and increasing its economies of scale. . . . (2) that the industry went on improving its equipment even though radical changes in technique were not as rapid as they could have been, given the accessible range of inventions; the fact is that even where technical change is unspectacular it tends to be continuous wherever there is a high rate of investment, for new machines tend to be better than their predecessors, even if they are not substantially different from them, so that a high rate of investment, which involves a high rate of introduction of new machines, generates a continuous flow of these minor improvements.

When the supply of labour became somewhat less elastic in the late 1840's and after, the industry's rate of growth slackened. The reasons for the tightening up of the labour supply were several. First of all there was the fact that certain pockets of technological unemployment—the hand-loom weavers constitute the classic case— were liquidated by depression and sheer starvation. Secondly, the social conscience was beginning to revolt against the callous exploitation of child and female labour and the shorter-hours legislation was gradually beginning to take effect. Thirdly, other industries were beginning to compete for labour, particularly when the railroad boom developed and stimulated trade and industry in general, and when the other textile trades began seriously to mechanize. These factors slowed the rate of expansion of the industry but accelerated the growth of incomes from employment in the industry. Between 1845 and 1870, for example, the cotton industry's output roughly doubled, that is to say it grew at about half the pace of the preceding 25 years, but the workers' share in the incomes which it generated grew a little faster than the total. By this time cotton had no claim to be the leading sector in the industrial revolution or to be setting the pace for national economic growth.

To sum up, then, it is not difficult to see why and how the cotton industry grew from insignificance to principal manufacture within little more than a generation and became the first British industry to adopt labour-saving power-driven machinery on a large scale and to produce for an international market. There is no doubt that its spectacular success captured the imagination of contemporaries and set an example which may well have been an important factor in encouraging technical change in other industries. But it is possible, nevertheless, to exaggerate the direct influence of this industry in the first industrial revolution. The fact is that its connections with other important British industries were not large enough to set off powerful secondary repercussions. In so far as it directly and immediately induced technological change in other industries it was in the textile processing trades which, taken over-all, did not constitute a very significant industrial sector. The principal raw material was entirely imported, so that the links in this direction were with non-British rather than British industries. It was a long time before cotton manufacture began to use much coal. The industry was highly localized so that it did not create a spreading demand for new transport and building facilities. To begin with, machinery was made of wood and was produced at the factories by factory labour. It was not until the second quarter of the nineteenth century that a textile-machinery industry developed on any scale. In short, the industry's links with other major producing sectors were quite limited and its repercussions on the rest of the economy were indirect rather than direct. In particular its remarkable expansion was not sufficiently powerful or pervasive in itself to stimulate the English industrial revolution, though it was certainly an important part of it. In order to complete the picture we need to examine the process of technological change in other industries which were independently transformed over the period 1780–1850.

The Iron Industry

The other British industry whose technology was revolutionized in the last quarter of the eighteenth century was the iron industry. As with cotton, the effect of the technological transformation was to satisfy a long-established need with the production of a commodity which was so different, both in quality and in price, from what had hitherto been produced in Britain that it was virtually a new commodity.

In certain other respects the changes in the iron industry's system of production which were involved in the industrial revolution were less radical than the changes in the cotton industry. The textile industries were transformed in organization as well as in technology. There the domestic-handicraft type of manufacture gradually changed into a capitalistic factory industry. But the iron industry was already capitalistically organized. Its development in the sixteenth century was one of the outstanding examples of technological and organizational change which Professor Nef adduced to support his argument that the origins of the industrial revolution lie in the period 1540–1640. Professor Ashton makes the point forcibly in his study of the iron industry in the Industrial Revolution:

From the earliest period of which we have exact information, iron-making in this country has been conducted on capitalistic lines—capitalistic not only in that the workers are dependent upon an employer for their raw material and market, but also in that they are brought together in a "works," are paid wages and perform their duties under conditions not dissimilar to those of any large industry of modern times. The scale of operations has increased enormously: the sapling has become an oak, deep-rooted and wide-spread; technique has been revolutionized. But in structure and organization there is no fundamental change.

Another feature of the industrial revolution in iron and steel which distinguishes it from that of the cotton industry is that the former expanded on the strength of domestic raw materials. The eighteenth-century innovations enabled British industries to turn from charcoal (a dwindling resource) to coal (which was abundantly available) and from imported to native ores. Whereas the cotton industry achieved its spectacular economies largely by saving labour, the iron industry did so by economizing in raw materials, that is by using materials that were abundant and cheap in place of materials that were scarce and dear.

The third distinguishing characteristic of the industrial revolution in iron is that its final breakthrough seems to have depended at least as much on an invention that was external to the industry as on the inventions of the iron industry proper. Abraham Darby had successfully smelted iron with coke as early as 1709. In a sense this was the beginning of the end of the charcoal-iron industry. But it was only the beginning. Even when the iron-masters had learned first to select the types of iron ore and coal so as to produce an acceptable quality of pig-iron, and then to get rid of impurities in the final cast-iron by resmelting the pig in foundry furnaces, the innovation was still not profitable enough to persuade existing producers to move from their woodlands to the coalfields. Coke was a slow-burning fuel compared with charcoal and needed power to secure an adequate blast. Water-power was used, of course, but was subject to seasonal variations. It was not until Boulton and Watt had developed an efficient steam-engine, around 1775, that the furnaces were able to generate a blast strong enough and continuous enough to make coke-smelting a manifestly more efficient way of producing pig-iron in any circumstances. Till then the use of coke was confined to only a few furnaces while the majority still used charcoal. Even in Darby's own iron-works at Coalbrookdale in Shropshire coke was not exclusively used.

Finally there was a fourth reason why we might expect the iron industry to have played a very different role to that played by cotton in the British industrial revolution. This is the fact that iron was primarily a producer's good, subject to a derived rather than a direct demand and, partly in consequence, was subject to an inelastic demand. The expansion of a producers' good industry depends on economic conditions in general or on the growth of industries which consume its products. In some ways the iron industry was able to widen its market when its price dropped, to create new demands by replacing other products—iron began to be used widely in construction work (bridges, and building for example), in the last quarter of the eighteenth century, and in 1784 the plant of a London flour-mill was built entirely of cast-iron. But until towards the middle of the nineteenth century when the demand for iron to construct railroads, locomotives, ships, machinery, gas and sanitation systems greatly expanded the range of its outlets, the industry's expansion was severely limited by factors on the side of demand. So that although the changes in its production function were radical enough and its price fell steeply, demand was too inelastic to permit a *corresponding* rise in the amount sold. There had to be some progress in industrialization before the iron industry could develop and sustain an accelerating momentum comparable to that of the cotton industry.

These four characteristics of the iron industry in the last quarter of the eighteenth century—its traditions of capitalistic large-scale organization, its new demand for domestically produced raw materials, its dependence on the steam-engine, and its inelastic demand—rendered the role it played in the British industrial revolution very different from that of cotton. Whether it was less or more important in this respect is a matter of legitimate doubt. Professor Rostow, who gave cotton the role of leading sector in his model of the British take-off, apparently considered iron less important, but this view seems to be largely a consequence of the rather rigid frame of thought imposed by his "stages of growth" analysis. If it is necessary to think of the Industrial Revolution, as Rostow does, in terms of a specific period of two to three decades within which the crucial changes in methods of production had *decisive* consequences, then the fact that he ascribes the British industrial revolution to the period following 1783 and the fact that the cotton industry did (and the iron industry did not) reach a relatively massive proportion within the British economy in that period, lead inevitably to the conclusion that cotton must have been the leading sector. If, on the other hand, we regard the Industrial Revolution as having effec-

tively evolved over a longer and less rigidly defined span of years—roughly within the period 1770–1850—and judge an industry's importance in the process by the weight and range of its repercussions on the rest of the economy, then the iron industry's claim to have played the key role is quite impressive. Here surely in its forward and backward linkages with the rest of the economy—in the demand for coal and iron and extensive transport and capital facilities on the one hand, and in the reduction of costs for a wide range of manufactured goods as well as in the building and transport industries on the other—we can see the iron industry playing a more powerful and pervasive role in the process of British industrialization than did cotton.

But it is not really necessary, or even useful, to persist in the attempt to identify a single industry to which can be ascribed the leading part in precipitating the British industrial revolution. A more satisfying and convincing, if less dramatic, case can be made for the view that the first industrialization was the result of a cluster of innovations in Schumpeter's sense of the term. Some of the relevant *inventions* belong to an earlier period: but it is the *innovations,* the general adoption of the inventions, that counts. This cluster of innovations was decisive for three main reasons: (1) because they occurred at roughly the same period of time, (2) because they came when Britain's naval supremacy and commercial contacts enabled her to take advantage of rising European and North American incomes, and (3) because they reinforced each other in certain important respects. The concentration of the cluster was all-important. It made the process of industrialization a great deal more profitable than it would otherwise have been, and gave the British economy a lead over its rivals which ensured that the process would go on being profitable so long as the lead was maintained. . . .

In short, the iron industry played a role in British industrialization that was both pervasive and stimulating. It provided cheaply and abundantly the commodity on which, more than on any other single material except coal, modern industry was to depend for its essential equipment. Nineteenth-century industrialization may indeed have been started by the textile innovations of the end of the eighteenth century. But continuous industrialization depended on the availability of coal and iron, and would have been inconceivable without the steam-engine and the technical progress in the iron industry which also took effect in the last three decades or so of the eighteenth century. Even today underdeveloped countries seeking a means of escape from economic stagnation are inclined to see the establishment of a steel industry as a first step. They may not always be right in this assessment of their current problem but it is not difficult to see why they drew this lesson from nineteenth-century British experience.

The Chronology of Innovation

The process of industrialization which gathered momentum in Britain during the second half of the eighteenth century and initiated the sustained upward movement of real incomes that the western world now takes for granted, involved revolutionary changes in the structure and organization of the economy. The origins of some of these changes can be traced to earlier centuries. Some of them are still working themselves out. It is generally agreed, however, that the crucial transformation occurred fairly rapidly—certainly within the century between 1750 and 1850, probably in a considerably shorter time. The temptation to time it narrowly, to identify a relatively short period of time within

which the crucial change can be said to have taken place, is very strong. The discontinuities of history are more dramatic than its continuities, and it is natural to want to give them a precise time reference.

So the chronology of the industrial revolution has become a fruitful source of controversy. There are those who would like to trace its beginnings back to the beginnings of organized manufacturing industry itself and others who insist that it is not over yet, even for a fully industrialized country like Britain. There are those who find overwhelming evidence for significant discontinuity in the last quarter of the eighteenth century: and others like Clapham and Schumpeter who are equally convinced that "if one wishes to refer the industrial revolution to a definite historical epoch it can be located more justifiably in the second quarter of the nineteenth than in the end of the eighteenth century."

What answer one gives to this kind of problem of interpretation depends of course on what precise question one is asking of the data: in particular, in this context, what one means by the "crucial" changes. Crucial in what sense? Was it the very beginnings of organized industry that constituted the significant change? If so, one must go back like Nef to Tudor times and earlier and give up all hope of ascribing the industrial revolution to a definite epoch. Was it when technical change assumed a distinctively modern character, involving the substitution of machinery for man-power, of mineral for biological sources of energy, of factory organization for domestic industry? If so, presumably it is the cluster of innovations which took effect in the last three decades of the eighteenth century which must engage our attention. Was it when modern industry grew massive enough to shape the structure of the national economy, to set the pace of economic growth, to determine standards of life and ways of living for people in general? If so, we should probably focus on the beginnings of the railway age in the second quarter of the nineteenth century.

More recently Professor Rostow has given added interest to the problem of identifying and of timing the British industrial revolution by making it the basis of his theory of the stages of economic growth; that is, viewing it as the prototype of the take-off, "that decisive interval in the history of a society when growth becomes its normal condition." This of course is going much further than his predecessors have done in the ancient controversy over the chronology of the industrial revolution. What they were trying to do was to suggest a chronology of British industrialization which could be useful in the attempt to analyse the causes, character and consequence of the central process. What Professor Rostow has tried to do is to interpret British economic history in a way that has immediate policy implications for those concerned with the problems of today's pre-industrial economies, and this leads him to view the industrial revolution as something nearer to an *event* than to a *process*. So that although he claims that his is a return to an "old fashioned way of looking at economic development" it is indeed a highly novel way of looking at economic history. If he is right and it *is* possible to identify, in the history of those countries which have successfully industrialized, a period of two or three decades within which the transformation was sufficiently decisive to ensure a continuance not only of the process of industrialization but also of the growth in average productivity and standards of living, then it is certainly important for today's policy makers to understand the mechanics of the change. For presumably in principle the changes which

took place spontaneously in past "take offs" can be induced by appropriate government action in today's underdeveloped countries.

Examination of the historical record for particular countries in the light of the "take-off" as formalized by Professor Rostow has proved immensely fruitful in focusing the attention of economists and economic historians on the significant discontinuities implied in the fact of an industrial revolution. However, it is clear that the concept of the "take-off" is a dramatic simplification which does not stand up to a systematic attempt to relate it to the known facts in any detail or to give it a definite chronology. In the British case, for example, the choice of the period 1783–1802 as the one in which the process of industrialization became in some sense irreversible is, while understandable, not justified by detailed analysis. The period contained some significant developments in the cotton and iron industries, it included the canal mania, it saw an acceleration in the pace of enclosures and of population growth and above all it was characterized by a sharp upsurge in the amount of overseas trade entering and leaving British ports. Each of these developments, however, formed part of a historical continuum in which the period 1783–1802 was not unique. Population, for example, and enclosures had begun their acceleration earlier and reached their peak later. The canal mania was preceded by an earlier burst of activity in canal construction which, if it was less powerful was certainly unprecedented; and it was followed a generation later by the more spectacular and important railway mania. The cotton and iron industries had begun to transform their techniques in earlier decades and by 1802 were still too small in part of total economic activity to carry the national economy along by their own weight. The most significant change of trend which fits this period is that for overseas trade and any estimate of national output which is heavily dependent on the foreign-trade series suggests an acceleration in the national rate of growth during this period. On the other hand, overseas trade was highly vulnerable to the fortunes of war, and the upsurge of the 1780's and 1790's can easily be explained by war conditions; the growth of trade in the 1780's, for example, can be seen as a rebound from the abnormally low levels to which it had been pushed by the American War, and the prolonged growth of the 1790's must have owed a good deal to the fact that Britain's main continental competitors were so largely kept off the seas by the French wars. If we allow for these special circumstances, the upsurge in foreign trade which characterized the period 1783–1802 is not as spectacular as it might appear at first.

What all this amounts to, in effect, is that we cannot justify the choice of such a tightly specified and narrow period as 1783–1802 to represent the span of years within which the industrial revolution took the kind of shape that made continuing future industrialization inevitable. Yet the questions raised by Professor Rostow's attempt to give a time reference to the crucial changes in the industrial revolution remain interesting and important. We know, for example, that some of today's underdeveloped countries have begun to industrialize and have failed either to maintain their original impetus or to generate sustained economic growth. If we knew more about the mechanics of past industrial revolutions, in particular if we could say whether there was an identifiable stage in the process beyond which growth seemed to be inevitable, it might help us to understand the conditions of successful industrialization. In this connection the first industrial revolution, because it was spontaneous, has a special interest.

One thing that is clear about modern economic growth is that it depends on, more that anything else, a continuing process of technical change. What the industrial revolution did was to increase substantially the flow of innovations embodied in the nation's economic activity and to turn it into a continuous, if fluctuating, flow. In a pre-industrial economy technical progress tends to be exceptional and intermittent. In an industrialized economy it is accepted as part of the normal order of things. Each generation expects to be able to improve on the productive techniques of its fathers. Each new machine is expected to be in some way more efficient than the machine it replaces in the production process.

The analysis of the effect of the Industrial Revolution has divided historians into "pessimists," and "optimists." This book's first pair of pessimists and optimists is a German, FRIEDRICH ENGELS (1820–1895) and an Englishman, G. R. PORTER (1792–1852). Engels was twenty-four years old when he wrote *The Conditions of the Working Class in England in 1844,* from which a selection is taken. It resulted from his two-year visit to England to learn the textile business in some firms in which his father was a partner. He met Karl Marx for the first time just before he left for England in 1842, but the meeting was far from friendly. This book, as much as anything, initiated their life-long collaboration, which included, among other works, *The Communist Manifesto.* The book was to have a great influence on socialist and nonsocialist alike.

For his part, Porter spent most of his adult life heading the statistical department of the Board of Trade. The most important of his numerous books on economic matters was *The Progress of the Nation* (1838), which enjoyed two revised editions and from which a selection is given here. The views of both Engels and Porter have been superceded by more accurate accounts. In the light of the later selections in this book, which of these two contemporary accounts is the more penetrating?

Friedrich Engels, G. R. Porter

A Contemporary Pessimist and Optimist

Friedrich Engels, *Deterioration of Living and Working Conditions Under Industrialization**

Let us see what pay for his work society gives the working-man in the form of dwelling, clothing, food, what sort of subsistence it grants those who contribute most to the maintenance of society; and, first, let us consider the dwellings.

Every great city has one or more slums, where the working-class is crowded together. True, poverty often dwells in hidden alleys close to the palaces of the rich; but, in general, a separate territory has been assigned to it, where, removed from the sight of the happier classes, it may struggle along as it can. These slums are pretty equally arranged in all the great towns of England, the worst houses in the worst quarters of the towns; usually one or two-storied cottages in long rows, perhaps with cellars used as dwellings, almost always

*Friedrich Engels, *The Conditions of the Working Class in England in 1844* (London, 1892), pp. 26–27, 69, 72–74, 98–99, 101–102, 105–108, 150–151, 160–161, 166–167, 178–180. Footnotes omitted.

irregularly built. These houses of three or four rooms and a kitchen form, throughout England, some parts of London excepted, the general dwellings of the working-class. The streets are generally unpaved, rough, dirty, filled with vegetable and animal refuse, without sewers or gutters, but supplied with foul, stagnant pools instead. Moreover, ventilation is impeded by the bad, confused method of building of the whole quarter, and since many human beings here live crowded into a small space, the atmosphere that prevails in these working-men's quarters may readily be imagined. Further, the streets serve as drying grounds in fine weather; lines are stretched across from house to house, and hung with wet clothing.

Let us investigate some of the slums in their order. London comes first, and in London the famous rookery of St. Giles which is now, at last, about to be penetrated by a couple of broad streets. St. Giles is in the midst of the most populous part of the town, surrounded by broad, splendid avenues in which the gay world of London idles about, in the immediate neighbourhood of Oxford Street, Regent Street, of Trafalgar Square and the Strand. It is a disorderly collection of tall, three or four-storied houses, with narrow, crooked, filthy streets, in which there is quite as much life as in the great thoroughfares of the town, except that, here, people of the working-class only are to be seen. A vegetable market is held in the street, baskets with vegetables and fruits, naturally all bad and hardly fit to use, obstruct the sidewalk still further, and from these, as well as from the fish-dealers' stalls, arises a horrible smell. The houses are occupied from cellar to garret, filthy within and without, and their appearance is such that no human being could possibly wish to live in them. But all this is nothing in comparison with the dwellings in the narrow courts and alleys between the streets, entered by covered passages between the houses, in which the filth and tottering ruin surpass all description. Scarcely a whole window-pane can be found, the walls are crumbling, doorposts and window-frames loose and broken, doors of old boards nailed together, or altogether wanting in this thieves' quarter where no doors are needed, there being nothing to steal. Heaps of garbage and ashes lie in all directions, and the foul liquids emptied before the doors gather in stinking pools. Here live the poorest of the poor, the worst paid workers with thieves and the victims of prostitution indiscriminately huddled together, the majority Irish or of Irish extraction, and those who have not yet sunk in the whirlpool of moral ruin which surrounds them, sinking daily deeper, losing daily more and more of their power to resist the demoralising influence of want, filth, and evil surroundings.

Nor is St. Giles the only . . . slum. . . .

So much for the dwellings of the workers in the largest cities and towns. The manner in which the need of a shelter is satisfied furnishes a standard for the manner which all other necessities are supplied. That in these filthy holes a ragged, ill-fed population alone can dwell is a safe conclusion, and such is the fact. The clothing of the working-people, in the majority of cases, is in a very bad condition. The material used for it is not of the best adapted. Wool and linen have almost vanished from the wardrobe of both sexes, and cotton has taken their place. Shirts are made of bleached or coloured cotton goods; the dresses of the women are chiefly of cotton print goods, and woolen petticoats are rarely to be seen on the washline. The men wear chiefly trousers of fustian or other heavy cotton goods, and jackets or coats of the same. Fustian has become the proverbial costume of the working-men, who a

alled "fustian jackets," and call them-
lves so in contrast to the gentlemen who
ear broadcloth, which latter words are
sed as characteristic for the middle-
ass. . . .

The whole clothing of the working-class,
ven assuming it to be in good condition, is
ttle adapted to the climate. The damp
ir of England, with its sudden changes of
mperature, more calculated than any
ther to give rise to colds, obliges almost
ie whole middle-class to wear flannel
ext the skin, about the body, and flannel
arfs and shirts are in almost universal
se. Not only is the working-class deprived
 this precaution, it is scarcely ever in a
osition to use a thread of woollen cloth-
ig; and the heavy cotton goods, though
icker, stiffer, and heavier than woollen
othes, afford much less protection against
old and wet, remain damp much longer
cause of their thickness and the nature
 the stuff, and have nothing of the com-
act density of fulled woollen cloths. . . .
Ioreover, the working-man's clothing is,
 most cases, in bad condition, and there
 the oft-recurring necessity for placing the
st pieces in the pawnbroker's shop. . . .
As with clothing, so with food. . . . The
otatoes which the workers buy are usually
oor, the vegetables wilted, the cheese old
id of poor quality, the bacon rancid, the
eat lean, tough, taken from old, often dis-
sed, cattle, or such as have died a natu-
l death, and not fresh even then, often
lf decayed. . . . But they are victimised
 yet another way by the money-greed of
e middle-class. Dealers and manufactur-
s adulterate all kinds of provisions in an
rocious manner, and without the
ghtest regard to the health of the con-
mers. . . .
The habitual food of the individual
orking-man naturally varies according to
s wages. The better paid workers, espe-
illy those in whose families every mem-

ber is able to earn something, have good
food as long as this state of things lasts;
meat daily and bacon and cheese for supper. Where wages are less, meat is used
only two or three times a week, and the
proportion of bread and potatoes increases.
Descending gradually, we find the animal
food reduced to a small piece of bacon cut
up with the potatoes; lower still, even this
disappears, and there remain only bread,
cheese, porridge, and potatoes, until on the
lowest round of the ladder, among the Irish,
potatoes form the sole food. As an ac-
companiment, weak tea, with perhaps a
little sugar, milk, or spirits, is universally
drunk. Tea is regarded in England, and
even in Ireland, as quite as indispensable
as coffee in Germany, and where no tea is
used, the bitterest poverty reigns. But all
this pre-supposes that the workman has
work. When he has none, he is wholly at
the mercy of accident, and eats what is giv-
en him, what he can beg or steal. And, if
he gets nothing, he simply starves, as we
have seen. . . .

To sum up briefly the facts thus far
cited. The great towns are chiefly
inhabited by working-people, since in the
best case there is one bourgeois for two
workers, often for three, here and there for
four; these workers have no property whatsoever of their own, and live wholly upon
wages, which usually go from hand to
mouth. Society, composed wholly of atoms,
does not trouble itself about them; leaves
them to care for themselves and their families, yet supplies them no means of
doing this in an efficient and permanent
manner. Every working-man, even the
best, is therefore constantly exposed to loss
of work and food, that is to death by starvation, and many perish in this way. The
dwellings of the workers are everywhere
badly planned, badly built, and kept in
the worst condition, badly ventilated,
damp, and unwholesome. The inhabitants

are confined to the smallest possible space, and at least one family usually sleeps in each room. The interior arrangement of the dwellings is poverty-stricken in various degrees, down to the utter absence of even the most necessary furniture. The clothing of the workers, too, is generally scanty, and that of great multitudes is in rags. The food is, in general, bad; often almost unfit for use, and in many cases, at least at times, insufficient in quantity, so that, in extreme cases, death by starvation results. Thus the working-class of the great cities offers a graduated scale of conditions in life, in the best cases a temporarily endurable existence for hard work and good wages, good and endurable, that is, from the worker's standpoint; in the worst cases, bitter want, reaching even homelessness and death by starvation. The average is much nearer the worst case than the best. And this series does not fall into fixed classes, so that one can say, this fraction of the working-class is well off, has always been so, and remains so. If that is the case here and there, if single branches of work have in general an advantage over others, yet the condition of the workers in each branch is subject to such great fluctuations that a single working-man may be so placed as to pass through the whole range from comparative comfort to the extremest need, even to death by starvation, while almost every English working-man can tell a tale of marked changes of fortune. . . .

How is it possible, under such conditions, for the lower class to be healthy and long lived? What else can be expected than an excessive mortality, an unbroken series of epidemics, a progressive deterioration in the physique of the working population? Let us see how the facts stand.

That the dwellings of the workers in the worst portions of the cities, together with the other conditions of life of this class, engender numerous diseases, is attested on all sides. . . . Typhus, that universally diffused affliction, is attributed by the official report on the sanitary condition of the working-class, directly to the bad state of the dwellings in the matters of ventilation, drainage, and cleanliness. This report compiled, it must not be forgotten, by the leading physicians of England from the testimony of other physicians asserts that a single ill-ventilated court, a single blind alley without drainage, is enough to engender fever, and usually does engender it, especially if the inhabitants are greatly crowded. . . .

Another category of diseases arises directly from the food rather than the dwelling of the workers. The food of the labourer indigestible enough in itself, is utterly unfit for young children, and he has neither means nor time to get his children more suitable food. . . . Scrofula is almost universal among the working-class, and scrofulous parents have scrofulous children, especially when the original influences continue in full force to operate upon the inherited tendency of the children. A second consequence of this insufficient bodily nourishment, during the years of growth and development, is rachitis, which is extremely common among the children of the working-class. . . . The neglect to which the great mass of working-men's children are condemned leaves ineradicable traces and brings the enfeeblement of the whole race of workers with it. Add to this, the unsuitable clothing of this class, the impossibility of precautions against colds, the necessity of toiling so long as health permits, want made more dire when sickness appears, and the only too common lack of all medical assistance; and we have a rough idea of the sanitary condition of the English working-class. . . .

The result of all these influences is a general enfeeblement of the frame in the working-class. . . . Their enfeebled consti tutions are unable to resist disease, and are therefore seized by it on every occasion. Hence they age prematurely, and die early. On this point the mortality statistics supply unquestionable testimony.

According to the Report of Registrar-General Graham, the annual death-rate of all England and Wales is something less than 2¼ per cent. That is to say, out of forty-five persons, one dies every year. This was the average for the year 1839–40. In 1840–41 the mortality diminished somewhat, and the death-rate was but one in forty-six. But in the great cities the proportion is wholly different. I have before me official tables of mortality (*Manchester Guardian*, July 31st, 1844), according to which the death-rate of several large towns is as follows: In Manchester, including Chorlton and Salford, one in 32.72; and excluding Chorlton and Salford, one in 30.75. In Liverpool, including West Derby (suburb), 31.90, and excluding West Derby, 29.90; while the average of all the districts of Cheshire, Lancashire, and Yorkshire cited, including a number of wholly or partially rural districts and many small towns, with a total population of 2,172,506 for the whole, is one death in 39.80 persons. . . .

That this enormous shortening of life falls chiefly upon the working-class, that the general average is improved by the smaller mortality of the upper and middle-classes, is attested upon all sides. One of the most recent depositions is that of a physician, Dr. P. H. Holland, in Manchester, who investigated Chorlton-on-Medlock, a suburb of Manchester, under official commission. He divided the houses and streets into three classes each, and ascertained . . . that the mortality in the *streets* of the second class is 18 per cent greater, and in the streets of the third class 68 per cent greater than in those of the first class; that the mortality in the *houses* of

the second class is 31 per cent greater, and in the third class 78 per cent greater than in those of the first class; that the mortality in those bad streets which were improved, decreased 25 per cent. He closes with the remark, very frank for an English bourgeois:

When we find the rate of mortality four times as high in some streets as in others, and twice as high in whole classes of streets as in other classes, and further find that it is all but invariably high in those streets which are in bad condition, and almost invariably low in those whose condition is good, we cannot resist the conclusion that multitudes of our fellow-creatures, *hundreds of our immediate neighbours,* are annually destroyed for want of the most evident precautions.

The Report on the Sanitary Condition of the Working-Class [1842] contains information which attests the same fact . . . and no one need wonder that in Manchester . . . more than fifty-seven per cent of the children of the working-class perish before the fifth year, while but twenty per cent of the children of the higher classes, and not quite thirty-two per cent of the children of all classes in the country die under five years of age. . . .

The great mortality among children of the working-class, and especially among those of the factory operatives, is proof enough of the unwholesome conditions under which they pass their first year. These influences are at work, of course, among the children who survive, but not quite so powerfully as upon those who succumb. The result in the most favourable case is a tendency to disease, or some check in development, and consequent less than normal vigour of the constitution. A nine years old child of a factory operative that has grown up in want, privation, and changing conditions, in cold and damp, with insufficient clothing and unwholesome dwellings, is far from having the working force of a child brought up under healthier conditions. At nine years of age it is sent into the mill to work 6½ hours (formerly 8, earlier still, 12 to 14, even 16 hours) daily, until the thirteenth year; then twelve hours until the eighteenth year. The old enfeebling influences continue, while the work is added to them. It is not to be denied that a child of nine years, even an operative's child, can hold out through 6½ hours' daily work, without any one being able to trace visible bad results in its development directly to this cause; but in no case can its presence in the damp, heavy air of the factory, often at once warm and wet, contribute to good health; and, in any case, it is unpardonable to sacrifice to the greed of an unfeeling bourgeoisie the time of children which should be devoted solely to their physical and mental development, withdraw them from school and the fresh air, in order to wear them out for the benefit of the manufacturers. . . .

The influence of factory-work upon the female physique also is marked and peculiar. . . .

That factory operatives undergo more difficult confinement than other women is testified to by several midwives and accoucheurs, and also that they are more liable to miscarriage. Moreover, they suffer from the general enfeeblement common to all operatives, and, when pregnant, continue to work in the factory up to the hour of delivery, because otherwise they lose their wages and are made to fear that they may be replaced if they stop away too soon. It frequently happens that women are at work one evening and delivered the next morning, and the case is none too rare of their being delivered in the factory among the machinery. And if the gentlemen of the bourgeoisie find nothing particularly shocking in this, their wives will perhaps admit that it is a piece of cruelty, an infamous act of barbarism, indirectly to

force a pregnant woman to work twelve or thirteen hours daily (formerly still longer), up to the day of her delivery, in a standing position, with frequent stoopings. But this is not all. If these women are not obliged to resume work within two weeks, they are thankful, and count themselves fortunate. Many come back to the factory after eight, and even after three to four days, to resume full work. . . .

A pretty list of diseases engendered purely by the hateful money greed of the manufacturers! Women made unfit for childbearing, children deformed, men enfeebled, limbs crushed, whole generations wrecked, afflicted with disease and infirmity, purely to fill the purses of the bourgeoisie. And when one reads of the barbarism of single cases, how children are seized naked in bed by the overlookers, and driven with blows and kicks to the factory, their clothing over their arms, how their sleepiness is driven off with blows, how they fall asleep over their work nevertheless, how one poor child sprang up, still asleep, at the call of the overlooker, and mechanically went through the operations of its work after its machine was stopped; when one reads how children, too tired to go home, hide away in the wool in the drying-room to sleep there, and could only be driven out of the factory with straps; how many hundreds came home so tired every night, that they could eat no supper for sleepiness and want of appetite, that their parents found them kneeling by the bedside, where they had fallen asleep during their prayers. . . .

Further, the slavery in which the bourgeoisie holds the proletariat chained, is nowhere more conspicuous than in the factory system. Here ends all freedom in law and in fact. The operative must be in the mill at half-past five in the morning; if he comes a couple of minutes too late, he is fined; if he comes ten minutes too late, he is not let in until breakfast is over, and a quarter of the day's wages is withheld, though he loses only two and one-half hours' work out of twelve. He must eat, drink, and sleep at command. For satisfying the most imperative needs, he is vouchsafed the least possible time absolutely required by them. Whether his dwelling is a half-hour or a whole one removed from the factory does not concern his employer. The despotic bell calls him from his bed, his breakfast, his dinner.

What a time he has of it, too, inside the factory! Here the employer is absolute lawgiver . . . . And such rules as these usually are! For instance: 1. The doors are closed ten minutes after work begins, and thereafter no one is admitted until the breakfast hour; whoever is absent during this time forfeits 3d. per loom. 2. Every power-loom weaver detected absenting himself at another time, while the machinery is in motion, forfeits for each hour and each loom, 3d. Every person who leaves the room during working-hours, without obtaining permission from the overlooker, forfeits 3d. 3. Weavers who fail to supply themselves with scissors forfeit, per day, 1d. 4. All broken shuttles, brushes, oil-cans, wheels, window panes, etc., must be paid for by the weaver. 5. No weaver to stop work without giving a week's notice. The manufacturer may dismiss any employee without notice for bad work or improper behaviour. 6. Every operative detected speaking to another, singing or whistling, will be fined 6d.; for leaving his place during working-hours, 6d.: . . . It may be said that such rules are necessary in a great, complicated factory, in order to insure the harmonious working of the different parts; it may be asserted that such a severe discipline is as necessary here as in an army. . . . But these operatives are condemned from their ninth year to their death to live under the sword, physically

and mentally. They are worse slaves than the negroes in America, for they are more sharply watched, and yet it is demanded of them that they shall live like human beings, shall think and feel like men! Verily, this they can do only under glowing hatred towards their oppressors, and towards that order of things which place them in such a position, which degrades them to machines.

G. R. Porter, *Progress Shown by Population, Wage, and Consumption Statistics**

It must, of course, be of the first importance, as respects the progress of any people, that the productive part of its population should be large in proportion to the number of children on the one hand, and of aged persons on the other, who must, in some degree, be considered as dependent upon those in the active period of life. If we assume that this active period is to be found between the ages of fifteen and fifty, the comparative condition in this respect of the United Kingdom, in 1821 and 1841, [will show] . . . that, in each division of the kingdom, there was a larger proportion of the population between the ages of fifteen and fifty in 1841 than in 1821. . . .

The following table, taken from the reports of the Registrar-General, gives the number of deaths and the proportions occurring at different ages during each of the three years ending 30 June, 1839, and 1840, and during the entire years of 1841 and 1842. . . .

The numbers dying in proportion to the population during those years, as ascertained from actual registration, were [one in 46.63 in 1838–1839, one in 44.76 in 1839–1840, one in 44.73 in 1840–1841; for

*From G. R. Porter, *The Progress of the Nation* (London, 1847), pp. 16, 19–20, 23–24, 26–27, 455, 459–460, 532–534, 547–548, 552–555, 562–563, 572, 574, 580–582, 588, 590–591, 637–638. Footnotes omitted.

children under five, one in 38.92 in 1841 and one in 39.82 in 1842.] . . .

The estimated proportions of deaths in the course of the preceding century . . . [show] a continually diminishing mortality [from one in 39⅘ in 1700 to one in 47¾ in 1800.]

The Census Commissioners for 1841 have given a statement . . . of the ages of 348,018 persons, viz., 175,843 males and 172,175 females who were buried in the metropolis during the ten years, 1831 to 1840. . . .

[According to it] the proportion of persons dying under twenty years of age is thus seen to be still diminishing, this proportion during the ten years ending with 1840 having been 44⁶/₁₀ per cent.

It is not possible to state the numbers of persons who, at several periods, have inhabited that part of the metropolis which is included within the Bills of Mortality; no precise calculation can therefore be given as to the proportion of deaths to population occurring at different intervals.

It will appear . . . that the improvement in this respect which has been progressive since the middle of the last century, has become much more rapid since the beginning of the present. The difference observable between the proportionate number of deaths under twenty, in the decade commencing with 1751, and in that ending with 1800, two periods the extremes of which are separated from each other by a space of fifty years, shows an improvement of only 1⅛ per cent; while the difference experienced in the ten years that occurred between 1831 and 1840 shows an improvement of 7½ per cent as compared with 1751–60, and of 5¼ per cent as compared with 1791–1800. It must be borne in mind, that the improvement here spoken of is calculated upon the actual number of deaths among the population; and that to form a just estimate of the probability of

life among the young at the present time as compared with former periods, the number of deaths occurring under twenty should be calculated not upon the number who have died, but upon the number of the entire population. The estimate given above merely compares one improvement with another, or rather shows which of the classes, the young or the old, has participated most largely in the improvement which has taken place. In 1780, the annual mortality of England and Wales, according to the data then available, was 1 in 40; in 1801, it was 1 in 48; and in 1830, it had decreased to 1 in 58. Supposing these proportions, which have been established for the whole of England and Wales, to be applicable to London, we find the progressive decrease in the mortality of persons under twenty was . . . not much more than one-half of the proportion who died under twenty half a century ago. . . .

It has been supposed that the general healthiness and duration of life among the people must be diminished by their being brought together in masses, and in particular it has been objected to the factory system of this country, that by this means it has added to the sum of human misery. To combat this opinion, it will be sufficient at present to bring forward the case of Manchester, where the increase of population has been great beyond all precedent, owing to the growth of its manufacturing industry. . . .

The mortality of [the townships of Manchester and Salford] in the middle of the last century, as stated from the parish registers, was 1 in 25; in 1770, 1 in 28. In 1811, when the population had already very greatly increased, the rate of mortality had sunk considerably, and in the ten years ending with 1830 was not more than 1 in 49; a low rate, if we take into the account the fact that, in manufacturing towns, children are brought together in a much greater proportion than the average of the kingdom.

The decrease in the proportion of deaths among children in London has already been mentioned. It is not easy to determine satisfactorily the number of deaths of aged persons, in consequence of the prevailing custom of persons whose worldly circumstances allow of their doing so, to retire in the evening of their days from the crowded city to the country. We may mention, however, that for several years the bills of mortality have exhibited a continually and steadily increasing number of persons whose deaths can be ascribed to no particular disease, and who are stated to have vanished from the scene of life in consequence of "old age and debility."

The annual mortality of the county of Middlesex, the largest proportion of whose population belongs to the metropolis, was, according to the parish registers, in 1801, 1 in 35, having been computed at the beginning of the preceding century at 1 in 25; whereas in 1830 the rate of mortality had diminished to 1 in 45, and in 1840 was only 1 in 53, a rate much more favourable than that for the whole of France, and indeed of almost any other country in Europe, and materially less than the known rate of mortality of every populous city out of the United Kingdom. The greater mortality of cities, as compared with rural districts, has been attributed to "the constant importations from the country of individuals who have attained to maturity, but having been previously habituated to frequent exercise in a pure atmosphere, and to a simple regular diet, are gradually sacrificed to confined air, sedentary habits, or capricious and over-stimulating food." . . .

After many and long-continued efforts to that end, it is not possible here to bring forward many authentic or continuous statements of the rates of wages in this country. The following Table[1] comprises, indeed, nearly all that can be offered on the subject with confidence to the reader. Some details of the rate of wages paid to agricultural labourers might have been added, but owing to the vicious system which prevailed until lately through almost every part of the kingdom of paying a part of the wages of such labourers out of parochial rates, the addition would not have given any greater value to the statement. The last column contains the annual average price of wheat in each of the years. If the variations in the weekly earnings of artisans are examined in connexion with the variations in the price of this first necessary of life, it will at once be seen what violent alternations of misery and comparative plenty must have been experienced by the working classes in this country, and an additional argument will be thence afforded in justification of the repeal of the law which, by virtually excluding grain of foreign growth, aggravates such alternations.

The influence which these alternations have upon the moral character of the working classes is greater than would be conceived by any persons who have not had opportunities for observation or inquiry upon the subject. . . .

---

[1]The three pages of tables merely tabulate by trade, town, and year the average wage of 14 trades in several towns for 1800–1836. The data, sketchy and incomplete for workers in some towns and years and almost non-existent at the beginning and end of the period, show that wages generally tended upward through the end of the Napoleonic Wars and downward thereafter for the building trades, tailors, shoemakers, spinners, woolcombers, and laborers. Wages of hand-loom weavers experienced a sharper decline, while those of the printing trades remained stable and those of sailors rose through the entire period. Compared with wages, wheat prices fluctuated wildly in a generally downward trend, sharply rising to highs in 1801 and 1810–1813 and less spectacular ones in 1817 and 1824–1825. Wheat prices were considerably lower in the 1830s than they had been in the first two decades of the century.—Ed.

It will be apparent, from the examination of the foregoing tables, that although at certain seasons all those who live by daily wages must have suffered privation, yet with some exceptions their condition has, in the course of years, been much ameliorated. The exceptions here alluded to are hand-loom weavers, and others following analogous employments, conducted in the dwellings of the workmen. The diminution in the weekly earnings of other parties has been but small in any case, and certainly not commensurate with the diminished cost of most of the necessaries of life, comprehending in this list most articles of food, and every article of clothing. By this means they have acquired, with their somewhat diminished wages, a much greater command than formerly over some of the comforts of life.

It is true that the necessity under which most labouring men are placed, of purchasing in very small quantities from retail dealers who are themselves, perhaps, unable to purchase in the best markets, prevents their deriving in every case the full advantage of diminished prices; but it must be plain to everybody that at least in one respect the condition of the labouring poor is greatly mended. The reduction in the prices of all kinds of manufactured goods, accompanied as it is by improvement in their quality, has been such that few indeed are now so low in the scale of society as to be unable to provide themselves with decent and appropriate clothing. It cannot be necessary to adduce any evidence in support of this fact, which is obvious to every one who passes through the streets; so great indeed is the change in this respect, that it is but rarely we meet with any one that is not in at least decent apparel, except it be a mendicant, whose garb is assumed as an auxiliary to his profession. . . .

The improvement here noticed has no hitherto been extended in an equal degre to the dwellings of the working classe These, especially in large towns, are sti for the most part comfortless, and eve unwholesome, ill furnished and ill kep betraying a lamentable want of self-respec in their inmates, with a degree of reckles ness that speaks unfavourably for their mo al progress. The inquiries that have of la years been made on the subject by th London and the Manchester Statistical S cieties, and by the Central Society of Edu cation, have brought to light an amount debasement which is truly appalling, whil they have served to indicate the mea through which the evil may be remedie without even calling for any great pecun ary sacrifice on the part of those who ma apply themselves to the good work. It worthy of remark, that this comfortle condition of the dwellings of the poor is n seen in all localities. In some places whe no other appearances in the state of societ would seem to indicate it, there is to b found an extraordinary degree of respec ability in this particular. The town of She field, for instance, contains a large man facturing population, by no means r markable for orderly conduct. The tow itself is ill built and dirty, beyond the usu condition of English towns, but it is th custom for each family among the labou ing population to occupy a separate dwel ing, the rooms in which are furnished in very comfortable manner, the floors a carpeted, and the tables are usually mahogany; chests of drawers of the sam material are commonly seen, and so i most cases is a clock also, the possession which article of furniture has often bee pointed out as the certain indication prosperity and of personal respectabili on the part of the working man. It wou be difficult to account for this favourab peculiarity in the town of Sheffield, which, in this respect, offers a strong contrast to other manufacturing towns in the same county; but it is greatly to be desired that this peculiarity should be made to cease through the growing desire of other communities to surround themselves with the like comfortable emblems of respectability. . . .

The fact, the existence of which is shown in various ways in these pages, that the people at large have of late years, notwithstanding some occasional checks, obtained in England a continually increasing command of the necessaries of life, is proof sufficient that the amount of their individual industry must be greater, or, what is the same thing in effect, must be more skilfully applied than it formerly was when their numbers were not so great, and when, according to the popular (but ill-founded) belief, it must have been easier than it now is for each individual to provide for his comfortable subsistence. . . .

There are no means provided by which the consumption of the prime necessaries of life in this country can be traced at different periods. It is only with respect to those few articles of native production which have been subjected to the payment of duties that any provision has ever been made for ascertaining their quantity; and as the chief articles of food and clothing, when of native production, have never been directly taxed in England, we have always been ignorant in this respect regarding the quantities produced. . . .

In estimating the growth of wheat in England, it has not been possible to assume as data the breadth of land appropriated to its cultivation, and the average produce of the land per acre, both those elements of the computation being unknown; but the number of the consumers being known, the average consumption of each individual

has been assumed, and the total quantity consumed has been thence deduced. This average consumption has been variously estimated by different writers at from six to eight bushels during the year. . . . In former times a still further degree of uncertainty attended the estimate, from the fact of a considerable, but unascertained, proportion of the people not being habitual consumers of wheaten bread. Unless in years of scarcity, no part of the inhabitants of England, except perhaps in the extreme north, and there only partially, have now recourse to rye or barley bread, but a larger and increasing number are in a great measure fed upon potatoes, and it must be evident that any computation which assumes an average quantity in a case liable to so many disturbing influences, must be at best vague and unsatisfactory. . . .

The following Table,[2] which includes the whole kingdom, shows the quantity of sugar, and of molasses equivalent to crystalline sugar, retained for consumption in the United Kingdom in each year, from 1830 to 1845, together with the average price during the year, computed from the *Gazette* advertisements, and the average consumption of each individual stated in pounds and decimal parts of a pound.

If, by means of this statement, we trace from year to year the fluctuations in price, we shall find that they are attended by corresponding fluctuations in the consumption, and that with a degree of regularity more like the operations of a piece of machinery than as resulting from circumstances affecting in such various ways and in such different degrees our numerous population. With one exception only, that of the year 1835, every rise in price has been accompanied by diminished consump-

---

[2]The table shows per capita consumption to have been 19.94 lb. in 1830; 20.11 lb. in 1831; 19.21 lb. in 1835; and 20.33 lb. in 1845.—Ed.

tion, while every fall in the market has produced an increased demand.... But even under these circumstances of comparative ease the average consumption of 1835 did not attain the rate which it reached in 1830 or in 1831, when the market-price was from 8*s.* to 10*s.* per cwt. lower, but when the condition of the labouring population was not in other respects so prosperous as in 1835.

It will be observed that the last year of the series, 1845, is marked by a larger consumption than occurred in the year 1831, although the market-price was higher by 9*s.* 1*d.* per cwt., or nearly one penny per pound....

The quantities stated in the foregoing Table, as the yearly consumption of each individual, are average quantities, calculated on the assumption that the rich and the poor, the nobleman and the beggar, fare alike in their use of this condiment. It would be difficult to discover with accuracy the consumption of the various ranks into which the community is divided....

From inquiries carefully made, it appears probable that in the families of the rich and middle ranks the individual yearly consumption of sugar for all purposes is 40 lbs.; if then we assume that one-fifth of the families in the kingdom are so circumstanced as not to vary their mode of living with every fluctuation in the market-prices of provisions, we shall find that in 1831 the average consumption per head of the remaining four-fifths was 15 lbs. 2 ozs. In 1840 the average consumption was 15¼ lbs., or 76¼ lbs. for five persons, one of which taking the constant quantity of 40 lbs. left for each of the remaining four only 9 lbs. 1 oz. Every person serving on board one of Her Majesty's ships is allowed 1½ oz. of sugar per diem, or 34 lbs. 3 ozs. yearly; and the allowance given to aged paupers in the Union-houses is 1 oz. per diem, or 22¾ lbs. per annum....

The following comparative statement of the consumption [of tea] at the periods selected must therefore be considered to apply to Ireland as well as to Great Britain....[3]

The difference in the proportionate consumption at the above periods is small, when compared with the fluctuations experienced with other articles....

The consumption of tea has greatly increased since 1841....

The average consumption [of beer] per head in England and Wales [was 24.76 gal. in 1801, 25.19 gal. in 1811, 20.53 gal. in 1821, and 21.10 gal. in 1829]....

These figures do not afford a true statement of the consumption of beer by the people, because the duty was paid, and consequently the account was taken, only with reference to that which was brewed for sale, no duty having ever been charged on beer brewed in private families....

In great towns, and among the easy classes, and especially among our young men whose expenditure is least likely to be carefully regulated as regards minor luxuries, the smoking of tobacco is probably much greater now than it has been at any earlier period. The falling off in the consumption is principally experienced in Ireland, where the smoking of tobacco has long been a chief luxury among the working classes, and where, considering the few comforts that usually fall to their lot, its diminution betokens a great degree of privation. Contrasting 1839 with 1801, it will be seen that the average use of tobacco in Ireland is only one-half what it was at the beginning of the century.... In Great Britain, where the condition of the people generally has been more satisfactory than in Ireland, the consumption per head is now

---

[3]Porter inserts a table which shows per capita consumption to have been 1 lb., 3.75 oz. in 1801; 1 lb. 1.10 oz. in 1811; 1 lb., 0.52 oz. in 1821; 1 lb., 3.93 oz. in 1831; and 1 lb., 5.96 oz. in 1841.—Ed.

about equal to what it was at the beginning of the century. . . .

It is impossible to estimate, with anything approaching to exactness, the consumption of the metropolis. Accounts are given of the number of cattle and sheep sold in the markets, but we should greatly mislead ourselves by taking these accounts alone as our guide in the matter. A large quantity of slaughtered meat is brought for sale to the London markets from various and distant parts of the kingdom, and especially in the winter months, when meat killed at Newcastle and Edinburgh is so brought in great abundance. . . .

The steam-vessels from Berwick, Aberdeen, Dundee, and Inverness, bring also large numbers of live stock—oxen, sheep, and swine; and further numbers of these animals are brought by sailing-vessels. . . .

Even the live animals which are included in the returns do not comprise all which are brought to be slaughtered, many both of oxen and sheep being sold in London and the immediate suburbs before they reach the markets; and, on the other hand, butchers who carry on their business in some of the neighbouring towns are accustomed to attend at Smithfield market to make their purchases. With all this uncertainty, it would be idle to expect that any accurate statement can be offered on this subject. . . .

It may be thought an easy thing to ascertain the consumption of food by families, and thence to determine the average quantities used by individuals, and the aggregate for the whole kingdom. Any one who may attempt to procure this information will, however, soon find greater difficulties in his way than he has anticipated. Very few persons keep any adequate records of their expenditure; and with those who do preserve them, such a variety of circumstances must be taken into consideration before the experience of individual families, placed in some circumstances or other of peculiarity, can be assumed as affording a test of the average expenditure, that a very rough approximation to the fact is all that we can reasonably expect to attain. . . .

It has been shown, in the preceding sections of this volume, that since the beginning of the present century this kingdom has made the most important advances in population, in wealth, and in various arts of life which are capable of ministering to man's material enjoyments. It is now proposed to consider whether equal advances have been made in regard to his moral condition and to the general tone of society. . . .

An inquiry of this nature, honestly and fearlessly conducted, would, in all likelihood, lead us to conclusions of a mixed and partial character. . . .

It must be owned that our multiplied abodes of want, of wretchedness, and of crime—our town populations huddled together in ill-ventilated and undrained courts and cellars—our numerous workhouses filled to overflowing with the children of want—and our prisons (scarcely less numerous) overloaded with the votaries of crime, do indeed but too sadly and too strongly attest that all is not as it should be with us as regards this most important branch of human progress.

The next pair of pessimists and optimists wrote their works almost a century after those of Engels and Porter. The British JOHN L. (1872–1949) and BARBARA HAMMOND (1873–1961), pessimists and husband and wife, collaborated on a number of working-class studies of the Industrial Revolution. This selection comes from one of their more general accounts. Their books had their greatest influence in the 1920s and 1930s. They have been criticized for overemphasizing the drearier features of life during the Industrial Revolution, but their view is upheld by E. P. Thompson in another selection in this book. Perhaps their most influential critic was T. S. ASHTON (1889–1968), long-time professor of economic history at the University of London. His specialized studies of the iron, steel, and coal industries as well as his *Economic History of England, the Eighteenth Century* (1955) and *The Industrial Revolution* (1948) established him as the dean of historians of the Industrial Revolution. He argues that the plight of the worker needs to be seen as an unfortunate by-product of economic forces rather than as a result of capitalism.

J. L. and Barbara Hammond, T. S. Ashton

Pessimism and Optimism Reworked

J. L. and Barbara Hammond, *Nineteenth-century Capitalist Attitudes at Fault**

Rome imported slaves to work in Italy: Englishmen counted it one of the advantages of the slave trade that it discouraged the competition of British colonists with British manufacturers, and that it supplied British manufactures with a market. For the slaves wore cotton clothes and they were most suitable for industries like sugar planting, in which Englishmen at home were not engaged. Thus it might be ar-

gued that England had escaped the fate of Rome and that she so used the slave trade as to make it a stimulus rather than a discouragement to native energy and skill.

Yet England did not escape the penalty. For it was under this shadow that the new industrial system took form and grew, and the immense power with which invention had armed mankind was exercised at first under conditions that reproduced the degradation of the slave trade. . . . The factory system was not like war or revolution a deliberate attack on society: it was the

*From J. L. and Barbara Hammond, *The Rise of Modern Industry* (London: Methuen & Co., Ltd., 1926), pp. 194–204, 206–208, 217–224, 226–232. Footnotes omitted.

effort of men to use will, energy, organization and intelligence for the service of man's needs. But in adapting this new power to the satisfaction of its wants England could not escape from the moral atmosphere of the slave trade: the atmosphere in which it was the fashion to think of men as things. . . .

In the days of the guilds the workman was regarded as a person with some kind of property or status; the stages by which this character is restricted to a smaller and smaller part of the working classes, and more and more of the journeyman and apprentices fall into a permanently inferior class have been described by historians. In the early nineteenth century the workers, as a class, were looked upon as so much labor power to be used at the discretion and under conditions imposed by their masters; not as men and women who are entitled to some voice in the arrangements of their life and work. The use of child labor on a vast scale had an important bearing on the growth of this temper. . . .

Infant man soon became in the new industrial system what he never was under the old, the basis of a complicated economy.

Most children under the old domestic system worked at home under their parents' eyes, but in addition to such children there were workhouse children, who were hired out by the overseers to every kind of master or mistress. Little care was taken to see that they were taught a trade or treated with humanity by their employers, and though London magistrates like the Fieldings did what they could to protect this unhappy class, their state was often a kind of slavery. The number of children on the hands of the London parishes was largely increased in the latter part of the eighteenth century, because an Act of Parliament, passed in 1767 in consequence of the exertions of Jonas Hanway, com-

pelled the London parishes to board out their young children, and to give a bonus to every nurse whose charge survived. Until this time few parish pauper children grew up to trouble their betters.

The needs of the London workhouses on the one hand, and those of the factory on the other, created a situation painfully like the situation in the West Indies. The Spanish employers in America wanted outside labor, because the supply of native labor was deficient in quantity and quality. The new cotton mills placed on streams in solitary districts were in the same case. The inventions had found immense scope for child labor, and in these districts there were only scattered populations. In the workhouses of large towns there was a quantity of child labor available for employment, that was even more powerless and passive in the hands of a master than the stolen negro, brought from his burning home to the hold of a British slave ship. Of these children it could be said, as it was said of the negroes, that their life at best was a hard one, and that their choice was often the choice between one kind of slavery and another. So the new industry which was to give the English people such immense power in the world borrowed at its origin from the methods of the American settlements. . . .

How closely the apologies for this child serf system followed the apologies for the slave trade can be seen from Romilly's description of a speech made in the House of Commons in 1811.

Mr. Wortley, who spoke on the same side, insisted that, although in the higher ranks of society it was true that to cultivate the affections of children for their family was the source of every virtue, yet that it was not so among the lower orders, and that it was a benefit to the children to take them away from their miserable and depraved parents. He said too that it would be highly injurious to the public to put a stop to the binding so many apprentices to the cotton manufacturers, as it must necessarily raise the price of labor and enhance the price of cotton manufactured goods.

It was not until 1816 that Parliament would consent to reform this system of transportation. In that year a Bill that had been repeatedly introduced by Mr. Wilbraham Bootle passed both Houses, and it was made illegal for London children to be apprenticed more than forty miles away from their parish. But by this time the problem had changed, for steam-power had superseded water-power and mills could be built in towns; in these towns there were parents who were driven by poverty to send their children to the mills. In the early days of the factory system there had been a prejudice against sending children to the mill, but the hand-loom weaver had been steadily sinking from the beginning of the century into deeper and deeper poverty, and he was no longer able to maintain himself and his family. Sometimes too an adult worker was only given work on condition that he sent his child to the mill. Thus the apprentice system was no longer needed. It had carried the factories over the first stage and at the second they could draw on the population of the neighborhood.

These children, who were commonly called "free-labor children," were employed from a very early age. Most of them were piecers: that is, they had to join together or piece the threads broken in the several roving and spinning machines. But there were tasks less skilled than these, and Robert Owen said that many children who were four or five years old were set to pick up waste cotton on the floor. Their hours were those of the apprentice children. They entered the mill gates at five or six in the morning and left them again at seven or eight at night. They had half an hour for breakfast and an hour for dinner, but even during meal hours they were often at work cleaning a standing machine; Fielden calculated that a child following the spinning machine would walk twenty miles in the twelve hours. Oastler was once in the company of a West Indian slave-master and three Bradford spinners. When the slave-master heard what were the children's hours he declared:

I have always thought myself disgraced by being the owner of slaves, but we never in the West Indies thought it possible for any human being to be so cruel as to require a child of nine years old to work twelve and a half hours a day.

This terrible evil fastened itself on English life as the other fastened itself on the life of the Colonies. Reformers had an uphill struggle to get rid of its worst abuses. The first effort was made in 1802 when, after strong representations from a great Manchester doctor, Percival, Sir Robert Peel, father of the statesman, prompted by Owen and a Manchester merchant named Gould, carried a Bill limiting the hours of apprentices to twelve a day, forbidding night work and providing for visits to the mills by parsons and magistrates. The Act was a dead letter from the first. A second Act, passed in 1819, applying to all children in cotton mills, forbidding employment under nine and limiting working hours of children between nine and twelve to twelve a day, was equally ineffective. An Act passed in 1831 brought all persons under eighteen within the provision for a 12 hours' working day, but the first Act that had any considerable effect was the Act passed in 1833 which provided for State inspection. This Act, applying to woolen as well as to cotton mills, forbade the employment of children under nine, limited the working hours of children between nine and twelve to 9 a day and 48 a week, and those of persons under eighteen to 12 a day or 69 a week. But though this

Act was a notable advance, because it introduced the principle of inspection, it was easily evaded. The work of the children and that of adults was so closely connected that it was in practice impossible to protect the children except by a measure that would in fact limit the working hours of the whole mill. This was the plan that had been urged by the advocates of the ten hours' day. The struggle from 1829, when Sadler first adopted this scheme, was between those who thought it so important to rescue the children that they were ready to limit the working hours of the mill, and those who held that it was so important to let the mill work to the utmost of its capacity that it was necessary to overlook the consequences to child life. The struggle ended at last in 1847 with the passing of the Ten Hours Bill, which limited the actual work of all between nine and eighteen to 10 hours a day, exclusive of meal times. The chief names associated with this reform are Sadler, Fielden, Oastler, and Shaftesbury.

Throughout this long struggle the apologies for child labor were precisely the same as the apologies for the slave trade. Cobbett put it in 1833 that the opponents of the Ten Hours Bill had discovered that England's manufacturing supremacy depended on 30,000 little girls. This was no travesty of their argument. The champions of the slave trade pointed to the £70,000,000 invested in the sugar plantations, to the dependence of our navy on our commerce, and to the dependence of our commerce on the slave trade. This was the argument of Chatham in one generation and Rodney in another. When Fox destroyed the trade in 1806 even Sir Robert Peel complained that we were philosophizing when our looms were idle, and George Rose, that the Americans would take up the trade, and that Manchester, Stockport and Paisley would starve. They

could point to Liverpool, which had been turned from a small hamlet into a flourishing port by the trade. For Liverpool was the center of the commerce that throve on this trade. She shipped cheap Manchester goods to Africa, took thence slave cargoes to the West Indies and brought back sugar and raw cotton. . . .

The argument for child labor followed the same line. In the one case the interests of Liverpool, in the other those of Lancashire, demanded of the nation that it should accept one evil in order to escape from another. Cardwell, afterwards the famous army reformer, talked of the great capital sunk in the cotton industry and the danger of the blind impulse of humanity. Sir James Graham thought that the Ten Hours Bill would ruin the cotton industry and with it the trade of the country. The cotton industry had taken the place in this argument that had been held by the navy in the earlier controversy. Our population, which had grown so rapidly in the Industrial Revolution, was no longer able to feed itself: the food it bought was paid for by its manufactures: those manufactures depended on capital: capital depended on profits: profits depended on the labor of the boys and girls who enabled the manufacturer to work his mills long enough at a time to repay the cost of the plant and to compete with his foreign rivals. This was the circle in which the nation found its conscience entangled. . . .

The Industrial Revolution did not create the quarrels of class, nor did it create the wrongs and discontents that are inevitable in any relationship, where interests are sharply opposed and power is mismatched. But it made the disproportion of power much greater, and the immense extension of industrial life which followed came at a time when there was a general disposition to regard the working-class world as idle and profligate, and to regard industry as a system that served men by ruling them. Consequently the Industrial Revolution, if it did not introduce all the evils that were so acute in the earlier factories, gave them a far greater range and importance.

What happened at the Industrial Revolution was that all the restraints that the law imposed on workmen in particular industries, were standardized into a general law for the whole of the expanding world of industry, and all the regulations and laws that recognized him as a person with rights were withdrawn or became inoperative. The workman, as we have seen, lost one by one the several Acts of Parliament that give him protection from his master in this or that industry. His personal liberty was circumscribed by a series of Acts, beginning with the Act of 1719, which made it a crime for him to take his wits and his skill into another country: a law that applied to the artisan but not to the inventor. At the end of the century the masters were given complete control of their workmen, by a Combination Act which went far beyond the Acts against combinations already on the Statute book. By the Combination Act of 1799 any workman who combined with any other workman to seek an improvement in his working conditions was liable to be brought before a single magistrate—it might be his own employer—and sent to prison for three months. This Act, of which the chief authors were Pitt and Wilberforce, was modified next year, when Parliament decided that two magistrates were necessary to form a court, and that a magistrate who was a master in the trade affected should not try offenses, but these modifications did not affect in practice the power that the law gave to employers. Under cover of this Act it often happened that a master would threaten his workman with imprisonment or service in the fleet in or-

der to compel him to accept the wages he chose to offer. In 1824 Place and Hume, taking advantage of the reaction from the worst of the panics produced by the French Revolution, managed to carry the repeal of the Combination Laws. Next year, after their repeal had been celebrated by an outburst of strikes, a less stringent law was put in their place. But the view of the new system as a beneficent mechanism which the mass of men must serve with a blind and unquestioning obedience was firmly rooted in the temper of the time, and thus anybody who tried to think of Englishmen in the spirit of Burke's description of a man, found himself strangely out of tune in a world where the workman was refused education, political rights and any voice in the conditions of his employment.

At Tyldesley [it was said in a pamphlet published during a strike] they work fourteen hours per day, including the nominal hour for dinner; the door is locked in working hours, except half an hour at tea time; the workpeople are not allowed to send for water to drink, in the hot factory: and even the rain water is locked up, by the master's order, otherwise they would be happy to drink even that.

In this mill a shilling fine was inflicted on a spinner found dirty, or found washing, heard whistling or found with his window open in a temperature of 84 degrees. The men who were thrust into this discipline, however hard and bare their lives, had been accustomed to work in their own homes at their own time. The sense of servitude that was impressed on the age by this discipline, by the methods of government, the look of the towns and the absence of choice or initiative in the lives of the mass of the workpeople, was strengthened by the spectacle of the new power.

While the engine runs [wrote an observer] the people must work—men, women, and children are yoked together with iron and steam. The animal machine—breakable in the best case, subject to a thousand sources of suffering—is chained fast to the iron machine which knows no suffering and no weariness.

. . . For a people passing through such changes as those that accompanied the Industrial Revolution, this question, whether and at what point the claim of the capitalist to uncontrolled exercise of his power should be withstood, became the most important question in public life. England was on the eve of a great expansion of resources, numbers, wealth and power. What were the new towns to be like? What their schools, their pleasures, their houses, their standards of a good life, their plans for cooperation and fellowship? What the fate of the mass of people who did not feel or force their way through the doors thrown open to enterprise? To all these questions the Industrial Revolution gave the same answer: "Ask Capital." And neither Conservative nor Radical, the man defending or the man attacking bad laws and bad customs, thought that answer wrong. But that answer meant that the age had turned aside from making a society in order to make a system of production. . . .

The effect of this concentration is seen in the towns of the age. They were left, like everything else, to the mercy and direction of the spirit of profit. . . .

Mankind did not admire wealth for the first time; but the rich merchant of Bruges, Genoa or Norwich, like the rich Pope or the rich noble of the Middle Ages, or the rich Senator of the Roman Empire, had regarded the beauty and culture of his town as a sign of his own importance and success. . . . The private citizen who gave Bordeaux an aqueduct costing £160,000, or the benefactor who spent £80,000 on the walls of Marseilles, the soldier who provided free baths for slave girls at Suessa Senonum, the civic dignitaries who gave

temples and theaters, these typical figures of the early Roman Empire would have been astonished to learn that in the districts of South Wales, where men had risen in a few years to such wealth as would have rivaled the wealth of Atticus or Herodes, the poorer classes had to go a mile for water, waiting in a queue a great part of the night; that the chief town of this rich district had neither public lighting nor drainage.

Yet the Industrial Revolution which had given these men their fortunes had made it much easier to supply the needs of the towns that sprang up beside their great establishments. One of the products of that revolution was gas lighting; the Soho Works were lighted with gas in 1802 to celebrate the Peace of Amiens. Great factories at Manchester and Leeds soon followed the example of Boulton and Watt. Another product was the cheap waterpipe. At the end of the American War English ironmasters were exporting waterpipes to Paris and New York. The Romans had no cheap water-pipes made by the help of mechanical power, but they could supply their towns with clean water, whereas the people of Merthyr Tydfil, their streets echoing by day and night with the clamor of forge and furnace, had to drink whatever the river brought them. . . .

This concentration led to the complete neglect of the most urgent of the tasks of the age. In the first twenty years of the nineteenth century the population of Manchester increased from 94,000 to 160,000; of Bolton from 29,000 to 50,000; Leeds more than doubled its population between 1801 and 1831; Bradford, which had 23,000 inhabitants in 1831, grew grass in its streets at the end of the eighteenth century. Oldham, which had 38,000 inhabitants in 1821, had three or four hundred in 1760. In the twenty years from 1801 to 1821 the population of Lancashire grew from 672,000 to 1,052,000; in the next twenty years it grew to 1,701,000. The population of Merthyr increased from 7,700 to 35,000 between 1801 and 1841, and that of the two counties of Glamorgan and Monmouth from 126,000 to 305,000. Industry was accumulating dense masses of people into particular districts, where the workman was shut up in melancholy streets, without gardens or orchards. England was passing from a country to a town life, as she passed from a peasant to an industrial civilization. What this meant is clear if we compare the state of the towns, as revealed in the health statistics, with that of the country districts. In 1757 Dr. Percival put the death-rate for Manchester at 1 in 25, for Liverpool at 1 in 27. In Monton, a few miles from Manchester, the ratio was at that time 1 in 68, at Horwich between Bolton and Chorley, 1 in 66, at Darwen, three miles from Blackburn, 1 in 56. The Industrial Revolution was to spread the conditions of town life over places like Monton, Horwich and Darwen.

The problem of arranging and controlling the expansion of the towns was thus the most urgent of the problems created by the Industrial Revolution. Its importance was illustrated by a picture of some cottages near Preston published by the Health of Towns Commission in 1844. These cottages stood in two rows, separated by little back yards, with an open sewer running the whole length. The picture was given as an example of dangerous and disgusting drainage. But this is not its chief significance. One would suppose that these huddled cottages, without gardens of any kind, were built in a crowded town, where not an inch of space was available for amenities. They were in fact in the open country. Clearly then there was more here than a problem of drainage, for if it were left to private enterprise to develop this district, under the guidance of an uncontrolled sense for profit, these rows would spring up all round, and Preston would have another slum on her hands. This is what happened in the new industrial districts. When the Health of Towns Commission investigated towns like Manchester, they were told that the worst evils were not the evils of the past, for new Manchester was reproducing the slums and alleys of the old, and spreading them, of course, over a far wider surface. Of no other problem was it so true that neglect by one generation tied the hands and the mind of the next. . . .

In 1840 a Committee of the House of Commons recommended a series of reforms of a drastic and far-reaching character, and the Government of the day, represented at the Home Office by Normanby, a Minister who was in earnest, introduced Bills to give effect to its proposals. This Committee regretted that there was no general building law in force at the beginning of the century, "the fulfillment of one of the first duties of a humane government," and called for a general building law, a general sewage law, the setting up of a Board of Health in every town, with instructions to look after water supply, burial grounds, open spaces and slums. Cellar dwellings and back-to-back houses were to be forbidden. The importance of preserving amenities, footpaths, and something of the look of the country was impressed on Parliament. The most significant comment on the neglect of these proposals is to be found in the recurring complaint that runs through all the Reports on Health and Housing that were issued in the nineteenth century. The most urgent of the tasks of a humane government remained undischarged throughout that time. Town planning never found its way into an Act of Parliament until the twentieth century, and back-to-back houses (made illegal in 1909) were built in great numbers two generations after Normanby's Bill had proposed to make them illegal. The Commission which sat in 1867 found in existence the main evils that were revealed by the Committee of 1840; the Commission of 1884 found in existence the main evils that had been revealed by the Commission of 1867. In many towns the death-rate was higher in 1867 than in 1842, and Cross, speaking as Home Secretary in 1871, could match the terrible revelations by which Chadwick had tried to rouse the indignation and fear of the Parliaments of Melbourne and Peel.

Before each Commission the large towns disclosed the same difficulties. The law did not enable them to control expansion, or to prevent the creation on their circumference of the evils they were trying to suppress at the center. The Committee of 1840 had pointed out that back-to-back houses were being introduced into towns that had been free from them. Town Clerks told the Commission of 1867 that whole streets were still being built on "a foundation composed of old sweepings, refuse from factories, old buildings and other objectionable matter." Parliament passed Public Health Acts and set up authorities with sharply limited powers, but the fatal blindness to the character of the problem, as a problem in the organization and planning of town life, which marked the early phases of the Industrial Revolution, persisted. England learnt sooner than other countries how to cleanse her towns, but towns still continued to grow at the pleasure of the profit seeker. Each generation looked wistfully back to its predecessor as living in a time when evil was still manageable, and over the reforms of the century could be inscribed the motto "the Clock that always loses." For the creed of the first age of the Industrial Revolution, that the needs of production must regulate the conditions of life, and that the incidence of profits must decide in what kind of town, in what kind of streets, and in what kind of houses a nation shall find its home, had

cast its melancholy fatalism over the mind of the generations that followed. . . .

The other task that became immensely more important with the Industrial Revolution was the task of education. Adam Smith had pointed out that the division of labor, though good for production, was bad for the mind of the laborer. Men, women and children lost range, diversity and incentive in their work, when that work was simplified to a single process, or a monotonous routine. Life was more versatile and interesting when craftsmanship was combined with agriculture. Under the new system a boy or youth learnt one process and one process only; a great part of his mind was never exercised; many of his faculties remained idle and undeveloped. Moreover, apprenticeship was declining, and thus an important method of education was passing out of fashion.

Nor were these the only reasons why popular education was needed more urgently in this than in previous ages. Men learn from their leisure as well as from their work. Now the common life of the time was singularly wanting in inspiration, comparing in this respect unfavorably with the life of the ancient or that of the medieval world. The Greeks and the Romans put a great deal of beauty into their public buildings; they made provision, in some cases barbarous provision, for public amusement; they did not isolate art and pleasure for the delight of a small class. . . .

Life in Manchester or Merthyr was very different. One observer, himself an enthusiast for the new industrial system, said after a visit to Manchester that he would rather "trust himself to the savages of New Zealand than to a race bred in such surroundings"; another that it was impossible not to notice the complete absence of public parks and gardens. The workmen put it that their sports had been converted into crimes, and their holidays into fast days. Rich men in the Roman Empire spent their money on things that were for common enjoyment as rich men in the Middle Ages spent their money on things that were for common salvation. . . .

But in the England of the early Industrial Revolution all diversions were regarded as wrong, because it was believed that successful production demanded long hours, a bare life, a mind without temptation to think or to remember, to look before or behind. Some Lancashire magistrates used to refuse on this ground to license public-houses where concerts were held. Long hours did not begin with the Industrial Revolution, but in the Middle Ages the monotony of industrial work was broken for the journeyman by frequent holidays, saints' days and festivals; for medieval Europe, like Rome, gave some place in common life to the satisfaction of the imagination and the senses. . . .

The need for popular education became in these circumstances specially urgent. The reading of print is one way of using and exercising the mind, and its value at any moment depends on circumstances. In the days of pageants and spectacles, when story-tellers went from village to village, when peddlers and pilgrims brought tales of adventure or war or the habits of foreign countries, a man might be unable to read or write, and yet take a share in the culture of the time. Buildings, plays, music, these may be greater influences on the mind than book or pamphlet or newspaper. But the youth of the early nineteenth century who found no scope for initiative or experiment or design in his work, found no stimulus or education for his fancy from the spectacles and amusements provided for his recreation. Science was improving the mechanical contrivances of life, but the arts of life were in decline. To take advantage of these improvements, the power to read and write was essential. In a world depending on newspapers the man who cannot read lives in the darkest exile;

when the factory was taking the place of the craft, the newspaper the place of the pageant, illiteracy was the worst disfranchisement a man could suffer.

Horner, reporting in 1829 that a population of over a hundred thousand persons in a district of Lancashire comprising Oldham and Ashton was without a single public day-school for poor scholars, the Commissioner who said of South Wales in 1842 that not one grown male in fifty could read, both spoke of an age in which the story-teller had left the village, and the apprenticeship system was leaving the town. Adam Smith had argued that as the division of labor deprived the worker of opportunities of training his mind, the State ought to provide opportunities by public education. The ruling class argued, on the contrary, that with the new methods of specialization, industry could not spare a single hour for the needs of the men who served it. In such a system education had no place. A few far-seeing men, like Price, Paine, Whitbread and Brougham, had pressed for the public provision of education. Whitbread carried a Bill through the Commons in 1807 under which each parish would have had its elementary school. Brougham incessantly urged the claims of education. But politicians were prepared to leave the nation to a hopelessly inadequate provision made by voluntary societies, and it was not until 1839 that education received any help from the public funds. The great majority of the ruling class believed, as one of them put it, that the question to ask was not whether education would develop a child's faculties for happiness and citizenship, but whether it "would make him a good servant in agriculture and other laborious employment to which his rank in society had destined him."

Thus England asked for profits and received profits. Everything turned to profit. The towns had their profitable dirt, their profitable smoke, their profitable slums, their profitable disorder, their profitable ignorance, their profitable despair. The curse of Midas was on this society: on its corporate life, on its common mind, on the decisive and impatient step it had taken from the peasant to the industrial age. For the new town was not a home where man could find beauty, happiness, leisure, learning, religion, the influences that civilize outlook and habit, but a bare and desolate place, without color, air or laughter, where man, woman and child worked, ate and slept. This was to be the lot of the mass of mankind: this the sullen rhythm of their lives. The new factories and the new furnaces were like the Pyramids, telling of man's enslavement, rather than of his power, casting their long shadows over the society that took such pride in them.

T. S. Ashton, *Economics Responsible for Living Conditions**

What happened to the standard of life of the British working classes in the late decades of the eighteenth and the early decades of the nineteenth centuries? Was the introduction of the factory system beneficial or harmful in its effect on the workers? These, though related, are distinct questions. For it is possible that employment in factories conduced to an increase of real wages but that the tendency was more than offset by other influences, such as the rapid increase of population, the immigration of Irishmen, the destruction of wealth by long years of warfare, ill-devised tariffs, and misconceived measures for the relief of distress. Both questions have a bearing on some political and economic disputes of our own day, and this makes it difficult to consider them with complete objectivity.

Reprinted from T. S. Ashton in F. A. Hayek (ed.), *Capitalism and the Historians* by permission of The University of Chicago Press. Copyright © 1954 by The University of Chicago. Pp. 33–51, 123–124, 127, 129–132, 139–140, 147–148, 152–155. Footnotes omitted.

An American scholar (so it is said) once produced a book entitled *An Impartial History of the Civil War: From the Southern Point of View.* If I seek to emulate his impartiality, I ought also to strive to equal his candor. Let me confess, therefore, at the start that I am of those who believe that, all in all, conditions of labor were becoming better, at least after 1820, and that the spread of the factory played a not inconsiderable part in the improvement. . . .

It may be well to begin by making a rapid survey of the economic and demographic landscape. In these early decades of the nineteenth century population was increasing rapidly. Whether it is good or ill that more human beings should experience the happiness and misery, the hopes and anxieties, the ambitions and frustrations of life, may be left for the philosopher or the theologian to determine. But the increase in numbers was the result not of a rise of the birth rate but of a fall of the death rate, and it might be thought that this was indicative of an improved quality of life. . . .

The growth of population, and, in particular, the increase in the number of people of working age, might well have resulted in a fall of wages. But there took place simultaneously an increase in the supply of other factors of production. Estimates of the national income for this period are few and unreliable. But the statistics of output, expenditure, and consumption all suggest that over the period as a whole it was growing somewhat more rapidly than population. Is there any reason to believe that the proportion of this increased income that went to the workers diminished and that other classes obtained a larger share? This is a question to which no sure answer can be given; all that is possible is to estimate probabilities. In attempting this, it is important to distinguish between the period of the war, the period of deflation and readjustment, and the succeeding period of economic expansion.

During the war[1] heavy government expenditure of an unproductive nature produced a high level of employment but a low standard of comfort. Difficulties of obtaining foodstuffs from abroad led to an extension of the margin of cultivation, and the profit of the farmer and the rent of the landowner increased. Wartime shortages of timber, bricks, glass, and other materials limited the construction of houses; high rates of interest and a burdensome property tax reduced the incentives to build. With a growing population and an increased proportion of people of marriageable age the demand for homes increased; urban rents, like agricultural rents, rose. The growth of the national debt led to an expansion of the number of bondholders. The high rates at which loans were floated swelled the income of the passive investor, and, since the tax system was highly regressive, the gain to the rentier was largely at the expense of the poor. Prices in general rose, and, though rates of wages also moved up, they did so more slowly. This, as Earl Hamilton has argued, put additional resources at the disposal of the entrepreneur, and the tendency was reinforced by other, institutional factors. The trader's or manufacturer's token, the "long pay," and the truck system[2] had existed at earlier times. But it is probable that the shortage of coin, which became acute during the period of inflation, led to an extension of these and other devices, the effect of which was to shift purchasing power from the workers to their employers. During the war, then, there took place a whole series of transfers of income—to landlords, farmers, houseowners, bondholders, and entrepreneurs—and these almost certainly worsened the economic status of labor.

The five or six years that followed the peace brought little alleviation. The landlords obtained legislation that enabled them to perpetuate their windfall gains. House rents remained high. Rates of interest fell but slightly. And, though wage rates were less affected than profits, the reduction of government expenditure, the contraction of the currency, banking failures, and a general reluctance to embark on long-term investment reduced the level of activity. Any gains that may have come from the lag of wage rates behind falling prices were probably offset by high unemployment. It is difficult to believe that these years of deflation and civil tumult saw any marked improvement in the condition of the wage-earners.

After 1821, however, economic forces bore less harshly on labor. The gold standard had been restored. A larger quantity of silver and copper was available for the payment of wages. Reforms of the fiscal system were in train. A series of conversions reduced the burden of the national debt, and by 1824 the gilt-edge rate was down to its prewar level of 3.3. Wartime scarcities had disappeared. A more ample supply of bricks and timber combined with cheap money to stimulate the building of factories and dwellings. By the early thirties rents (in the north at least) had fallen about 10 per cent, and, in spite of a number of disturbing reports on conditions in the towns, it is fairly clear that the standard of housing was improving. The fall of prices—less marked than in the years immediately after the war—now represented not depression but a reduction of real costs. All in all, the economic climate had become more genial; it was possible for the workers to look forward to better conditions of life and work. . . .

It is time . . . to say something about such figures as we have relating to wage

---

[1]The wars of the French Revolution and Napoleon, 1793–1815.—Ed.

[2]The payment of wages in goods instead of money.—Ed.

and the cost of living. The outstanding contribution to our knowledge of the first of these was made forty years ago or more by A. L. Bowley and G. H. Wood.[3] It is based mainly on printed sources, but it is unlikely that further research will invalidate it in any serious way. Nevertheless, it is greatly to be hoped that it may be supplemented by data derived from the wages books which . . . still exist in many scattered factories up and down England. In the hands of careful students these records may be made to yield much information not only about rates of payment but also about actual earnings and sometimes about hours of work and the rents of working-class houses. Until the task is performed, it will continue to be impossible to speak with assurance on the topic. . . .

For information about the cost of living we are dependent almost entirely on the work of American scholars.[4] . . .

[3] Their widely accepted studies of wages in agriculture, 24 towns and coal fields, and over 30 industries indicate that wages rose 75 per cent during the French Revolutionary and Napoleonic wars. From this high they fell 10 per cent by the mid-1820s and 15 per cent by the 1840s. Their results, in the form of tables, may be found in J. H. Clapham, *An Economic History of Modern Britain* (London, 1930 and 1939), vol. 1, pp. 128, 561.—Ed.

[4] In the deleted portion of the original article Ashton questions the cost of living indices of N. J. Silberling (1923), E. W. Gilboy (1936), and R. T. Tucker (1936). According to Ashton, Silberling's index falls short because he relied on the wholesale, rather than retail, prices of only fifteen commodities (several of which were raw materials and not finished consumer products), did not include the effect of tariffs on raising prices, neglected consumer spending on rent, potatoes, and beer, underestimated spending on bread, and overestimated spending on meat, butter, and sugar. While Gilboy gave a more accurate estimate for bread, her reliance on London contract prices of hospitals, schools, etc., prevented her index from reflecting regional or retail prices. While Tucker relied on retail prices and added new commodities to his index as the worker's living standard improved, he perhaps overestimated spending on rent and services and, like Gilboy, limited himself to London. For a further discussion on the usefulness of these indices in determining the standard of living, see the selections by Hobsbawm (pp. 84–95), Hartwell (pp. 96–106) and Taylor (pp. 107–118).—Ed.

[Their studies] point to the difficulties of measuring arithmetically changes in the standard of living. The pioneers, as so often happens, have attempted too much. We must restrict our ambitions, realize the limitations of our bag of tricks, and refrain from generalizations. We cannot measure changes in real wages by means of an index of wholesale or institutional prices. We cannot apply the price data of one area to the wage data of another. We cannot safely draw up a table to cover a long series of years during the course of which changes may have occurred not only in the nature and variety of the goods consumed but also in human needs and human wants. We require not a single index but many, each derived from retail prices, each confined to a short run of years, each relating to a single area, perhaps even to a single social or occupational group within an area.

I cannot hope at this stage to meet these requirements. All I have to offer are three short tables exhibiting the changes in the cost of staple articles of diet in the area that is often spoken of as the cradle of the factory system. Such virtue as they possess derives from the fact that they are based on retail prices recorded by contemporaries. . . .

I have resisted the temptation to throw these three figures together so as to offer a single index of the cost of provisions from 1791 to 1831, partly because of slight differences of area and of the range of commodities but mainly because the data are not derived from a common source. The outlines are, however, clear. Following a fall after the famine of 1800–1801, the upward movement of prices continued, to a peak in 1812. Thereafter food prices fell to about 1820 but rose again during the following decade. In 1831 the standard diet of the poor can hardly have cost much less than in 1791. If this was so, it would seem that any improvement in the standard of living must have come either from a rise in money wages or from a fall in the prices of things not included in this index. One of the striking features of domestic production was the wide variations in the prices offered for labor. . . . Generally, for reasons set forth by Adam Smith, the price of labor rose when the cost of provisions fell and years of dearth were usually years of low wages. In these circumstances the standard of life of the worker was subject to violent fluctuation. One of the merits of the factory system was that it offered, and required regularity of employment and hence greater stability of consumption. During the period 1790–1830 factory production increased rapidly. A greater proportion of the people came to benefit from it both as producers and as consumers. The fall in the price of textiles reduced the price of clothing. Government contracts for uniforms and army boots called into being new industries, and after the war the products of these found a market among the better-paid artisans. Boots began to take the place of clogs, and hats replaced shawls, at least for wear on Sundays. Miscellaneous commodities, ranging from clocks to pocket handkerchiefs, began to enter into the scheme of expenditure, and after 1820 such things as tea and coffee and sugar fell in price substantially. The growth of trade-unions, friendly societies,[5] savings banks, popular newspapers and pamphlets, schools, and nonconformist chapels—all give evidence of the existence of a large class raised well above the level of mere subsistence.

There were, however, masses of unskilled or poorly skilled workers—seasonally employed agricultural workers and hand-loom weavers in particular—whose incomes were almost wholly absorbed in paying for the bare necessaries of life, the prices of which, as we have seen, remained high. My guess would be that the number of those who were able to share in the benefits of economic progress was larger than the number of those who were shut out from these benefits and that it was steadily growing. But the existence of two groups within the working class needs to be recognized. . . .

The student of English economic history is fortunate in having at his disposal the reports of a long series of Royal Commissions and Committees of Inquiry beginning in the eighteenth century but reaching full stream in the 1830's, 1840's, and 1850's. These reports are one of the glories of the early Victorian age. They signalized a quickening of social conscience, a sensitiveness to distress, that had not been evident in any other period or in any other country. Scores of massive folios provided statistical and verbal evidence that all was not well with large numbers of the people of England and called the attention of legislators and the reading public to the need for reform. The economic historians of the succeeding generations could do no other than draw on their findings; and scholarship, no less than society, benefited. There was, however, loss as well as gain. A picture of the economic system constructed from Blue Books[6] dealing with social grievances, and not with the normal processes of economic development, was bound to be one-sided. It is such a picture of early Victorian society that has become fixed in the minds of popular writers and is reproduced in my scripts. A careful reading of the reports would, indeed, lead to the conclusion that much that was wrong was the result of laws, customs, habits, and forms of organization that belonged to earlier periods and were rapidly becoming obsolete. It would

[5]The not always successful mutual aid societies which paid sickness, accident, and death benefits from the fees of the members.—Ed.

[6]The reports of these Royal Commissions and Committees of Inquiry.—Ed.

have brought home to the mind that it was not among the factory employees but among the domestic workers, whose traditions and methods were those of the eighteenth century, that earnings were at their lowest. It would have provided evidence that it was not in the large establishments making use of steam power but in the garret or cellar workshops that conditions of employment were at their worst. It would have led to the conclusion that it was not in the growing manufacturing towns or the developing coal fields but in remote villages and the countryside that restrictions on personal freedom and the evils of truck were most marked. But few had the patience to go carefully through these massive volumes. It was so much easier to pick out the more sensational evidences of distress and work them into a dramatic story of exploitation. The result has been that a generation that had the enterprise and industry to assemble the facts, the honesty to reveal them, and the energy to set about the task of reform has been held up to obloquy as the author, not of the Blue Books, but of the evils themselves. Conditions in the mills and the factory town were so bad, it seemed, that there must have been deterioration; and, since the supposed deterioration had taken place at a time when machinery had increased, the machines, and those who owned them, must have been responsible.

At the same time the romantic revival in literature led to an idyllic view of the life of the present. The idea that agriculture is the only natural and healthy activity for human beings has persisted, and indeed spread, as more of us have escaped from the curse of Adam—or, as the tedious phrase goes, "become divorced from the soil." . . . Bear with me while I read some passages with which Friedrich Engels (who is usually acclaimed a realist) opens his account of *The Condition of the Working Classes in England in 1844. . . .* Engels' book opens with the declaration that "the history of the proletariat in England begins with the invention of the steam-engine and of machinery for working cotton." Before their time, he continues,

the workers vegetated throughout a passably comfortable existence, leading a righteous and peaceful life in all piety and probity; and their material condition was far better than that of their successors. They did not need to overwork; they did no more than they chose to do, and yet earned what they needed. They had leisure for healthful work in garden or field, work which, in itself, was recreation for them, and they could take part beside in the recreation and games of their neighbours, and all these games—bowling, cricket, football, etc. contributed to their physical health and vigour. They were, for the most part, strong, well-built people, in whose physique little or no difference from that of their peasant neighbours was discoverable. Their children grew up in fresh country air, and, if they could help their parents at work, it was only occasionally; while of eight or twelve hours work for them there was no question.

It is difficult to say whether this or the lurid picture of the lives of the grandchildren of these people presented in later pages of the book is more completely at variance with the facts. Engels had no doubt whatsoever as to the cause of the deterioration in the condition of labor. "The proletariat," he repeats, "was called into existence by the introduction of machinery." "The consequences of improvement in machinery under our present social conditions," he asserts, "are, for the working-man, solely injurious, and often in the highest degree oppressive. Every new advance brings with it loss of employment, want and suffering."

Engels has had many disciples, even among those who do not accept the historical materialism of Marx, with which such views are generally connected. Hostility to the machine is associated with hostility to its products and, indeed, to all innovation in consumption. One of the outstanding accomplishments of the new industrial age is to be seen in the greatly increased supply and variety of fabrics offered on the market. Yet the changes in dress are taken as evidence of growing poverty: "The clothing of the working-people in a majority of cases," Engels declares, "is in a very bad condition. The material used for it is not of the best adapted. Wool and linen have almost vanished from the wardrobes of both sexes, and cotton has taken their place. Skirts are made of bleached or coloured cotton goods, and woollen petticoats are rarely to be seen on the wash-line." The truth is that they never had been greatly displayed on the wash line, for woolen goods are liable to shrink. The workers of earlier periods had to make their garments last (second or third hand as many of these were), and soap and water were inimical to the life of clothing. The new, cheap textiles may not have been as hard-wearing as broadcloth, but they were more abundant; and the fact that they could be washed without suffering harm had a bearing, if not on their own life, at least on the lives of those who wore them.

The same hostility is shown to innovation in food and drink. Generations of writers have followed William Cobbett in his hatred of tea. One would have thought that the enormous increase in consumption between the beginning of the eighteenth and the middle of the nineteenth century was one element in a rising standard of comfort; but only a few years ago Professor Parkinson asserted that it was "growing poverty" that made tea increasingly essential to the lower classes as ale was put beyond their means. (This, I may add, unfortunately meant that they were forced to consume sugar, and one must suppose that this practice also led to a fall in the standard of living.) Similarly, Dr. Salaman has recently assured us that the introduction of the potato into the diet of the workers at this time was a factor detrimental to health and that it enabled the employers to force down the level of wages—which, it is well known, is always determined by the minimum of food required for subsistence.

Very gradually those who held to these pessimistic views of the effects of industrial change have been forced to yield ground. The painstaking researches of Bowley and Wood have shown that over most of this period, and later, the course of real wages was upward. The proof is not at all easy, for it is clear that there were sections of the working classes of whom it was emphatically not true. In the first half of the nineteenth century the population of England was growing, partly because of natural increase, partly as the result of the influx of Irish. For those endowed with little or no skill, marginal productivity, and hence earnings, remained low. A large part of their incomes was spent on commodities (mainly food, drink, and housing), the cost of which had hardly been affected by technical development. That is why so many of the economists, like McCulloch and Mill, were themselves dubious about the beneficial nature of the industrial system. There were, however, large and growing sections of skilled and better-paid workers whose money incomes were rising and who had a substantial margin to spend on the products of the machine, the costs of which were falling progressively. The controversy really rests on which of the groups was increasing most. Generally it is now agreed that for the majority the gain in real wages was substantial.

But this does not dispose of the controversy. Real earning might have risen, it was said, but it was the quality of life and not the quantity of goods consumed that mattered. In particular, it was the evil conditions of housing and the insanitary conditions of the towns that were called as evidence that the circumstances of labor had worsened. "Everything which here arouses horror and indignation," wrote Engels of Manchester in 1844, "is of recent origin, belongs to the industrial epoch"— and the reader is left to infer that the equally repulsive features of cities like Dublin and Edinburgh, which were scarcely touched by the new industry, were, somehow or other, also the product of the machine. . . .

Now, no one who has read the reports of the Committee on the Sanitary Condition of the Working Classes of 1842 or that of the Commission on the Health of Towns of 1844 can doubt that the state of affairs was, from the point of view of modern Western civilization, deplorable. But equally, no one who has read Dorothy George's account of living conditions in London in the eighteenth century can be sure that they had deteriorated. Dr. George herself believes that they had improved, and Clapham declared that the English towns of the mid-century were "less crowded than the great towns of other countries and not, universally, more insanitary." The question I wish to raise, however, is that of responsibility. Engels, as we have seen, attributed the evils to the machine; others are no less emphatic in attributing them to the Industrial Revolution, which comes to much the same thing. No historian, as far as I know, has looked at the problem through the eyes of those who had the task of building and maintaining the towns.

There were two main aspects: the supply of houses in relation to the demand and the technical matters of drainage, sani-

tation, and ventilation. In the early nineteenth century, according to one of these scripts, "the workers were pressed into back-to-back houses, like sardines in a rabbit warren." Many of the houses were certainly unsubstantial and insanitary, and for this it is usual to blame the industrialist who put them up, a man commonly spoken of as the jerry-builder. I had often wondered who this man was. When I was young, the parson of the church I attended once preached a sermon on Jerry, who, he asserted with complete conviction, was at that very moment burning in hell for his crimes. I have searched for records of him, but in vain. It appears from Weekley's *Etymological Dictionary of Modern English* that "jerry" is a corruption of "jury"—a word of nautical origin applied to any part of a ship contrived for temporary use, as in "jury mast" and "jury rig," and extended to other things, such as "jury leg" for "wooden leg." "Jerry," then, means temporary, or inferior, or makeshift; and no doubt other uses of the word as a makeshift in an emergency will come to the mind. According to Partridge's *Dictionary of Slang and Unconventional English,* it was first used in Liverpool about 1830. The place and time are significant. Liverpool was the port for the rapidly developing industrial area of southeastern Lancashire; it was the chief gate of entry for the swarms of Irish immigrants. It was probably here that the pressure of population on the supplies of accommodation was most acute. Houses were run up rapidly, and many of them were flimsy structures. . . .

It is necessary to take account of the organization of the industry. The typical builder was a man of small means, a bricklayer or a carpenter, who bought a small plot of land, carried out himself only a single operation, such as that of laying the bricks, and employed craftsmen on contract for the other processes of construction.... The jerry-builders were not, in the usual sense of the word, capitalists but workingmen....

In Liverpool the builders of so-called "slop houses," or scamped houses, were usually Welshmen, drawn largely from the quarrymen of Caernarvonshire. They were backed by attorneys who had land to dispose of on lease but were not themselves willing to become builders. They bought their materials, which were of a cheap and shoddy type, on three months' credit. They tended to employ a high proportion of apprentices, and so, it was said, workmanship was of low quality. They needed credit at every stage: to obtain the building lease, to purchase the materials, and to meet the claims of the joiners, plasterers, slaters, plumbers, painters, etc., who performed their special tasks as contractors or subcontractors. The price of money was an important element in building costs. Under the operation of the usury laws it was illegal to offer, or demand, more than 5 per cent, and this meant that, at times when the state itself was offering 4½ or more per cent, it was impossible for the builders to obtain loans at all. By allowing the rate of interest to rise to 4½ or 5 per cent on the public debt, and prohibiting the industrialist from offering more, the state had been successful in damping down the activities of the builders for more than twenty years and so had deflected to itself the resources of men and materials required for the prosecution of the war against Napoleon. After 1815 the rate of interest fell tardily; it was not until the early twenties that the builders could resume operations. They were faced with a demand that had swollen enormously as the result of a vast increase of population, which now included an abnormally large number of young adults seeking homes of their own.

They were faced also by an enormous increase in costs. In 1821, according to Silberling's index number, wholesale prices in general stood about 20 per cent above the level of the year 1788. In the same period the price of building materials had risen far more: bricks and wainscot had doubled; deals had risen by 60 per cent and lead by 58 per cent. The wages of craftsmen and laborers had gone up by anything from 80 to 100 per cent. The costs of a large number of specific operations are given annually in the *Builders' Price Books* published in London. They show an increase in the cost of plain brickwork of 120 per cent. Oak for building purposes had gone up by 150 per cent, and fir by no less than 237 per cent. The cost of common painting had doubled, and that of glazing with crown glass had increased by 140 per cent.

It was not, in the main, the producer of materials who was responsible. During the war the duties levied by the state on bricks and tiles, stone, slate, and wallpaper had increased enormously. At this time the cost of timber was the chief element in the total cost of building materials, amounting, according to one estimate, to fully a half of the whole. Almost prohibitive duties had been laid on the supplies of timber and deals from the Baltic, and the builders of working-class houses had to make use of what were generally said to be inferior woods, brought at great cost across the Atlantic from Canada. Joseph Hume declared, in 1850, that, if the duties on bricks and timber were removed, a cottage which cost £60 to build, as things were, could be put up for £40.

All these charges had to come out of rents. But the occupier of a house had to bear further burdens imposed by the state. Windows had been subject to taxation from the time of William III (1696). Before the outbreak of the French wars, all houses paid a fixed rate of 6s. a year and those with seven or more windows additional duties, increasing with the number of windows. There was much stopping-up of lights to avoid the duties. The number of houses chargeable was less in 1798 than in 1750. It is true that the houses of the very poor were excused and that those with fewer than eight windows were exempted in 1825. But these concessions brought no relief to the poor of such cities as London, Newcastle, Edinburgh, and Glasgow, where many of the workers lived in large tenements, which remained liable to the impost. In addition, there was the heavy weight of local taxation. In the case of working-class houses the rates were paid by the landlord but were recovered from the tenants by addition to the rent. Local rates were rising at an alarming rate. Here again, it is true, there were exemptions. It was left to the discretion of the justices of the peace to remit the rates on occupiers who were considered to be too poor to pay them. By the middle of the century about one-third of the houses in the rural counties of Suffolk and Hampshire and one-seventh of those in industrial Lancashire (where poverty was less acute) had been excused the payment of rates. But, it was argued with some force, the exemption was of little benefit to the poor, since it enabled the landlords to charge more for the houses than they would otherwise have done. In any case it led to an increase in the poundage on houses not exempt, and for this reason it was said that "the ratepayers disliked the builders of cottages and thought them public enemies." The odium rested on "Jerry."

In the years that followed the long war,

then, the builders had the task of making up arrears of housing and of meeting the needs of a rapidly growing population. They were handicapped by costs, a large part of which arose from fiscal exactions. The expenses of occupying a house were loaded with heavy local burdens, and so the net rent that most workingmen could afford to pay was reduced. In these circumstances, if the relatively poor were to be housed at all, the buildings were bound to be smaller, less substantial, and less well provided with amenities than could be desired. It was emphatically not the machine, not the Industrial Revolution, not even the speculative bricklayer or carpenter that was at fault. Few builders seem to have made fortunes, and the incidence of bankruptcy was high. The fundamental problem was the shortage of houses. Those who blame the jerry-builder remind one of the parson, referred to by Edwin Cannan, who used to upbraid the assembled worshipers for the poor attendance at church. . . .

If the towns were ridden with disease, some at least of the responsibility lay with legislators who, by taxing windows, put a price on light and air and, by taxing bricks and tiles, discouraged the construction of drains and sewers. Those who dwell on the horrors that arose from the fact that the products of the sewers often got mixed up with the drinking water, and attribute this, as all other horrors, to the Industrial Revolution, should be reminded of the obvious fact that without the iron pipe, which was one of the products of that revolution, the problem of enabling people to live a healthy life together in towns could never have been solved.

For a while quantitative critique of the Hammonds by Ashton and others virtually demolished the credibility of the pessimists' case. But a change came largely as a result of the work of E. J. HOBSBAWM, who wrote a section appearing earlier in this book. By casting much doubt on the optimists' position with its own weapon, the quantitative method, he revived the pessimists' cause. Hobsbawm's article was persuasive enough to bring forth an optimistic reply from R. M. HARTWELL, fellow of Nuffield College and reader in recent social and economic history at Oxford University as well as co-editor of *The Economic History Review*. The two men continued the debate by commenting on each other's articles in "The Standard of Living during the Industrial Revolution: A Discussion," *The Economic History Review*, XVI (1963), 120–146. The two selections reprinted here illustrate the difficulties of the quantitative method.

E. J. Hobsbawm, R. M. Hartwell

A Debate on the Quantitative Approach

E. J. Hobsbawm, *Inadequacy of Quantitative Evidence in Support of the Optimists' Case**

The debate about the standard of living under early industrialism has now continued for some thirty years. . . .

It is today heterodox to believe that early industrialization was a catastrophe for the labouring poor of this or other countries, let alone that their standard of living declined. This article proposes to show that the currently accepted view is based on insufficient evidence, and that there is some weighty evidence in favour of

the old view. So far as possible, I proposed to refrain from using the type of evidence (Royal Commissions, observers' accounts) which has been criticized as biased and unrepresentative. I do not in fact believe it to be unreliable. It is dangerous to reject the consensus of informed and intelligent contemporaries, a majority of whom, as even critics admit, took the dark view. It is illegitimate to assume that even reformers who mobilize public support by drawing attention to dramatic examples of a general evil, are not in fact attacking a general

*From Chapter 5, pp. 64–88, "The British Standard of Living 1790–1850," *Labouring Men* by E. J. Hobsbawm, ©1964 by E. J. Hobsbawm. Basic Books, Inc., Publishers, New York, and Weidenfeld & Nicolson Ltd., London. Footnotes omitted.

evil. But the classical pessimistic case can be based, to some extent, on quantitative evidence, and, in order to avoid irrelevant argument, I shall rely mainly on it. . . .

I

An initial observation is perhaps worth making. There is no *a priori* reason why the standard of living should rise markedly under early industrialism. An initial rise must almost certainly take place, on demographic grounds, but it may be very slight indeed and need not be lasting once the new rhythm of population increase has been set up. It should be remembered that the decrease in mortality which is probably primarily responsible for the sharp rise in population need be due not to an *increase* in per capita consumption per year, but to a *greater regularity of supply*; i.e., to the abolition of the periodic shortages and famines which plagued pre-industrial economies and decimated their populations. It is quite possible for the industrial citizen to be worse fed in a normal year than his predecessor, so long as he is more regularly fed.

This is not to deny that the increase in production, which greatly exceeded that of population, in the long run brought about an absolute improvement in material living standards. Whatever we may think of the relative position of labourers compared to other classes, and whatever our theory, no serious student denies that the bulk of people in North-western Europe were materially better off in 1900 than in 1800. But there is no reason why living standards should improve at all times. Whether they do, depends on the distribution of the additional resources produced among the population. But we know that under early industrialism (a) there was no effective mechanism for making the distribution of the national income more equal and sev-

eral for making it less so, and (b) that industrialization under then prevailing conditions almost certainly required a more burdensome diversion of resources from consumption than is theoretically necessary, because the investment mechanism was inefficient. A large proportion of accumulated savings were not directly invested in industrialization at all, thus throwing a much greater burden of savings on the rest of the community. In countries with an acute shortage of capital a depression of popular living standards was almost inevitable. In countries such as Britain, where plenty of capital was theoretically available, it was likely, simply because much of what was available was not in fact pressed into the most useful investment. At best, therefore, we should expect improvements in the standard of living to be much slower than they might have been, at worst we should not be surprised to find deterioration.

There is no reason to assume that in countries with a rapidly rising population and a large reserve of rural or immigrant labour, shortage as such is likely to push up real wages for more than limited groups of workers. It may be argued that industrialization and urbanization automatically improve living-standards in any case, because industrial wages normally tend to be higher than non-industrial or rural ones, and urban consumption standards than village ones. But (a) we are not merely concerned with the incomes of one section of the labouring poor, but of all. We must not isolate any group of the labouring poor, whether better or worse off, unless it forms a majority of the population. Moreover (b) the argument is not always correct. Thus while in many continental countries social indices, like mortality and literacy, improve faster in town than country, in Britain this was not always so. Lastly (c)

we must beware of interpreting the qualitative differences between urban and rural,
industrial and pre-industrial life *automatically* as differences between "better" and
"worse." Unless we bring imponderables
into the argument, townsmen are not necessarily better off than countrymen; and
as the Hammonds showed, imponderables
can also be thrown on the pessimistic side
of the scale.

One final point must be made. Optimists often tend to exonerate capitalism
from blame for such bad conditions as they
admit to have existed. They argue that
these were due to insufficient private enterprise, to hangovers from the pre-industrial past or to similar factors. I do not
propose to enter into such metaphysical arguments. This chapter is concerned primarily with fact, and not with accusation,
exculpation or justification. What would
have happened if all citizens in Europe in
1800 had behaved as textbooks of economics told them to, and if there had been
no obstacles or frictions, is not a question
for historians. They are, in the first instance, concerned with what did happen.
Whether it might have happened differently, is a question which belongs to another
argument.

II

We may now consider the views of the
"optimistic" school. Its founder, Clapham,
relied primarily on calculations of real
wages which showed them to rise in the
period 1790 to 1850 at times when contemporaries, and the historians who followed them, assumed that the poor were
getting poorer. On the money side these
calculations depended mainly on the well-
known collections of wage-data by Bowley
and Wood. On the cost-of-living side they
depended almost wholly on Silberling's index. It is not too much to say that

Clapham's version of the optimistic view
stood or fell by Silberling.[1]

It is now generally realized that the statistical basis of Clapham's conclusions is
too weak to bear its weight; especially as
the argument for the period 1815–40 odd
turns largely on the question whether the
curve of the cost-of-living sloped downwards more steeply than that of money-
wages, it being admitted that both tended
to fall. Clearly in extreme cases, e.g., when
prices fall and wages rise or the other way
round, even a thin index may be reliable.
In this case, however, the possibilities of error are much greater.

Now our figures for money-wages are
chiefly time-rates for skilled artisans
(Tucker, Bowley). About piece-workers we
know very little. Since we also know little
about the incidence of unemployment,
short-time, etc., our figures cannot be regarded as a reliable reflection of actual
earnings. . . . For large sections of the "labouring poor"—the unskilled, those whose
income cannot be clearly expressed in
terms of regular money-wages, we are almost completely in the dark. We therefore
possess nothing which would be regarded
as an adequate index of money-wages today. The weakness of the cost-of-living figures is equally great. Silberling has been
criticized by Cole, by Judges, and most recently by Ashton, the most eminent of the
"optimists." For practical purposes it is no

---

[1]To a slight extent it also depended on the choice of
period. Today, when most economic historians would
place the turning-point between the post-Napoleonic
period of difficulties and the "golden age" of the Vic-
torians rather earlier than was once fashionable—in
1842–3 rather than in 1848 or thereabouts—few
would deny that things improved rapidly in Britain
(though not in Ireland) from the earlier forties on, the
crisis of 1847 interrupting a period of progress rather
than initiating it. But the admission that the middle
and later forties were a time of improvement does not
imply that the whole of the period 1790–1842 or
1815–42 was. . . .

longer safe to generalize about the working-class cost-of-living on this basis. Indeed, practical, as distinct from methodological, doubt has been thrown on such attempts to construct real wage indices for the first half of the nineteenth century. Thus Ashton's figures for retail prices in some Lancashire towns, 1790–1830, show nothing like the post-war fall which Silberling would lead one to expect. Tucker's index of London artisan real wages shows the major improvement in their position in the period 1810–43 to have occurred in 1813–22. But, as we shall see, these were years of stagnant or falling per capita consumption of meat in London, and of sugar and tobacco nationally; facts which hardly support the assumption of rising real wages.

In defence of Clapham it ought to be said that he was more cautious in his conclusion than some of the optimistic vulgarizers have been. Thus Silberling's index itself shows living-costs to have remained fairly steady for about twenty years after 1822, rising and falling about a level trend. Not until after 1843 did they drop below the 1822 level. Tucker's, a later index, shows that between 1822 and 1842 the real wages of London artisans rose above the 1822 level in only four years, the average improvement for the whole period, even for them, being only about 5 or 6 per cent. The two decades of, at best, relative stagnation of real wages—which R. C. O. Matthews confirms for the 1830s—are significant, though often omitted from the argument. In fact, one is bound to conclude that Clapham has had a surprisingly easy passage, thanks largely to the extreme feebleness of the reply of his chief opponent, J. L. Hammond, who virtually accepted Clapham's statistics and shifted the argument entirely on to moral and other non-material territories.

However, today, the deficiencies of Clapham's argument have been admitted and the most serious of the optimists, Professor Ashton, has in fact abandoned it, though this fact has not always been realized. Instead, he relies on arguments or assumption of three types. First, on various theoretical arguments designed to prove that a rise in real wages must have taken place. Second, on factual evidence of rising material prosperity—such as improvements in housing, food, clothing, etc. Third, on the—so far as one can judge—unsupported assumption that the part of the labouring population whose real wages improved must have been larger than the part whose real wages did not. It is admitted that conditions for part of the working population did not improve. I do not propose to discuss the first lot of arguments, since, if there is evidence that the standard of living did not improve significantly or at all at the relevant periods, they automatically fall to the ground. . . .

The evidence is certainly too sketchy to sustain the assumption, which today appears to be fundamental to the optimistic view, that the proportion of the labouring population whose conditions improved must have been larger than the rest. There is, as we have seen, no theoretical reason for making this assumption about the period 1790–1840 odd. It is, of course, impossible to verify owing to the absence of adequate data on the British income structure at the time, but what we know about this structure in later periods (and in admittedly better-off periods at that) does not support it. As I have attempted to show at greater length elsewhere, about 40 per cent of the industrial working class in later periods lived at or below the poverty-line, i.e., at or below subsistence level on the prevailing definitions of this concept. Perhaps 15 per cent belonged to a favoured stratum which was in a clear position to improve its real wages at almost all times. That is, the first group lived in what amounted to a permanently glutted labour market, the second in one of permanent relative labour scarcity, except during bad slumps. The rest of the labouring population was distributed between the two groups. Only if we assume *either* that in 1790–1850 the favoured stratum was markedly larger, the poor stratum markedly smaller than later *or* that at least five-sevenths of the intermediate stratum were more like than unlike the labour aristocracy, does the optimistic view, insofar as it is based on assumptions about income structure, hold good. This is not very plausible, and until there is more evidence for the optimistic assumption, there is no reason for making it. For the sake of brevity, I do not propose to enter further into the complex discussion of social stratification among the "labouring poor" here.

It thus seems clear that the optimistic view is not based on as strong evidence as is often thought. Nor are there overwhelming theoretical reasons in its favour. It may, of course, turn out to be correct, but until it has been much more adequately supported or argued, there seems to be no major reason for abandoning the traditional view. In view of the fact that there is also statistical evidence tending to support that view, the case for its retention becomes stronger.

III

We may consider three types of evidence in favour of the pessimistic view: those bearing on (a) mortality and health, (b) unemployment and (c) consumption. In view of the weaknesses of wage and price data, discussed above, it is best not to consider them here; in any case actual consumption figures shed a more reliable light on real wages. However, we know too little about the actual structure of the population to isolate the movements of working-class indices from the rest of the "labouring poor" and of other classes. But this would be troublesome only if the indices showed a fairly marked rise, which they do not. Since the "labouring poor" clearly formed the majority of the population, a general index showing stability or deterioration is hardly compatible with a significant improvement of their situation, though it does not exclude improvement among a minority of them. . . .

[*A. Social indices*]

The general movement of mortality rates is fairly well known. On theoretical grounds, such as those discussed by McKeown and Brown,[2] it is almost inconceivable that there was not a real fall in mortality rates due to improvements in living standards at the beginning of industrialization, at least for a while. General mortality rates fell markedly from the 1780s to the 1810s and thereafter rose until the 1840s. This "coincided with a change in the age-distribution favourable to a low death-rate, namely an increase in the proportion of those in healthy middle life."[3] The figures therefore understate the real rise in mortality rates, assuming the same age-composition throughout the period. The rise is said to have been due chiefly to higher infantile and youth mortality, especially in the towns, but figures for Glasgow 1821–35 suggest that there it was due primarily to a marked increase in the mortality of men of working age, greatest in the age-groups from 30 to 60. Social conditions are the accepted explanation for this. Ed-

[2] T. McKeown and R. G. Brown, "Medical Evidence relating to English population changes," *Population Studies*. IX (1955) [Extended footnote—Ed.]

[3] T. H. Marshall, "The Population Problem during the Industrial Revolution," *Economic History* (1929), p. 453.

monds, who discusses the Glasgow figures, observed (1835) that "this is just what might be expected to occur, on the supposition of the rising adult population possessing a lower degree of vitality than their immediate predecessors." On the other hand we must not forget that mortality rates did not improve drastically until very much later—say, until the 1870s or 1880s—and may therefore be less relevant to the movement of living standards than is sometimes supposed. (Alternatively, that living standards improved much more slowly after the 1840s than is often supposed.) Nevertheless, the rise in mortality rates in the period 1811–41 is clearly of *some* weight for the pessimistic case, all the more as modern work, especially the studies of Holland during and after World War II, tend to link such rates much more directly to the amount of income and food consumption than to other social conditions.[4]

B. Unemployment

There is room for much further work on this subject, whose neglect is rather inexplicable. Here I merely wish to draw attention to some scattered pieces of information which support a pessimistic rather than a rosy view.

Little as we know about the period before the middle 1840s, most students would agree that the real sense of improvement among the labouring classes thereafter was due less to a rise in wage-rates, which often remained surprisingly stable for years, or to an improvement in social conditions, but to the up-grading of labourers from

very poorly to less poorly paid jobs, and above all to a decline in unemployment or a greater regularity of employment. In fact, unemployment in the earlier period had been heavy. Let us consider certain components and aspects of it.

We may first consider *pauperism*, the permanent core of poverty, fluctuating relatively little with cyclical changes—even in 1840–2. The trends of pauperism are difficult to determine, owing to the fundamental changes brought about by the New Poor Law [1834], but its extent is sufficiently indicated by the fact that in the early forties something like 10 per cent of the total population were probably paupers. For the sake of comparison, between 1850 and 1880 the ratio of paupers to total population was never higher than 5.7 per cent (1850). It averaged 4.9 in the 1850s and 4.6 in the 1860s. The paupers of the period with which we are concerned were not necessarily worse off than the rest, for Tufnell, in the Second Annual Report of the Poor Law Commissioners, estimated that farm-labourers ate perhaps 30 per cent less in crude weight of foodstuffs than paupers. This was also the case in depressed towns like Bradford-on-Avon, where in 1842 the average working-class consumption of meat was not two-thirds of the workhouse minimum.

The impact of *structural* unemployment cannot be measured. Those who were most affected by it were often precisely those independent small craftsmen, out-workers or part-time workers whose sufferings, short of absolute catastrophe, were reflected in falling piece-prices, in under-employment, rather than in cessation of work. The sufferings of the largest group among them, those working the half-million or so hand-looms (which may have represented perhaps one and a quarter million or more citizens) have been amply documented. If,

---

[4]Prof. McKeown of Birmingham has drawn my attention to these. The rise of Dutch death and sickness rates during and their fall after the war must have been due exclusively to variations in food consumption, since other social conditions—e.g., housing—did not improve seriously during the period when the rates declined.

taking the more modest figures of Gayer, Rostow and Schwartz, we bear in mind that in the course of the 1830s well over half these weavers abandoned their looms, we have some measure of the possible impact of structural unemployment in this occupation, though this is, of course, no guide to any other.

As to the impact of cyclical slumps or other periods of acute depression, we have a good deal of evidence for two of these (1826 and 1841–2) and scattered evidence for other dates. The figures we possess naturally tend to some extent to overstate the distress, for particularly bad areas were more likely to attract attention than less hard-hit ones; especially in 1826, when our source is a relief committee. Nevertheless, the figures are so startling that they can bear a good deal of deflation. They suggest that in the hard-hit areas of Lancashire between 30 and 75 per cent of the total population might have been destitute in the course of this slump; in the woollen areas of Yorkshire, between 25 per cent and 100 per cent; in the textile areas of Scotland, between 25 per cent and 75 per cent. In Salford, for instance, half the population was wholly or partly out of work, in Bolton about one third, in Burnley at least 40 per cent.

For the slump of 1841–2, which was almost certainly the worst of the century, our figures are more representative, for a great deal of information was collected at this time, not only for purposes of relief, but for purposes of political argument (notably by the Anti-Corn Law League). Moreover, several of these enquiries command confidence, being evidently based on serious and detailed surveys by hard-headed, statistically-minded local businessmen.

Ashworth's survey of Bolton . . . [in 1842 showed] that unemployment of ironworkers in this industrial centre was [36 per cent] higher than the national average for the Ironfounders' Union, which was then about 15 per cent.

Again, in the Vauxhall Ward of Liverpool a little over 25 per cent of smiths and engineers were unemployed, in Dundee somewhat over 50 per cent of the mechanics and the shipbuilders. Slightly under 50 per cent of the Liverpool shoemakers, over half the Liverpool tailers, two-thirds of the London tailors were unemployed, only 5 out of 160 Dundee tailors were in full work. Three-quarters of the plasterers, well over half the bricklayers in Liverpool, almost five-sixths of the masons, three-quarters of the carpenters, slaters, plumbers, etc., in Dundee had no work. Neither had half the "labourers" and almost three-quarters of the women workers in the Liverpool ward. . . . The list could be prolonged. . . .

Such figures mean little, unless we remember what they implied for the standard of living. Clitheroe (normal population, 6,700, normal employment in the five main factories, 2,500) had 2,300 paupers in 1842; the Brontes' Haworth (population 2,400), 308. 20 per cent of the population of Nottingham was on the Poor Law, 33 per cent of that of Paisley on charity. 15–20 per cent of the population of Leeds had an income of less than *one shilling* per head per week; over one-third of the families in the Vauxhall Ward of Liverpool had an income of less than five shillings a week, indeed most of them had no visible income at all. 3,196 of the 25,000 inhabitants of Huddersfield had an average income of 8*d* per person per week. In Bradford, even in January 1843, "many of the most respectable have long since pawned their watches and other valuables, and they have been unable to redeem them; and the clothes pawned are now seldom redeemed." In Stockport (where . . . unem-

	1839	1841	(in £s)
13 provision dealers	70,700	47,300	
14 butchers	27,800	17,200	
10 grocers	63,800	43,300	
13 drapers, etc.	35,400	22,300	

ployment ran at 50 per cent) the average weekly income of those *fully* employed was 7s. 6¼d., the average of those partly employed 4s. 7½d.

The effect of such depressions on consumption can fortunately be measured. It was profound. In the Vauxhall ward of Liverpool total earnings had halved since 1835, meat consumption had halved, bread consumption had remained stable, oatmeal consumption had doubled, potato consumption had risen by more than a third. In Manchester the decline can be measured even more precisely. Between 1839 (not an outstanding year by any means) and 1841 the receipts of 50 Salford shopkeepers went down [as shown in the above table]. . . . However, one particularly gruesome, though admittedly exceptional case may be quoted, combining the effects of secular decline and cyclical depression: Bradford on Avon, in the dying West of England woollen area (whose support of the extremes of physical-force Chartism is thus explained only too convincingly). In this tragic town, in the 13 weeks from October 1st to December 1st 1841, the 8,309 inhabitants consumed 9,497 lb of meat and 9,437 quartern loaves. But of this amount, 6,000 lb was eaten by 2,400 of the more prosperous citizens and the 409 inmates of the workhouse, leaving 3,088 lb of meat (or 8⅜ ozs per week) for the other 5,909. The consumption of bread and meat since 1820 had fallen by 75 per cent.

Since all but a minority of workers possessed no reserves whatever to meet such contingencies, unemployment was likely to plunge them into destitution. They could and did pawn their property. But this might be negligible. Thus in Ancoats and Newtown (Manchester), 2,000 families (8,866 persons) in 1842 held between them 22,417 pawn-tickets; but the average value of these per family amounted to a mere £1 8s. A larger sample of 10,000 families, which is less biased towards the very poorest, held an estimated average of £2 16s. in pawn-tickets each. (12,000 destitute families then represented a third of the population.) What this represented in domestic equipment can be guessed: at the prevailing rates, a mattress, bed-quilt, blankets and two sheets could be pawned for a total of 11s. 11½d. However, if we assume a family income of 10s., even £3 in pawnable property would hardly maintain an unemployed family for more than six weeks.

But how long did unemployment last? In 1841–2 it could last for more than a year, as is shown by various counts made in 1843. But even if we suppose a man to have been unemployed for 6 months, and to be capable of surviving on his domestic possessions for 6 weeks, he would either have to go on relief, or into debt, or both. And supposing his credit with local shopkeepers to be good for two months, he would still have to repay, say, £8 in debts when back in full work, which (at a weekly rate of repayment or redemption of 2s.) would prolong the effects of unemployment on his standard of living for another 18 months. Such calculations are, of course, speculative, but they may serve to suggest the effect of the periodic cataclysms which were likely to hit the early nineteenth-century worker.

Except in years like 1839–42 it is, of course, likely that the effects of unemployment or short-time were unevenly spread, being always worst among the unskilled and the workers in declining trades, least among the skilled in non-cyclical occupations. Thus in Burnley 83 per cent of the destitute on charity in 1842–3 were composed of weavers' and labourers' families. While in London (October 1841) almost two-thirds of the capital's 26,000 tailors were said to be out of work, normally rarely more than one-third were unemployed even in the bad season, though this figure is high enough for a trade which had been 100 per cent unionized in 1830 and had been capable of resisting all wage reductions since 1815. Among the unemployed working on the Manchester roads in 1826, 356 were labourers, mostly Irish, and only 89 in the textile trade, though this doubtless indicates the greater reluctance of "respectable" men to declass themselves. On the other hand, in a sample of the "poorest class of operatives" analysed by relief workers in Glasgow during the 1837 slump there was rather more than one "trade unionist" for every two "weavers."

Unfortunately the scattered statistics of trade unions . . . do not help us, partly because the unions with the best statistics were too small to be representative, partly because such unions would normally contain an abnormally prosperous sector of their trades. Thus, the average of unemployment for the Ironfounders for 1837 to 1842 inclusive was just over 13 per cent (1841: 18.5 per cent). Bad as this is for a skilled trade in a normally extremely prosperous occupation, and over a period of no less than six years, it pretty certainly understates the severity of unemployment in 1841–2; and perhaps also the minimum of

permanent unemployment in such a trade at the peak of a boom (as in 1836), which stood at 5 per cent. Moreover, even such as they are, these figures are misleading, for they take no account of the average *length* of unemployment per member. Fortunately the union's expenditure on tramp relief (which reflects this length, because payments represent unemployed days and not merely unemployed men) indicates the degree of such error. Thus, while the relationship between unemployment in 1835 and 1842 is roughly as between 1 and 2, the relationship between tramp relief in 1835 and 1842 is as between 1 and 14. No discussion which overlooks the massive waves of destitution which swamped large sections of the labouring poor in every depression, can claim to be realistic. . . .

Whether further study can give us more adequate figures about unemployment in the first half of the century is a matter for debate. It will certainly be unable to measure adequately the occasional, seasonal or intermittent unemployment and the permanent bulk of under-employment, though no estimate of real wages is worth much which neglects this. . . . However, it is perhaps worth quoting the general estimate of a contemporary observer of proved acuteness and a good sense of statistical information.

Henry Mayhew is not a negligible informant. And if, as E. P. Thompson has lately reminded us again, in his valuable discussion of the standard-of-living problem, the "controversy really depends on a 'guess' as to which group was increasing most—those 'who were able to share in the benefits of economic progress' and 'those who were shut out'—then Mayhew's guess is worth our attention."

Estimating the working classes as being between four and five million in number, I think we may safely assert . . . that . . . there is barely sufficient work for the *regular* employment of half our labourers, so that only 1,500,000 are fully and constantly employed, while 1,500,000 more are employed only half their time, and the remaining 1,500,000 wholly unemployed, obtaining a day's work *occasionally* by the displacement of some of the others.

I would not place too much weight on this or any other guess, until it can be verified by reliable figures. Unfortunately this is not yet—and may never be—possible, for our data are too scattered to allow us to deflate any real wage index which we choose to construct. All we can say is that cyclical unemployment was plainly much higher before the mid-forties than after, for the trade union figures which become available after 1850 (and which are reasonably representative for at least part of the skilled engineering, metal and shipbuilding workers) can show nothing like the catastrophes recorded above. . . .

I V

C. Consumption figures

The discussion of these neglected sources . . . shows that, from the later 1790s until the early 1840s, there is no evidence of any major rise in the per capita consumption of several foodstuffs, and in some instances evidence of a temporary fall which had not yet been completely made good by the middle 1840s. If the case for deterioration in this period can be established firmly, I suggest that it will be done on the basis of consumption data.

Tea, sugar and tobacco, being wholly imported, furnish national consumption figures which may be divided by the estimated population to give a crude index of per capita consumption. However, we note that Clapham, though an optimist and aware of the figures, wisely refused to use them as an argument in his favour since absolute per capita consumption in this period was low, and such increases as occurred were disappointingly small. Indeed, the contrast between the curve before and after the middle 1840s when it begins to rise sharply, is one of the strongest arguments on the pessimistic side. All three series show a slowly rising trend and after the 1840s a much sharper rise, though tobacco consumption fell (probably owing to increased duties) in the 1810s. The tobacco series includes Irish consumption after the middle 1820s and is thus difficult to use. The tea series is also hard to interpret, since it reflects not merely the capacity to buy, but also the secular trend to abandon older beverages for a new one. The significance of tea-drinking was much debated by contemporaries, who were far from considering it an automatic sign of improving living standards. At all events it only shows four periods of decline—1815–16, 1818–19, a dramatically sharp fall in 1836–7 after a sharp rise, and a slighter fall in 1839–40. Tea seems to have been immune to the slumps of 1826 and, more surprisingly, 1841–2, which makes it suspect as an index of living-standards. Tobacco does not reflect the slump of 1836–7, but does reflect the others, though not much. Anyway, this article shows virtually stable consumption. Sugar is the most sensitive indicator though—owing to various outside factors—it does not always reflect trade-cycle movements. It shows the slumps of 1839–40 and 1841–2 well. Broadly speaking, there is no tendency for sugar consumption to rise above the Napoleonic peak until well into the 1840s. There is a sharp post-war decline, a sharp rise to rather lower levels after 1818, a slow rise—almost a plateau—until 1831, and then an equally slow decline or stagnation until 1843 or 1844. Tea, sugar and tobacco indicate no marked rise in the standards of living, but beyond this little can be deduced from the crude series.

The case of *meat* is different. Here we

possess at least two indices, the Smithfield figures for London for the entire period, and the yield of the excise on hides and skins for the period up to 1825. The Smithfield figures show that, while London's population index rose from 100 in 1801 to 202 in 1841, the number of beef cattle slaughtered rose only to 146, of sheep to 176 in the same period. . . .

The increase in beef lagged behind that in population in all decades until the 1840s. Mutton also lagged—though less— except in the first decade. On the whole a per capita decline in London meat consumption up to the 1840s is thus almost certain.

The excise on hides and leather yields somewhat cruder figures. . . . The . . . table [on page 95] summarizes what little we can get from them. Without going further into the somewhat complex discussion of the sources, it seems clear that the figures do not indicate a major rise in per capita meat consumption.[5]

About *cereals* and *potatoes,* the staple of

[5]In a long appendix Hobsbawm discusses the limitations of the Smithfield and Excise figures: 1. Although the Smithfield figures do not include pork, for which there are no figures to indicate an increasing or decreasing use, and underestimate sheep, which were increasingly marketed at the Newgate market, Smithfield did not lose any ground to other London beef markets until 1850. 2. Because of the lateness of effective steamer or rail shipping Scottish-slaughtered meat did not significantly affect the Smithfield figures until the 1840s when everyone agrees that the living standard was improving anyway. 3. While most country-killed meat was sold at Newgate, there are no quantitative data for it and a good bit of it may have been sold at Smithfield (if so, the Smithfield figures are optimistically high). 4. The figures for 1821 on the excise table are too low thanks probably to evasion. 5. And the laboring poor's share of these figures probably was much lower than a per capita share. Even with these limitations, however, Hobsbawm believes that the Smithfield and Excise figures are, while incomplete, the most representative ones presently available to us. He also points out that "optimistic" historians such as B. R. Mitchell and Phyllis Deane have subscribed to the Smithfield index and Deane and W. A. Cole to the Excise one.—Ed.

the poor man's diet, we can also find out some things. The fundamental fact is that, as contemporaries already knew, wheat production and imports did not keep pace with the growing population, so that the amount of wheat available per capita appears to have fallen steadily from the late eighteenth century until the 1840s or 1850s, the amount of potatoes available rising about the same rate. The best figures for the rise in wheat productivity show fairly stable yields up to 1830, a modest rise of about 10 per cent in the 1830s and a startlingly large one of 40 per cent after 1840, which fits in with the picture of very rapid improvement in living standards after the effects of the 1842 depression had worn off. It follows that, whatever the literary evidence, some people *must* have shifted away from wheat, presumably to potatoes. The simplest view would be that the major change from brown to white bread had already taken place by, say, the 1790s, and that the drift from wheat took place thereafter; but this would not explain the almost certain later drift from brown to white bread in the North and West. But this may have been "paid for" by a decline of per capita consumption elsewhere. This is technically possible. . . . However it is not my purpose to suggest explanations. All we can say is, that a rise in the per capita consumption of white bread in this period *at nobody's expense* is out of the question. Wheat consumption may have fallen with or without additional potato consumption, or some areas may have seen it rise at the expense of others (with or without a rise in potatoes). . . .

A notable increase in consumption is, however, recorded for *fish.* In Birmingham per capita consumption—negligible in 1829—had more than doubled by 1835 and continued to grow at a rapid rate until 1840. Undoubtedly this improved the nu-

Yield of Excise on Hides and Skins in London and
Rest of Country 1801 (1800–1 for Excise) = 100

Date	Population	Country yield	London yield
1801	100	100	100
1811	114.5	122	107
1821	136	106	113
1825	150	135	150

tritive value of the poor man's diet, though it may not indicate that they *felt* themselves to be eating better; for the poor had always had a marked prejudice against this cheap and abundant food, and "the lower class of people entertain a notion that fish is not substantial enough food for them, and they prefer meat." They may well have moved to fish because they could not afford enough meat. . . .

The discussion of food consumption thus throws considerable doubt on the optimistic view. However, it should be pointed out that this does *not* mean that early nineteenth-century Britons had an "Asiatic" standard of living. This is nonsense, and such loose statements have caused much confusion. Britain was almost certainly better fed than all but the most prosperous peasant areas, or the more comfortable classes, in continental countries; but then it had been so as Drummond and Wilbraham pointed out long before the Industrial Revolution. The point at issue is not whether we fell as low as other countries, but whether, by our own standards, we improved or deteriorated, and in either case, how much.

V

There is thus no strong basis for the optimistic view, at any rate for the period from c. 1790 or 1800 on until the middle 1840s. The plausibility of, and the evidence for

deterioration are not to be lightly dismissed. It is not the purpose of this chapter to discuss the evolution of living standards in the eighteenth century, since the major discussion on living standards has been about the period between the end of the Napoleonic Wars and "some unspecified date between the end of Chartism and the Great Exhibition." It is altogether likely that living standards improved over much of the eighteenth century. It is not improbable that, sometime soon after the onset of the Industrial Revolution—which is perhaps better placed in the 1780s than in the 1760s—they ceased to improve and declined. Perhaps the middle 1790s, the period of Speenhamland and shortage, mark the turning-point. At the other end, the middle 1840s certainly mark a turning-point.

We may therefore sum up as follows. The classical view has been put in Sidney Webb's words: "If the Chartists in 1837 had called for a comparison of their time with 1787, and had obtained a fair account of the actual social life of the working-man at the two periods, it is almost certain that they would have recorded a positive decline in the standard of life of large classes of the population." This view has not been so far made untenable. It may be that further evidence will discredit it; but it will have to be vastly stronger evidence than has so far been adduced.

R. M. Hartwell, *The Standard of Living
Quantitatively Higher**

I

... The *exact* measurement of the standard of living in the years 1800 to 1850
may be impossible, but, eschewing prejudice and pre-conceived theories, a firm
statement about the trend of living standards can be derived from the mass of
evidence that has survived, and from an
analysis of the likely changes in income
distribution during a long period of economic growth. This article argues for an upward trend in living standards during the
industrial revolution; in section II, from an
examination of national income and other
aggregate statistics that have survived (or
can be calculated or guessed with some
certainty), from wage-price data, and from
analogy; in section III, from an analysis of
consumption figures; and in section IV,
from the evidence of vital statistics, from a
comparison with eighteenth century living
standards, and from details of the expansion after 1800 of social and economic opportunities. Briefly the argument is that,
since average per capita income increased,
since there was no trend in distribution
against the workers, since (after 1815)
prices fell while money wages remained
constant, since per capita consumption of
food and other consumer goods increased,
and since government increasingly intervened in economic life to protect or raise
living standards, then the real wages of the
majority of English workers were rising in
the years 1800 to 1850.

I I

Economic growth implies an increase in
per capita national income, and, if distribution leaves labour with at least the same

relative share of the increasing product, an
increase in the average standard of living.
Generally, as the historical analyses of economic development have shown, an increase in per capita income has been accompanied by a more equal income distribution.[1] In Britain, contemporary estimates
of the national income between 1800 and
1850 indicate that average real income
doubled in this period, and, although the
upward trend was uneven, with stagnation
during the war and a possible small decline
in the thirties, average per capita income had already increased fifty per cent
by 1830. No juggling of the figures could
suggest deterioration, but the estimates are
inadequate both in their methods of com-
pilation and in their statistical bases, so
that they can be used only as an indication
of trend, and not as a measure of change.
This probable increase, of uncertain size,
in per capita income becomes more plausible, however, when three other phenomena are taken into account: the increase
in the output of manufacturing industry
relative to the increase in population; the
increasing and substantial proportion of
manufacturing income in the national income; and the increasing and substantial
proportion of the total working population
employed in manufacturing industry. According to W. Hoffmann, the rate of
growth of industrial output between 1782
and 1855 was 3 to 4 per cent per annum
(except during the war years when the
rate was about 2 per cent); over the same
period the annual rate of growth of population varied from 1.2 to 1.5 per cent, with
the highest rate between 1811 and 1831,
and a declining rate thereafter. This,

---

*From R. M. Hartwell, "The Rising Standard of
Living in England, 1800–1850," *Economic History Review,* XIII (1961), 397–416. Reprinted by permission
of the Economic History Society. Footnotes omitted.

[1]See S. Kuznets, "Economic Growth and Income
Inequality," *American Economic Review,* March 1955.
Theoretically there may be an increase in inequality
in the early stages of growth to allow for larger savings and more investment. This possibility is discussed
below.

however, would have been of little signifi-cance if industrial output was so small a part of national income that changes in it could not have affected the average stan-dard of life. But the contribution of manu-facturing industry to the national income increased from about one fifth in 1770, to one quarter in 1812, to one third in 1831. Census figures for 1841 and 1851 show that about one third of the occupied popu-lation of England and Wales was engaged in manufacturing industry and that the 1851 proportion "was not exceeded until 1951." In 1850, M. Mulhall estimated, manufacturing industry provided £269 millions (about 40 per cent) of a British national income of £690 millions. It is prob-able, therefore, that by 1830 manufactur-ing had a similar role as income producer as it has had since 1850, and that the growth of manufacturing output substan-tially affected living standards.

Of the factors that raised per capita out-put the most important were capital for-mation, technical progress, and improved labour and managerial skills. It is neces-sary, from a combination of those, to ex-plain the shift between 1760 and 1840 from a situation where population and in-comes were rising very slowly to one where population was increasing at the annual rate of c. 1.5 per cent, and incomes at c. 3 per cent. . . .

The rate of capital formation certainly increased over the period, but to deter-mine accurately its effect on real income it would be necessary to know both the sav-ings ratio and the capital output ratio, neither of which can be determined. . . .

Modern analyses of underdeveloped economies in process of growth often as-sume low savings and low capital income ratios. In the England of the industrial revo-lution, likewise, the rate of saving was necessarily relatively low in a society where average incomes were still not much above subsistence, and where the capital market was imperfect; and the replace-ment of men by machines, of wind and water by steam power, and of the home by the factory, marked an increase in produc-tivity that was often spectacular. But where-as the productivity of much new indus-trial equipment was high, its cost was often low. Thus the comparatively low capital output ratio was not incompatible with ris-ing real incomes. By 1800 improvements in techniques and management were al-ready making capital more fruitful, and it is certain that over the whole period the rate of growth of output depended as much on the rate of technical progress as on the rate of capital accumulation, on the quality as much as on the quantity of investment. The productivity effect of better machin-ery during the industrial revolution was both large and rapid in impact, and the growth of output, because the output-in-crement per unit of investment was large, was rapid. As Robert Owen declared in 1816: "in my establishment at New Lan-ark . . . , mechanical powers and opera-tions superintended by about two thousand young persons and adults . . . . now com-pleted as much work as sixty years before would have required the entire working population of Scotland."

The employment effect, however, was also potentially large. Many of the new machines required less labour per unit of output, so that, theoretically, the conse-quent labour displacement could have been large enough to have prevented real wages from rising. On the other hand, be-cause the new machines generally reduced costs, including the cost of goods consumed by the workers, there was at the same time a tendency for real wages to rise. It is be-cause of this tendency, J. R. Hicks has sug-gested, that capital accumulation in the nineteenth century was so favourable to the standard of living.[2] Moreover, money wages were stable between 1820 and 1850, a period of falling prices, indicating that there was insufficient competition from underemployed and unemployed labour to pull down wages. In spite of pockets of technological underemployment, the displacement of labour by machinery did not result in a decline in average real wages. And the existence of groups of wage-earners whose real wages were stable or declining—industrial groups like the handloom weavers, or national groups like the Irish—bias the averages downwards and disguise the gains in the growing sectors of the economy. Indeed, to some extent, the displacement of labour was theoretical: the new machines required less labour per unit of output than did old plant making the same products; but much new plant was an addition to total plant, not a displacement of existing plant, and when this was so, the net effect on the total demand for labour was an absolute increase. Thus, for example, railways did gradually displace canals, but the displacement effect on canal labour was insignificant compared with the massive labour requirements for railway construction and maintenance. There was in this period a continually increasing demand for industrial labour, a demand that caused a differential between agricultural and industrial wages, and a consequent continuous migration towards the industrial areas. As a spokesman of the agricultural labours declared bitterly, "it is well known that in the great trading towns, such as Manchester, Sheffield, Birmingham, etc., four days work in a week

amply supply the dissolute and the drunken."

But factories have to be administered, and machines have to be tended, and even the best equipment is of little value without able entrepreneurs and skilled labourers. The industrial revolution was as much a revolution in industrial organization as in technology. Entrepreneurs increasingly centralized production into factories, worked out the problems of factory management, accounting, financing, merchanting and labour-relations. Not the least problem was to change craft and agricultural labourers into factory workers, with their different skills, different rhythm of work, different incentives, different social attitudes, and different way of life. This necessary transformation was certainly painful but it was gradually achieved without political revolution, and with labour simultaneously increasing its opportunities, its industrial skill and its bargaining strength. The quantitative effect of such changes on output cannot be measured accurately, but they certainly tended to increase productivity.

... Theoretically it is possible that economic growth could result in reduced real incomes in the short run, but it is quite unreasonable to assume, over a long period of a half century, during which per capita national income was rising, that the rich were getting richer and the poor poorer.

There is some evidence that the distribution of income in England in 1850 was less unequal than it had been in 1800. C. Clark, for example . . . reckons that income distribution was more unequal in 1812 than in 1848;[3] income tax assessments of 1812 and 1848 show, also, that the number of assessments between £150 and £500 increased more than those over £500; a com-

<hr>

[2] J. R. Hicks, *Value and Capital* (Oxford University Press, 1939), p. 292. "The fact that the things whose production has been facilitated have been particularly articles of mass consumption has worked in the same direction. If there are any goods in terms of which wages have fallen as a result of the accumulation of capital, they are not goods of much importance to the wage-earner."

[3] C. Clark, *The Conditions of Economic Progress* (London: Macmillan, 2nd ed., 1951), pp. 534, 538.

parison of fundholders of 1831 and 1848 reveals that the largest increase was in those receiving dividends of under £5. These figures, however, are no conclusive proof of a significant change in distribution. . . . There has been generally the simultaneous rise, at not dissimilar rates of growth, of capital stock, output, and real incomes. Study of the long-term trends in the wage-share of the national income show that since about 1860 that share has remained almost constant. If this stability has a longer history, the wage bill would have been increasing proportionately with the national income from some earlier date, possibly from the beginning of the industrial revolution. It is not unlikely, however, that the share of wages was less in 1780–1800 than in 1860, and thus, that wages were rising between those dates more quickly than national income. That this was probable is indicated by the continuous increase over the period of those employed in manufacturing industry. Agricultural wages lagged behind industrial wages, and as more workers transferred to higher productivity occupations, average real wages increased. Census figures show that the percentage proportions of agricultural to all families in 1811 and 1831 were 35.2 and 28.2 and that the percentage proportions of adult males employed in agriculture to all male workers in 1831, 1841 and 1851 were 31.7, 25.7 and 21.1. Further confirmation is provided by the increasing proportion over these years of total population engaged in commerce, finance and the professions, "a fairly precise measurement of the degree of economic advancement." Occupational statistics before 1841, except in broad categories, are not very helpful, but other evidence shows that there were large increases in the numbers employed in services—in transport, commerce and finance, in government,

and in the professions—between 1780 and 1850. . . .

At the same time the proportion of gainfully occupied in the population increased, as the under-employed labour of the predominantly agricultural economy of pre-industrial Britain was gradually absorbed into fuller employment in industry and services. Thus, for example, the much publicised and criticized employment of women and children, though common in the farms and domestic industries of pre-industrial revolution England, was certainly more productive and generally more humane during the industrial revolution.

The workers' standard of living is affected by the redistribution of income by government, especially through taxation and expenditure on social welfare. The tax structure between 1800 and 1850 was certainly regressive, although there was income tax during the war (the heaviest of the century) and again after 1842 when it yielded £5 millions annually. Government revenue came mainly from indirect taxation, of which customs revenue provided an increasing proportion until 1840, and thereafter a stable one. The reduction of tariffs after 1824, and especially after 1840, gave general benefit by lowering the price of many goods of common consumption and by encouraging the demand for goods which hitherto had been considered luxuries. Other taxation, also mainly indirect, was reduced after the war, and remained relatively stable at £3–4 millions between 1825 and 1856. Total government revenue also declined after 1815 both absolutely (until 1843) and as a proportion of national income, and in terms of average per capita contributions. On the expenditure side, the national debt service was the largest and most regressive item, but its incidence remained stable in money terms, varying from £33.9 to £28.1 millions between 1815 and 1845, so that it was a decreasing proportion of national income even though in real terms its incidence increased in the period of falling prices. . . . "Social services" cost from £2 to £5 millions, increasing after 1830, but the benefit to the worker must have been very small. Much more important was the expenditure for the relief and maintenance of the poor through the poor and county rates, which increased to £7.9 millions in 1818, varied from £5.7 to £7.0 millions from 1818 to 1832, fell to £4.0 millions in 1834, and increased to £6.2 millions in 1848. All that can be said in summary about these collections and disbursements of government is that there was no marked trend, although there was a reduction in the average contributions, and an increase in the average receipts, of the labouring poor. In another way, however, government action was important. Government legislation which involved private expenditure in improving the condition of the working classes was considerable. Such legislation included protective acts like the factory and truck acts [1830s–1840s], enabling acts such as the legislation for savings banks [1817] and friendly societies [1793–1829] and acts of general benefit such as those improving municipal government [1835]. Under such legislation, for example, hours of work were reduced in factories and limits were set to the age at which children were allowed to work, women and children were excluded from mines, some educational facilities were enforced for factory children, and the provision of water and the disposal of sewage by municipal authorities were facilitated. Such legislation, J. M. Ludlow and L. Jones declared [1867], secured "the primary elements of health, safety and well-being" for the people at large, and enable them "to become a better fed, better clothed, better housed, more healthy, more orderly, more

saving, more industrious, more self-reliant, better educated population. . . ."

III

Evidence of the condition of the working class during the industrial revolution can be found also in the statistics of savings, wages and consumption. After the establishment of savings banks in 1817 deposits increased to £14.3 millions by 1829, and to almost £30 millions by 1850, when the number of depositors totalled 1,112,999. "The £30 millions of deposits in 1847 were predominantly the savings of wage-earners, among whom domestic servants and artisans occupied the most prominent places."[4] Friendly and Benefit Societies, of which there were 20,000 in 1858 with a membership of about two millions had also accumulated £9 millions. Other societies catering for working-class savings, such as Building and Land Societies (after 1816) and Co-operative Societies (after 1844), did not advance with such rapidity, although their foundation in this period is evidence of the increasing ability of the working class to save.

A large and long economic expansion like the industrial revolution was possible only with a large extension of the market, with the creation or discovery of increasing and accessible markets with consumers willing and able to buy the expanding output of goods and services. For a shorter period, however, it is relevant, in an inquiry into living standards, to know how much of the increased production went into savings and investment rather than into consumption,

[4]H. O Horne, *A History of Savings Banks* (Oxford University Press, 1947), p. 116. The trend of savings was upwards except for the years 1828–9, 1830–2, and 1847–8. The range of depositors is best seen in examples: of the 14,937 depositors of the Manchester and Salford Savings Bank in 1842, 3,063 were domestic servants, 3,033 were children whose parents saved for them, 2,372 were tradesmen, clerks, warehousemen, porters, artists, and teachers, and the remainder were labourers and industrial workers. . . .

and how much went abroad without immediate repayment in other goods. But, whatever the amount of savings and exports in the short run, in the long run capital accumulation would have increased productivity, and sales abroad would have resulted in increased imports. In any case neither capital accumulation nor exports, nor the two together, could have completely absorbed the increase in production in this period: capital accumulation was not so large as to make exorbitant demands on current output; and exports, as a proportion of national income, increased from 12 per cent in 1820 to 15 per cent in 1850 (retained imports meantime increasing from 12 to 18 per cent), while the balance of merchandise trade became increasingly *unfavourable*. . . . There was, however, the period of the war, when much production went either into unproductive war effort at home, or into loans and subsidies for allies abroad. As G. W. Daniels has pointed out, 'the increased power of production, instead of improving the material welfare of the community, had to be devoted to the prosecution of the war.'[5] The failure of living standards to rise much before 1815 was due, therefore, not to industrialization, but to war. The extension of the market was made possible more by reduced prices than by increased money wages. While money wages after the war remained relatively constant, the prices of manufactured and agricultural goods declined. The goods

of the industrial and agricultural revolutions tended to be cheap and plentiful, for the new entrepreneurs were fully aware that great expansion of production was possible only by supplying goods suitable for mass markets. . . . If only manufactured goods had fallen in price, however, the gain in real wages to a working class that spent a high proportion of its income on food and fuel would not have been large. But food prices also declined after 1815, along with the prices of most other consumer goods. R. S. Tucker's index of consumer goods prices—for food, fuel and light, and clothing, the most important items in working class budgets—shows a downward trend from 1813–15 to 1845, as also does Miss E. B. Schumpeter's index for 22 articles of food and drink, and nine articles of fuel, light and clothing. Money wages, in contrast, rose slightly less than prices during the war, and remained stable, or fell less than prices after the war, as the wages indices that have been compiled for this period show. The facts that aggregate money national income increased substantially, money wages remained stable, and prices of key foodstuffs remained stable or fell, suggest clearly that food supplies at least kept pace with population. When other commodities are taken into consideration, the implication is clear: an increase in real wages, at least after 1815, which it would be irresponsible to deny, and which, indeed, has been confirmed by the industrial histories of the period.

Although consumption statistics before 1850 are inadequate and unreliable, they do indicate modest though fluctuating increases in the consumption of most foodstuffs and other consumption goods. M. G. Mulhall, for example, has reckoned that between 1811 and 1850 the per capita consumption of meat, sugar, tea, beer and eggs increased, while that of wheat de-

---

[5] G. W. Daniels, *The Early English Cotton Industry* (Manchester University Press, 1920), pp. 147–8. The memory of war hardships persisted throughout the nineteenth century resulting, for example, in such statements as that of J. E. Thorold Rogers: "Thousands of homes were starved in order to find the means for the great war . . . the resources on which the struggle was based, and without which it would have speedily collapsed, were the stint and starvation of labour, the overtaxed and underfed toils of childhood, the underpaid and uncertain employment of men" (*Six Centuries of Work and Wages,* London, 1884, p. 505). . . .

creased somewhat between 1830 and 1850, increasing thereafter.[6] Import statistics are the most accurate of the measures of consumption in this period, and these show important long-term gains in a wide range of commodities; for example, in tea, "from about 1815 there is a secular rise, notably accelerated in the last decade of the period"; in tobacco also a "persistent upward trend"; and in sugar, "the trend movement is upward."[7] By 1840, to take one source of imports, steamships were pouring into England an almost daily stream of Irish livestock, poultry, meat and eggs. During "the hungry forties" there were increases in the average per capital consumption of a number of imported foodstuffs: butter, cocoa, cheese, coffee, rice, sugar, tea, tobacco, currants. For this reason Peel, in his election letter to the electors of Tamworth in July 1847, noting the large increase in the import of non-essential foodstuffs between 1841 and 1846, declared: "Can there be a doubt that if the consumption of articles of a second necessity has been thus advancing, the consumption of articles of first necessity, of meat and of bread for instance, has been making at least an equally rapid progress?" Certainly, when P. L. Simmonds considered national eating habits in the 1850's he concluded "how much better an Englishman is fed than anyone else in the world."

There are, unfortunately, no adequate statistics for bread and meat consumption. The main statistical uncertainties in the case of bread are the acreage and the yield of cereal crops, especially wheat. There is no convincing evidence for Dr. Hobsbawm's statement that, "The fundamental fact is that, as contemporaries already knew, wheat production and imports did not keep pace with the growth of population so that the amount of wheat available per capita fell steadily from the late eighteenth century until the 1850s, the amount of potatoes available rising at about the same rate." On the contrary, as T. Tooke, G. R. Porter, J. R. McCulloch and even J. S. Mill pointed out, agricultural output increased faster than population. When F. M. Eden wrote in 1797, barley, oat and rye breads were common especially in the north; when McCulloch discussed bread in his commercial dictionary in 1859 he commented on the disappearance of barley and oat breads, the inconsiderable use of rye bread, and the universal consumption in towns and villages, and almost everywhere in the country, o wheat bread. Such a substitution in a rapidly growing population—and one usually associated with increasing living standards—would not have been possible without a large increase in the home production of wheat, for it cannot be accounted for by the increase in imports. In the century of the agricultural revolution however, this is not surprising: between 1760 and 1864 the common fields and wastes of England were enclosed, increasing both the area of, and yield from arable. Even without other improvements enclosure generally increased yields substantially. The largest increase in cultivation was during the war, and exactly how much increase there was after 1815 is no known. . . . On Drescher's estimates, wheat production just failed to keep pace with population. On other and reasonably plausible assumptions—for example, that yield were under 20 bushels per acre in 1800 and nearly 30 bushels in 1850—domestic wheat production (without wheat imports was keeping pace with population. Wheat and bread prices certainly support the view

---

[6]M. G. Mulhall, *The Dictionary of Statistics* (London, 1892), pp. 286, 542, 354, 281, 158, 120. Mulhall also gives statistics for increasing per capita consumption of soap, leather, linen, cotton and coal.
[7]A. D. Gayer, W. W. Rostow, and A. J. Schwartz, *The Growth and Fluctuation of the British Economy* (Oxford, 1953), II, 957–65. [Expanded note.—Ed.]

that there was no long-term shortage of wheat and flour. Wheat prices fell sharply after 1815 and were relatively stable, though with a discernible downward trend, after 1822. . . . The price of bread was also relatively stable in these years. . . .

Far less is known about potato consumption than wheat consumption, although R. N. Salaman reckoned that per capita daily consumption in England and Wales increased from 0.4 to 0.6 lbs. between 1795 and 1838. The theory that this increase was not a net addition to total diet, associated after 1815 with the increasing use of allotments by the working class, but a necessary substitution of an inferior vegetable for wheat bread, is based on the doubtful assumptions that bread consumption was declining, and that the potato was an inferior food. Prejudice against the potato stemmed partly from dislike of the Irish, and certainly the half million Irish in England in 1850 help to explain the increasing popularity of the root. But increasing consumption was due also to the simple facts that people liked potatoes and that they were good food, as Adam Smith demonstrated. Moreover the potato was but one of many vegetables and fruits whose consumption was increasing. Vegetables, that in 1800 had only been grown casually, like water-cress, were by 1850 commercialized; fruits that were not imported at all, or in very small quantities in 1800, were regularly imported by the 1830's—for example, cherries and apples—and in large quantities by 1850. In London, Covent Garden was rebuilt in 1827, and by 1850 there were in addition five other important markets supplying the metropolis with fruit and vegetables. By 1850 every large town had its market gardens and orchards, and for London, the largest and richest market, the movement was well under way which by 1870 had almost filled the Thames Valley with fruit trees and vegetable crops.

"Next to the *Habeas Corpus* and the Freedom of the Press," Charles Dickens wrote, "there are few things that the English people have a greater respect for and livelier faith in than beef." In the first fifty years of the nineteenth century, the English working class came to expect meat as a part of the normal diet. Above all other foods, wheat bread and meat were to them the criteria of increasing living standards and superiority over foreigners. "Until the 'Roast beef of old England' shall cease to be one of the institutions of the country— one of the characteristics whereby foreigners believe, at any rate, that they may judge us as a nation—butchers' meat will continue to be (with the exception of bread) the chief article in our commissariat," G. Dodd declared in 1856. The fifty years before had been a period of widespread livestock improvement. For example, the story of the English sheep in this period was one of substituting mutton for wool as the main criterion of breeding, a substitution firmly based on economic incentives; the flock owners were turning away from the ancient breeds to larger, stronger and quickly-maturing breeds like the New Leicester and the Southdown. As with sheep, so with cattle and pigs.

The only detailed statistics of meat consumption, however, are for London, based on killings at Smithfield, where, between 1800 and 1850, the slaughter of cattle increased 91 per cent and sheep 92 per cent while London population meantime increased 173 per cent. But these figures ignore any increase in carcass weight, and, also, the supply from other markets. Smithfield killings cannot be accepted as a reliable index for London meat consumption—as E. J. Hobsbawm does—for there were other fast growing markets—Newgate, Leadenhall, Farringdon and Whitechapel—in addition to a number of smaller markets, all of which were largely dependent on country-killed meat and on imported "preserved" meats, like bacon and salt pork. Even in the mid-eighteenth century, when London was smaller and Smithfield relatively more important, perhaps only two-thirds of the fresh meat for London went through Smithfield, "because the London butchers bought at the country markets and at fairs in Cambridge, Northampton and Norfolk as well as bringing carcases in."[8] In the nineteenth century the limitations of Smithfield and the growth of London led inevitably to the development of other sources of supply, other markets that increased in size more rapidly than Smithfield. Newgate had 13 principal salesmen in 1810, and by 1850, 200, who were handling half as many sheep, three-quarters as many cattle, and more calves and pigs than Smithfield; in 1850, 800 tons of country-killed meat arrived there weekly, mainly by railway. In the same year Poole estimated that the yearly sales at Newgate and Leadenhall amounted to 76,500 tons. Certainly the railways much increased the supply of country-killed meat to London, but well before their time increasing quantities had been transported in waggons and carts. At the same time the import of bacon, ham and salt pork increased. Little wonder, therefore, that McCulloch concluded that "the ... extraordinary increase in the supply of butchers' meat" was evidence of "a very signal improvement ... in the condition of the population, in respect of food." Nor, of course, was the increased supply confined to London. As a farmer noted significantly in 1836, the fat stock of Gloucestershire and Cumberland were then going, not to London as before, but increasingly to Birmingham, Liverpool and the other industrial towns. Increased

supply was reflected in prices, with steady prices generally from 1819 to 1841, and fluctuating prices in the forties.

Another important food whose consumption was increasing at this time was fish. Before 1815, except during gluts, fish was expensive, and appeared regularly only on the tables of the well-to-do. Early in the nineteenth century, consumption was small, partly because of religious prejudice, partly because of the difficulty of transporting such a perishable commodity, partly because of a preference for meat. After 1815 increasing supply and decreasing prices ... led to a large increase in consumption; but even in 1833 the clerk of Billingsgate declared that "the lower class of people entertain the notion that fish is not substantial food enough for them, and they prefer meat." Nevertheless the poor by this time were becoming large purchasers of fish, taking particular advantage of price fluctuations (which were much greater than for meat) to increase consumption. When, for example, mackerel and herring were cheap, the poor ate "a great deal of them" and at any time the news of cheap fish spread throughout London "with wonderful celerity." Official statistics, unfortunately, are confined mainly to the Scottish herring export industry. We know, however, that "a large proportion of the Fish caught upon the English coast [was] supplied by hand carriage to the London and Inland Markets," and, also, that the supply of fish increased after the abolition of the salt tax in 1825, and, after 1830, with technical innovations in fishing that increased yields, particularly the development of deep-sea trawling and of drift fishing; with improvements in the handling of fish, for example, the use of fast cutters, walled steamers and the railways, and the increasing use of ice; and with the discovery of new fishing waters, for example, the Great Silver Pitt, south of the

---

[8] G. E. Fussell and C. Goodman, "Eighteenth-Century Traffic in Live-Stock," *Economic History*, February 1936, p. 231.

Dogger, in 1837. By 1840 ice and fast transport were enabling trawlers to fish farther north, and were opening up new markets in the inland towns. The kipper was invented in 1843. By 1850 steamship and railway combined to transport catches quickly to the centres of consumption all over England: steamships linked the Channel, North and German Seas to the English ports; railways linked the ports to the internal towns and London. In season, herrings alone were arriving in London from Yarmouth at the rate of 160 tons an evening, and even the humble periwinkle, Simmonds estimated, was consumed at the rate of 76,000 baskets (or 1,900 tons) annually.

The conclusion from consumption figures is unquestionably that the amount and variety of food consumed increased between 1800 and 1850. . . .

Even allowing for contemporary exaggeration and enthusiasm, the consumption of *basic* foods in 1850 London was not wildly inferior to that of modern England.

I V

What conclusion follows from the evidence so far presented? Surely, since the indices point in the same direction, even though the change cannot be measured with accuracy, that the standard of living of the mass of the people of England was improving in the first half of the nineteenth century, slowly during the war, more quickly after 1815, and rapidly after 1840. And, if expectation of life depends partly on living standards, the increase in average life over these years is further proof of increasing well-being. As Macaulay argued, "that the lives of men should become longer while their bodily condition during life is becoming worse, is utterly incredible." The expectation of life at birth in 1840–50 was higher than in 1770–80; by the 1840's infantile mortality rates had

been reduced from "the terrifying levels of the eighteenth century," and "the death rate for ages 0–4 . . . was very low, at least for a highly urbanised country at that time."[9] McKeown and Brown have shown that medical improvements could have had little effect on life expectation before 1850, and suggest that it was an improvement in the economic and social environment that lengthened life. People lived longer because they were better nourished and sheltered, and cleaner, and thus were less vulnerable to infectious and other diseases (like consumption) that were peculiarly susceptible to improved living standards. Factory conditions also improved. . . .

But increasing life expectation and increasing consumption are no measures of ultimate well-being, and to say that the standard of living for most workers was rising, is *not* to say that it was high, *nor* is it to affirm that it was rising fast, *nor* that there was no dire poverty, and cyclical fluctuations and technological unemployment of a most distressing character. It is as foolish to ignore the sufferings of this period as to deny the wealth and opportunities created by the new industry. Moreover little understanding comes from trying to attribute blame for the suffering that did exist. The discomfort of the period was due in large part to an inability to handle new problems or old problems enormously magnified; problems of increasing population, of urbanization, of factory conditions, of fluctuating trade and employment. And the tensions of the period arose naturally from the rapidly changing social and economic relationships. As the Hammonds point out: "When . . . society is passing

[9]H. J. Habakkuk, "The Economic History of Modern Britain," *Journal of Economic History,* December 1958, p. 496; J. T. Krause, "Changes in English Fertility and Mortality," *Economic History Review,* August 1958, pp. 66–7.

through changes that destroy the life of customs, the statesman who seeks ... to command man's will and not merely his deeds and services has a specially difficult task, for these changes bring into men's minds the dreaded questions that have been sleeping beneath the surface of habit." On the easier practical problems, to take an example, municipal authorities did not have the knowledge, and usually not the adequate authority, to deal with the various problems of sanitation in rapidly growing cities. Such problems required study, experiment and experience, as well as a change of attitudes, before they could be solved, so that it was ignorance rather than avarice that was often the cause of misery. In any case, much of the ill that has been attributed solely to the industrial revolution existed also in the pre-industrial age. . . .

Thus much misunderstanding has arisen because of assumptions—mainly misconceptions—about England before the Industrial Revolution; assumptions, for example, that rural life was naturally better than town life, that working for oneself was better and more secure than working for an employer, that child and female labour was something new, that the domestic system (even though it often involved a house crammed with industrial equipment) was preferable to the factory system, that slums and food adulteration were peculiar products of industrialization, and so on; in other words, the perennial myth of the golden age, the belief that since conditions were bad, and since one did not approve of them, they could not have been worse, and, indeed, must once have been better! But, as Alfred Marshall pointed out:

"Popular history underrates the hardships of the people before the age of factories."

. . . One might well ask, however, as did the Hammonds. "Why did this age with all its improvements create such violent discontent?" But discontent is not merely a simple product of living standards. The vision of an age of plenty, stimulated by the obvious productivity of new machines that seemed to compete with labour, roused both anger and ambition. The breaking-up of the old social relationships was a liberating and stimulating experience that made possible, for the first time, an effective working class movement. And although the standard of living was rising, it was not rising quickly, and the individual was aware only that his wages were meagre and not sufficient to satisfy his wants and needs. As A. L. Bowley has pointed out: "The idea of progress is largely psychological and certainly relative; people are apt to measure their progress not from a forgotten position in the past, but towards an ideal, which, like an horizon, continually recedes. The present generation is not interested in the earlier needs and successes of its progenitors, but in its own distresses and frustration considered in the light of the presumed possibility of universal comfort or riches." Discontent, even disorder, were indeed understandable, and both, like suffering, it must be remembered, were also characteristic of the previous age. . . . And the important thing about suffering during the Industrial Revolution was that it brought with it its own solution: increasing productivity in industry and agriculture, and, in society, faith that social conditions should and could be improved, and that economic progress was inevitable.

If the selections by Hobsbawm and Hartwell were hard to understand and made it difficult to reach conclusions on the entire debate between pessimists and optimists, the next selection by A. J. TAYLOR should be a help. Professor of modern history at Leeds University, Taylor reviews the history of the standard-of-living controversy and evaluates the evidence of pessimists and optimists on all current aspects of the quantitative debate: the movement of real wages, the pattern of working-class consumption of food (be it bread, potatoes, meat, vegetables, and dairy products), clothing, and household articles, as well as the course of population growth and mortality. He then gives conclusions of his own and presents reasons for the condition of the working-class population during the Industrial Revolution. Although Taylor's article was written before Hartwell's, Taylor anticipates the latter's argument. His survey of the scene still remains a standard synthesis of the controversy.*

A. J. Taylor

An Attempt at Quantitative Synthesis

I

Did the condition of the working classes improve or deteriorate during the period of rapid industrial change between 1780 and 1850? The controversy is as old as the Industrial Revolution itself. For men like Andrew Ure and Thomas Carlyle, as for Porter and Engels, the issue was one of contemporary politics. While Ure, a nineteenth-century Dr. Pangloss, so admired the new industrial order that he could compare factory children to "lively elves" at play,[1] Carlyle saw the world of the mill-hand as "but a dingy prison-house, of rebellious unthrift, rebellion, rancour, indignation against themselves and against all men."[2] Even among the classical economists there was a sharp division of opinion. On the one hand were those like Porter, whose optimism had its roots in the doctrines of *The Wealth of Nations;* on the other those whose pessimism reflected the less sanguine approach of Malthus and Ricardo.

---

[1] A. Ure, *Philosophy of Manufactures* (1835), p. 301.
[2] T. Carlyle, *Chartism* (1839), p. 35.

---

*A. J. Taylor, "Progress and Poverty in Britain, 1780–1850: A Reappraisal," *History*, New Series, XLV (1960), 16–30. Reprinted by permission of *History*, the Journal of the Historical Association. Some footnotes omitted.

With the marked improvement in national prosperity which Britain experienced in the third quarter of the nineteenth century, the debate lost something of its early vigour and urgency. The statistical investigations of Leone Levi and Sir Robert Giffen[3] tended to confirm what the observation of contemporaries already suggested: that, in common with the nation at large, the working classes were enjoying a perceptibly higher standard of living in 1875 than twenty-five years earlier. The will to resist the tide of industrial growth was declining as its benefits became more apparent, and with the logic of time the controversy was passing from the hands of the publicists and reformers into those of the economic historians.

The transition was, however, by no means an immediate one. Thorold Rogers, an early historian of the Industrial Revolution, in 1884 welcomed the return of the political economist "to his proper and ancient function, that of interpreting the causes which hinder the just and adequate distribution of wealth."[4] To Rogers the years of rapid industrial change were a "dismal period" for the working classes, and the quarter century after 1790 "the worst time in the whole history of English labour."[5] Arnold Toynbee's verdict echoed that of Rogers. "We now approach," he said, "a darker period—a period as disastrous and as terrible as any through which a nation ever passed; disastrous and terrible because side by side with a great increase of wealth was seen an enormous increase of pauperism."[6] In both these interpretations the voice of the social reformer mingles with that of the historian: and the

view thus firmly expressed commanded general acceptance for more than a generation. It is to be found as much in the writings of Ashley and Cunningham as in those of the Webbs and the Hammonds.

It was not until after the first world war that a new and less dismal note was struck. Then within the short space of little more than a year the pessimists' interpretation was four times put to serious question. In her *London Life of the Eighteenth Century*, Mrs. Dorothy George argued, largely on the basis of mortality statistics, that the standard of life of the London labourer had improved considerably in the course of the eighteenth century. This thesis was reinforced and extended a year later in the work of Miss M. C. Buer[7] and G. Talbot Griffith.[8] Each found evidence of a declining death-rate in the country as a whole between 1750 and 1850, and from this drew the general conclusion that living standards were rising. At the same time an even more powerful "optimist" entered the lists. From the evidence of nineteenth-century wage statistics and commodity prices, Sir John Clapham concluded that the purchasing power of the English labourer in town and country had risen substantially between 1785 and 1850.[9]

This new turn in the controversy not only redressed the balance of forces, but by reintroducing the statistical weapon, revived methods of argument largely disused since the days of Rogers and Giffen. Where the Hammonds, like Engels before them, turned to the evidence of the blue books and the pamphleteers, Mrs. George and Griffith appealed to the bills of mortality, and Clapham to the wage books

---

[3]L. Levi, *Wages and Earnings of the Working Classes* (1885); R. Giffen, *Essays in Finance, Second Series* (1886), pp. 365–474.
[4]Thorold Rogers, preface to abridged version of *Work and Wages* (1885).
[5]*Ibid.*, pp. 140, 128.
[6]A. Toynbee, *The Industrial Revolution* (1884), p. 84.

[7]M. C. Buer, *Health, Wealth and Population in the Early Days of the Industrial Revolution* (1926).
[8]G. T. Griffith, *Population Problems of the Age of Malthus* (1926).
[9]J. H. Clapham, *Economic History of Modern Britain*, (1926), pp. 128, 466, 560–2.

Faced with so great a display of statistical force, J. L. Hammond conceded—though not uncritically—this part of the field.[10] He was content to rest his case on the written and verbal testimony of contemporaries to the physical and spiritual suffering which, he contended, had been the inevitable concomitant of the new order. Men might have more food for their bellies and cheaper clothing for their backs but the price exacted for these benefits was out of all proportion to the gains. "The spirit of wonder ... could not live at peace in treadmill cities where the daylight never broke upon the beauty and the wisdom of the world."[11]

As a *via media* between two hitherto irreconcilable viewpoints, Hammond's compromise was readily accepted by writers of general histories, and it has retained an unshaken place in their affections; but it could be no final settlement of the debate. Thirty years now separate us from the work of Clapham and Hammond. In those years discussion has continued sporadically but vigorously. Most recently T. S. Ashton and E. J. Hobsbawm, in particular, have opened up new fields of evidence and lines of enquiry. It is appropriate to ask how far their findings have changed the broad pattern of argument and interpretation.

I I

Of the twin sides of the debate that which relates to the qualitative aspects of the labourer's life has, not surprisingly, made least progress. The bleakness and degradation of much urban life in the early nineteenth century needs no underlining. The mean streets and insanitary houses still surviving in many industrial towns, and the mute desolation of large areas of South Wales and the West Midlands are as eloquent testimony to the drabness of nineteenth-century life as are the pages of the parliamentary reports. This was an England "built in a hurry" and with little thought for the health and wellbeing of its rapidly growing multitudes. But, as J. D. Chambers has observed:[12] "Whatever the merits of the preindustrial world may have been, they were enjoyed by a deplorably small proportion of those born into it." If the industrial towns carried the seeds of physical and spiritual death for some, they also brought new life and opportunity to others. Not only did the towns ultimately give enhanced possibilities of physical health and enjoyment to the many; they also provided those widening cultural opportunities which, side by side with more debasing attractions, have come to distinguish the urban societies of the modern world. The older generation perhaps suffered most in the upheavals and disorders of early industrial development: for the younger and more adaptable the transition may not all have been disenchantment. But at this point argument comes close to dogmatism, for the historian's assessment of gain and loss must inevitably be coloured by his personal value judgements and predilections.

This overriding difficulty is not entirely absent from the parallel controversy about material living standards; but here at least the historian can appeal to the statistics. Although this particular oracle is in no sense infallible—too often it is mute or, when vocal, ambiguous—it offers some firm foundations for argument. It is essential, therefore, at this point, that we examine, however briefly, the main types of statistical evidence available to the historian.

---

[10] J. L. Hammond, "The Industrial Revolution and discontent," *Econ. Hist. Rev.*, ii (1930), 215–28.

[11] J. L. and B. Hammond, *The Age of the Chartists* (1930), p. 365.

[12] J. D. Chambers, *The Vale of Trent 1670–1800* (Econ. Hist. Rev. Supplements, 3, n.d.), p. 63.

The most direct route to the assessment of changing living standards lies through the measurement of the movement of real wages. Real wages relate money earnings to retail prices, and their movement, therefore, reflects the changing purchasing power of the consumer. Clapham's calculation of the movement of real wages suggests that the purchasing power of the industrial worker rose by some 16 per cent between 1790 and 1840, and by 70 per cent over the slightly longer period from 1790 to 1850.[13] In the same periods the real earnings of farm-workers increased by 22 per cent and 60 per cent.[14] These assessments were based on the wage statistics assembled at the beginning of the present century by A. L. Bowley and G. H. Wood, and on a cost-of-living index computed by N. J. Silberling. Since Clapham's guarded findings were published, however, Silberling's index has been tested and found wanting, and its rejection has inevitably invalidated the conclusions which Clapham based upon it.

Where Silberling failed, others have ventured with little greater success.[15] But even were a satisfactory cost-of-living index established, and in the nature of things this would seem unlikely, it would still leave unsolved the equally complex problem of devising a satisfactory general index of working-class earnings. Here, as in the case of prices, the fundamental obstacle is the insufficiency and unreliability of the surviving evidence; but additional difficulties arise from the changing structure of the labour force—there were virtually no factory operatives in cotton in 1780, for example, and few surviving domestic workers in the

industry seventy years later—and the problem of assessing the incidence of rural and urban employment. Our knowledge of the extent and nature of mid-nineteenth century unemployment remains limited notwithstanding the light thrown upon the subject by recent investigations. For the eighteenth century even this modicum of evidence is lacking, and a basis for comparison between the two periods in consequence hardly exists.

It seems, therefore, that despite its attractiveness, the approach to the standard of living question through the measurement of real wages must be abandoned. The movement of real wages can be determined within acceptable limits of error only in the case of certain restricted occupational groups: for the working class as a whole the margin of error is such as to preclude any dependable calculation.

A more promising approach is provided by attempts to establish changes in the pattern of working-class consumption. The method has a long and respectable ancestry—it was employed, for example, by both Giffen and Levi—but its application to the period before 1840 has only recently been attempted. It is perhaps primarily on the basis of their investigations in this field that Professor Ashton reaches the conclusion that towards the end of the eighteenth century "in some important respects the standard of living was rising," and that Dr Hobsbawm arrives at the precisely opposite conclusion for the early nineteenth century. We may usefully investigate the basis of these generalizations.

Let us first consider food. In the middle of the nineteenth century, as half a century earlier, bread and potatoes were the staple items in the diet of every working-class family. It is impossible, on the evidence available to us, to calculate the changing levels of consumption of these commodities with any degree of accuracy; but it seems

---

[13]Based on Clapham, p. 561.
[14]Ibid., p. 128.
[15]E.g. E. W. Gilboy, "The Cost of Living and Real Wages in Eighteenth-Century England," *Rev. Econ. Statistics*, xviii (1936), 134–43; R. S. Tucker, "Real Wages of Artisans in London, 1729–1935," *Jour. Amer. Statistical Soc.* (1936), 73–84.

possible, as Dr. Hobsbawm suggests, that bread consumption was declining in the early decades of the nineteenth century. The implications of this development, however, are far from clear. In 1847 G. R. Porter noted that "a large and increasing number [of the population] are in a great measure fed upon potatoes," but at the same time he observed that "unless in years of scarcity, no part of the inhabitants of England except in the extreme North, and there only partially, have now re-course to barley or rye bread." It has been usual among dieticians and economic historians to interpret a shift from rye to wheaten bread as evidence of improvement, and a shift from bread to potatoes as evidence of deterioration in general living standards. Here the two processes are seen working themselves out side by side. How, if at all, is this seeming contradiction to be resolved?

The potato was still a relative newcomer to the diet of the average Englishman at the end of the eighteenth century. Its advance represented a minor dietetic revolution whose progress was determined not solely, and indeed perhaps not even primarily, by economic factors. Outside Ireland, the potato had made its greatest conquests in the English northwest. Cheapness and ease of growth commended its use to native as well as immigrant Lancastrians; but perhaps of equal importance was the variety which it gave to the working man's table. In Ireland the rising consumption of the potato was the mark of deteriorating living standards: in northern England the same phenomenon admits of a different explanation. Even if our statistical knowledge were increased, therefore, it is doubtful whether the case for an overall rise or decline in the standard of living could find any convincing basis in the changing consumption pattern of bread and potatoes. At best it suggests differences of experience between the agricultural and industrial communities.

Not so with meat. Here a decline in *per capita* consumption may well be taken as *prima facie* evidence of an overall deterioration in living standards. At this point the historian is more fortunate in his statistical sources. Both Professor Ashton and Dr. Hobsbawm have made important use of the Returns of the Collector of Beasts Tolls at Smithfield Market, the one to demonstrate a rise in meat consumption during the eighteenth century, the other to suggest its decline after 1800. The Smithfield returns present a continuous, though not necessarily always comprehensive, survey of the numbers of sheep and cattle brought to London for slaughter in the eighteenth and early nineteenth century, and in relation to population their trend is upward in the second half of the eighteenth, and downward in the first four decades of the nineteenth century. But, suggestive as they are of wider general tendencies, the Smith-field statistics must be approached with some caution. They do not take into account all classes of meat—the ubiquitous pig, for example, is omitted—nor do they allow for the weight, as distinct from the number, of beasts taken for consumption. The investigations of G. E. Fussell[16] thirty years ago disproved the once commonly held view that the weight of animals at market more than doubled during the course of the eighteenth century. His findings were that the Smithfield cow or sheep of 1800 was little heavier, though rather meatier, than its 1700 forbear: but it would be dangerous, without similar close investigations, to carry over this conclusion into the nineteenth century. Even more questionable is the extent to which London's experience may be said to reflect

---

[16]G. E. Fussell, "The Size of English Cattle in the Eighteenth Century," *Agricultural History*, iii (1929), 160–81.

that of the country as a whole. In its extremes of wealth and poverty London was no doubt a microcosm of the nation at large, but its economic progress ran a somewhat different course from that of either the industrial North or of the agricultural South. The evidence on meat, therefore, while it suggests a nineteenth-century decline and to that extent holds no comfort for the optimist, is of itself insufficient to establish any firm thesis of general deterioration.

When attention is turned from bread and meat to more quickly perishable foodstuffs like milk and green vegetables, historian and statistician part company. Contemporaries were virtually silent about the levels of consumption of these nutritively significant items of diet. It seems likely, however, that in the case of perishable commodities the years of rapid urbanization were years of declining consumption. Although cattle were grazing within a mile of Manchester Town Hall as late as 1850, and large-scale market gardening was developing on the fringe of the industrial areas, the carriage of fresh dairy produce and vegetables before the coming of the railway must have presented problems which could hardly fail to be reflected in shortages and high prices.

The conclusions to be drawn, therefore, from the evidence on food consumption are by no means clearly defined: but their general tenor is to suggest rising living standards towards the end of the eighteenth century and less certain progress or even decline thereafter. Food, however, though it remained the most important item of working-class expenditure and took up the greater part of every working-class budget, did not exhaust the worker's wants. We know less than we would wish about the movement of house rents, but perhaps sufficient to suggest that, in relation to the

labourer's wage, rent rose rather than declined between 1800 and 1850. Fuel, on the other hand, was increasing in availability and tending to fall in price with the greater exploitation of inland coalfields and improvements in transportation.

It was outside the field of necessities, in the narrow sense, that increasing consumption was most evident. Between 1785 and 1840 the production of cotton goods for the home market increased ten times more rapidly than did population. An equally well-attested, if somewhat more limited, increase is to be seen in the output of soap and candles; and it is possible to infer similar increases in the production of a wide range of household articles from pots and pans to furniture and furnishings. It would be unwise to interpret this general expansion in output as synonymous with an equivalent increase in working-class consumption. The upper and middle classes, no doubt, took a disproportionate share of the products as they did of the profits of industrialization: but it is clear that improving standards of comfort were slowly percolating down to the mass of the population. By the 1840s working-class houses in Sheffield were said [by Porter] to be "furnished in a very comfortable manner, the floors . . . carpeted, and the tables . . . usually of mahogany." Similar conditions were to be found in the mining districts of Northumberland and Durham. If these improvements were purchased in part at the expense of so-called necessities, and specifically of food, this was a matter of the consumer's choice. A society slowly growing more prosperous may well prefer to sacrifice near-necessities in the pursuit of new luxuries.

There remains for consideration one further possible approach to the measurement of changing living standards. As long ago as 1816 John Rickman, the census-taker, expressed the opinion that "human comfort is to be estimated by human health and that by the length of human life." Longevity is in general a useful yardstick of changing living standards, and for this reason among others the debate on living standards has tended to keep company with that on the causes and nature of population growth.

Between 1780 and 1850 the population of England and Wales rose from some $7\frac{1}{2}$ to 18 millions, a rate of growth wholly unprecedented in this country. Contemporaries were made increasingly aware of this development and sought its explanation in terms either of a rising birth-rate or of a declining death-rate. The followers of Malthus, perhaps even more than Malthus himself, put particular stress on a high birth-rate, and by implication discounted the significance of increased longevity. The contrary viewpoint, laying emphasis on a falling death-rate, was neither so firmly nor perhaps so coherently held, but indications of it are to be found in Rickman, among others. In the present century the issue has been no less vigorously debated. Griffith, in 1926, came down heavily on the side of a declining death-rate as the primary factor in population growth, but his thesis, though widely accepted, has never received the general endorsement of demographers. T. H. Marshall, for example, though giving full weight to the decline in the death-rate from 1780 onwards, insists that as much attention be given "to the forces which kept the birth-rate up as to those which pulled the death-rate down,"[17] and J. T. Krause goes even further in concluding that "the national [statistical] materials suggest strongly that a rising birth-rate was the major cause of

the growth of the English population in this period."[18]

When there is such disagreement about causes of first instance, it is not surprising that equal divergence of opinion is to be found about the underlying causes of population growth and their implication for the movement of living standards. Neither an increasing population nor a rising birth-rate is in itself evidence of improving living standards: indeed the experience of some Asiatic societies suggests that the reverse may often be the case. A declining death-rate, on the other hand, unless—an important proviso—it is merely the statistical reflection of a rising birth-rate, implies an increased expectation of life and may therefore be regarded as *prima facie* evidence of an improving standard of life.

It is generally agreed that the crude death-rate fell sharply—perhaps by a quarter—between 1780 and the end of the French Wars, and rose significantly, though slightly, over the next two decades; since when its course has been consistently downward. In so far as it is possible to regard the overall reduction of the death-rate as synonymous with increased longevity, this increase in expectation of life has been traced to a variety of causes: to a growth in medical knowledge and facilities, to the recession of specific virulent diseases, to improvements in personal hygiene and public health, to better and more plentiful supplies of food, and to a marked reduction in maternal and infant mortality. Griffith, for example, while touching on all these factors, perhaps lays most stress on improvements in medical knowledge and practice, and on environ-

---

[17]T. H. Marshall, "The Population Problem during the Industrial Revolution," *Economic History*, i (1929), 452. This article remains the classical statement of the population problem.

[18]J. T. Krause, "Changes in English Fertility and Mortality 1781–1850," *Econ. Hist. Rev.*, 2nd ser. xi (1958), 70. For another view, also broadly favourable to the birth-rate thesis, see H. J. Habakkuk, "English Population in the Eighteenth Century," *Econ. Hist. Rev.*, 2nd ser. vi (1953), 117–33.

mental factors—the latter to explain not only the decline in the death-rate before 1815 but also the temporary reversal of the trend in the post-war period. Marshall emphasizes the rapid decline in infant mortality before 1810 and its perceptible, if less marked, rise thereafter. More recently two medical investigators, T. McKeown and R. G. Brown,[19] have, for the eighteenth century at least, questioned the importance of improvements in medicine and treatment, and by implication given added weight to the significance of advances in nutritional standards.

These statistics and explanations are broadly consistent with those changes in living standards—upwards in the late eighteenth century and arrested to the point of decline thereafter—which have already been suggested by the evidence of food consumption. Yet, notwithstanding this coincidence, the ambiguity of the death-rate still makes it highly suspect as an instrument for the measurement of changing living standards. This is the more the case when it is borne in mind that the growth in population of these years was not solely a British nor even a European phenomenon. The fundamental cause of population increase would accordingly appear to lie outside the narrow confines of the new British industrial economy. This does not mean that industrialization played no part in determining the pattern of Britain's population growth; but it suggests that industrialization was at least as much a consequence as a cause of the increase in population. Where cause and effect are seemingly so inseparably intertwined, head is apt to chase tail in disconcerting fashion. The demographer would be the first to admit that he has problems of his own to solve in this period before he can effectively come to the aid of the economic historian.

III

Where so much remains legitimately controversial, the historian can at best draw only tentative conclusions. The evidence, however, would appear to permit two immediate generalizations. There is reason to believe that after an early upsurge in living standards in the first stages of rapid industrialization, the pace of advance slackened, and decline may even have set in, by the beginning of the nineteenth century. It is also evident, notwithstanding Porter's assertion to the contrary, that the progress of the working class lagged increasingly behind that of the nation at large. Had working-class incomes kept pace with the growth of the national income, the average worker could have expected to find himself some 50 per cent better off in real terms in 1840 than thirty years earlier.[20] Even the most sanguine of optimists would hardly claim that such was in fact the case.

To explain how this situation arose is in a measure to validate the facts themselves. Thorold Rogers, writing in the 1880s, attributed the poverty of the working classes in the earlier part of the century to a variety of causes: to the unrestricted employment, before the first effective factory act in 1833, of juvenile labour; to restrictions on, and the weakness of, trade unions; and to the attitude of employers and of the law. But, significantly, he added that, although "the sufferings of the working classes . . . might have been aggravated by the practices of employers, and were certainly intensified by the harsh partiality of the law . . . they were due in the main to

[19]T. McKeown and R. G. Brown, "Medical Evidence relating to English Population Changes," *Population Studies,* ix (1955), 119–41.

[20]Based on the national income estimates assembled by P. Deane, "Contemporary Estimates of National Income in the First Half of the Nineteenth Century," *Econ. Hist. Rev.,* 2nd ser. viii (1956), 339–54.

deeper causes." Chief among these, Rogers cited the protracted wars against France, the economic derangements which accompanied them, and the behaviour of successive governments, which were slow to remedy social evils, yet intervened unwisely to maintain the price of bread and to impede the development of trade unionism.

Modern historians have tended to endorse Rogers' findings, though with varying degrees of emphasis. They have also added two other factors, made evident by more recent economic experience: the effect of the claims of long-term investment on current consumption,[21] and the movement of the terms of trade. A brief examination of the interaction of these varied factors is relevant to our discussion of living standards.

In the early stages of rapid industrial growth, a society is obliged to make heavy investments not only in buildings, machinery, stocks and equipment, but also in communications and public utilities. Such investment must inevitably be made at the expense of current consumption, unless, as in the case of the United States, foreign investors are willing to prime the pump of economic development. Thus Soviet Russia declared a virtual moratorium on increased living standards while laying the foundations of her industrial greatness in the 1920s. Britain after 1780 was erecting textile-mills and iron-works, constructing a great network of canals and laying the nucleus of a greater railway system, and building reservoirs, gas-works and hospitals to meet the present and future needs of a rapidly growing urban population. Like Russia a century later, though less consciously, she was sacrificing present comfort to the pursuit of future wealth and prosperity. By 1850 this early investment was yielding abundant fruit, and future expansion, in terms of railways, steamships, steel-mills, and electrical plant, was no longer to be incompatible with rising living standards.

The needs of capital accumulation, therefore, supply a partial explanation of the relative depression of working-class living standards in this period of rising national wealth. It would be unwise to press this argument too hard, however. In Japan, for example, whose industrial growth after 1918 closely paralleled that of Britain in the early nineteenth century, it proved possible to reconcile industrial growth with a perceptible advance in living standards. We must, therefore, look further afield if we are to explain not only the slow but still more the inconstant rise of living standards in nineteenth-century England. It is here, in particular, that significance is to be attached to the effects of the French Wars and to the frequently adverse movement of the terms of trade.

The wars against revolutionary and Napoleonic France imposed a severe strain upon the resources of the nation, and offset, in part at least, the gains of industrial and commercial expansion. Large-scale borrowing by the state during the war, and the imposition of severely regressive taxation at its end, not only induced serious wartime inflation but tended further to redistribute the national income in favour of the men of property. War thereby, both directly and indirectly, acted on balance to the economic detriment of the nation at large and to that of the working class in particular.

The movement of the terms of trade also proved disadvantageous to the working-class consumer. During the first half of the nineteenth century the terms on which Britain dealt in foreign markets steadily worsened, more particularly between 1800

[21]For a recent restatement of this thesis, see S. Pollard, "Investment, Consumption and the Industrial Revolution," *Econ. Hist. Rev.*, 2nd ser. xi (1958), 215–26.

and 1815, and between 1830 and 1840. In order to pay for a given volume of imported goods, Britain had to export almost twice as much in 1840 as she had done in 1800. Specifically, the price of cotton exports fell much more rapidly after 1815 than did that of imported foodstuffs. In part—though only in part—cotton manufacturers and their employees were able to find compensation in a reduction of the price of their imported raw material: for the rest they had no alternative but to accept lower profit margins and reduced piece-rates. A significant share of the benefits of Britain's new industrial efficiency, therefore, went neither to her workers nor to her industrialists, but to the foreign consumer.

Behind these pervasive but temporary factors lay the insistent force of population pressure. In so far as population increase may be ascribed a determinant role in the economic growth of this period, it is easy to understand how the upward thrust of population, though it facilitated and encouraged industrial advance, also retarded the improvement in living standards which industrialization brought in its train. Since the value of labour, as of any other commodity, gains with scarcity, an overabundant supply of labour is plainly inimical to the advance of working-class living standards.

How plentiful then was the supply of labour in early nineteenth-century England? The question admits of no categorical answer. The rapid increase in population, the influx of Irish immigrants, particularly into industrial Lancashire and western Scotland, the readiness with which women and young children could be employed in mills and workshops, are all pointers to an abundant labour supply. But the supply of workers must be measured against the demands of employers. That the number of those seeking employment in a year of intense depression like 1842 was far in excess of demand is tragically evident; but we need to deepen our knowledge of employment conditions in boom years like 1835 before we can pass final judgement on the general state of the labour market. The relative immobility of labour, in terms both of geographical and of occupational movement, tended to create not one but a number of virtually independent "markets" for labour, in some of which workmen were in short, and in others in abundant supply. If a generalization is to be ventured it must be that, except at the level of the skilled worker or in years of exceptional demand, employers had little difficulty in finding hands; and to this extent the worker, lacking effective trade union organization, was generally placed in a weak position in his dealings with his employer.

To dwell thus upon these three major forces is not to deny the significance of more traditional explanations of working-class discontent; but it may serve to place these in a new perspective. That the scales were heavily weighted against the working classes is indisputable. There is no shortage of evidence, in the blue books and elsewhere, of capitalist excesses, some of them committed in the name of so-called sound economics, some of them less worthily motivated. In face of these, the worker could find little help from a state which made him the weaker partner in every contract and frustrated his efforts at collective self-help. But these evils, although they were the most apparent and the most easily remediable, were neither the only, nor probably the most important, causes of the failure of the working classes to derive early benefits from the rapid growth of industrial enterprise and productivity.

IV

We may now sketch in rather fuller detail the general movement of working-class living standards between 1780 and 1850. The limited evidence suggests that down to about 1795 working-class families were gaining at least a share in the benefits of quickening economic activity. Prices for manufactured goods in foreign markets were buoyant and industry was reaping the full reward of its increased productivity. Workers in the newly stimulated industries enjoyed rapidly rising living standards; this was above all the golden age of the Lancashire handloom weaver. From the mid-1790s a new and less happy trend is apparent. War, inflation, and worsening terms of trade spelt distress for all but limited sections of the working class. "Wages limped slowly behind the cost of living, the standard of living of the workers was lowered."[22] Recovery after 1815 was slow and interrupted. There were good years like 1825, when employment was high and earnings moved upwards, and even better ones like 1836, when a strong demand for labour went hand in hand with falling food prices. At such times working-class living standards, particularly in the industrial North, reached heights much above those of the best years of the eighteenth century. But there were also years, like 1817 and 1842, when work was scarce and food dear, and the position of the labourer, not least in the towns, was little if at all better than that of his predecessor in the leanest years of the earlier age. It is evident that by 1840 the material progress of half a century had not yet sufficed to insulate the working class against the worst effects of economic depression. The ebb and flow of working-class fortunes, as of those of the economy in general, had in some respects tended to become more marked with the growth of industrialism and of the nation's export trade. To this extent the labourer suffered more sharply under the pressure of industrial distress, though he gained equally substantially when business activity moved upward. In the exact calculation of gain and loss which a comparison with an earlier age involves, it is necessary to take account not only of both prosperous and depressed years but also perhaps of the new insecurity which the changing character of the business cycle brought with it. But the calculation, however nicely weighted, depends on the accuracy of the information at the historian's disposal, and the vagaries of the evidence must leave the ultimate question still an open one.

To say this may appear tantamount to suggesting that a generation of historians has laboured to bring forth a mouse. But the appearance is deceptive. Although the central issue may remain unresolved—and is perhaps likely to remain so—the area of controversy has been substantially and significantly reduced. Optimist and pessimist now agree in seeing the years before 1795 and from the early 1840s as periods of advance—the latter to be sustained until almost the end of the nineteenth century; each views the quarter century of war as a time of deterioration; and each also draws distinctions between the experiences of different types of worker.[23] It is common ground that the skilled enjoyed relative prosperity; and among these are to be numbered not only the craftsmen called into existence by the new order, but also the older artisan, now pressed into fuller and wider service. In this group are to be found machine-makers, iron-moulders, builders, printers and not least hewers of

---

[22]Ashton, *The Industrial Revolution, 1760–1830* (1948), p. 150.

[23]Cf. Ashton, *An Economic History of England: The Eighteenth Century* (1955), pp. 234–5; also "Standard of Life of the Workers in England," pp. 33–8, Hobsbawm, "The Labour Aristocracy in Nineteenth-Century Britain" in *Democracy and the Labour Movement* (ed. J. Saville), pp. 201–39 (especially pp. 205–8).

coal and ore. There is similar agreement that decline in living standards was the lot of the domestic worker in those industries where the machine had taken early command, in cotton weaving and hosiery knitting, for example. But in 1840 the majority of English workers, including the vast and varied army of farm-labourers and the smaller company of textile operatives, fell outside these two groups, and their experience in terms of gain or loss can be neither so easily nor so indisputably defined.

All this would suggest that the area of disagreement has contracted. Certainly it has become more clearly defined: and this is also true in a further sense. It is perhaps no more than an accident that Professor Ashton speaks of the Standard of Life of the Workers in *England* and Dr. Hobsbawm of the *British* Standard of Life. Neither makes great play with the implicit distinction; but from the point of view of the general controversy its importance can scarcely be exaggerated, a fact which Porter recognized a century ago, when he restricted his claim of improving living standards, in the first instance, to England. In 1841 the inhabitants of England outnumbered those of Ireland by only two to one.

Today, taking the same areas, the disproportion is almost ten to one. Ireland, politically integrated in the United Kingdom since 1801, loomed large in the British scene. Although in 1841 the tragedy of the Great Famine still lay in the future, the living standards of Ireland's eight millions were already close to the margin of subsistence. The 'Forties may not have been hungry in England; they were certainly so in Ireland. It would be too much to suggest that the pessimistic case rests on the inclusion, and the optimistic on the exclusion, of Ireland in the calculation of the nation's welfare; but the distinction between English and British is here clearly of more than marginal significance. The argument for declining living standards is patently strongest when the experience of Ireland is added to that of Great Britain, and correspondingly weakest when attention is confined to England and, more specifically, to its new industrial North and Midlands. If nothing else emerges from recent debate, therefore, it is evident that future controversialists will need to define their arguments in precise terms of date, area and the section of the population with which they are concerned.

In a book from which this selection is taken, E. P. THOMPSON examines the discontent that gave rise to the English working-class movement. Such an examination leads him to the standard-of-living question. While he takes the quantitative evidence into consideration, he ultimately concludes with Engels and the Hammonds that the qualitative or "literary" evidence tells us more about the rise of working-class discontent than the quantitative method does. In examining the standard of living in this way, Thompson offers a counter argument to Ashton's criticism of the Hammonds' use of the Blue Books, those reports of royal and parliamentary investigations of the conditions of the laboring poor. Thompson teaches in the Extra-Mural Department of Leeds University and wrote a biography of William Morris, the late-nineteenth-century English poet and socialist.*

E. P. Thompson

The Qualitative Method Continued

The controversy [over the standard of living] falls into two parts. There is, first, the very real difficulty of constructing wage-series, price-series, and statistical indices from the abundant but patchy evidence. . . . But at this point a further series of difficulties begins, since the term "standard" leads us from data amenable to statistical measurement (wages or articles of consumption) to those satisfactions which are sometimes described by statisticians as "imponderables." From food we are led to homes, from homes to health, from health to family life, and thence to leisure, work-discipline, education and play, intensity of labour, and so on. From standard-of-life we pass to way-of-life. But the two are not the same. The first is a measurement of quantities: the second a description (and sometimes an evaluation) of qualities. Where statistical evidence is appropriate to the first, we must rely largely upon "literary evidence" as to the second. A major source of confusion arises from the drawing of conclusions as to one from evidence appropriate only to the other. It is at times as if statisticians have been arguing: "the indices reveal an increased *per capita* consumption of tea, sugar, meat and soap, *therefore* the working class was happier," while social historians have replied: "the literary sources show that people were unhappy,

*Condensed from *The Making of the English Working Class*, by E. P. Thompson. © Copyright 1963 by E. P. Thompson. Reprinted by permission of Pantheon Books, a Division of Random House, Inc., and Victor Gollancz, Ltd. Pp. 210–212, 318–349.

therefore their standard-of-living must have deteriorated."

This is to simplify. But simple points must be made. It is quite possible for statistical averages and human experiences to run in opposite directions. A *per capita* increase in quantitative factors may take place at the same time as a great qualitative disturbance in people's way of life, traditional relationships, and sanctions. People may consume more goods and become less happy or less free at the same time. Next to the agricultural workers the largest single group of working people during the whole period of the Industrial Revolution were the domestic servants. Very many of them were household servants, living-in with the employing family, sharing cramped quarters, working excessive hours, for a few shillings' reward. Nevertheless, we may confidently list them among the more favoured groups whose standards (or consumption of food and dress) improved on average slightly during the Industrial Revolution. But the hand-loom weaver and his wife, on the edge of starvation, still regarded their status as being superior to that of a "flunkey." Or again, we might cite those trades, such as coal-mining, in which real wages advanced between 1790 and 1840, but at the cost of longer hours and a greater intensity of labour, so that the breadwinner was "worn out" before the age of forty. In statistical terms, this reveals an upward curve. To the families concerned it might feel like immiseration.

Thus it is perfectly possible to maintain two propositions which, on a casual view, appear to be contradictory. Over the period 1790–1840 there was a slight improvement in average material standards. Over the same period there was intensified exploitation, greater insecurity, and increasing human misery. By 1840 most people were "better off" than their forerunners had been fifty years before, but they had suffered and continued to suffer this slight improvement as a catastrophic experience. . . .

[Homes]

There were farm labourers at the end of the 18th century who lived with their families in one-roomed hovels, damp and below ground-level: such conditions were rarer fifty years later. Despite all that can be said as to the unplanned jerry-building and profiteering that went on in the growing industrial towns, the houses themselves were better than those to which many immigrants from the countryside had been accustomed. But as the new industrial towns grew old, so problems of water supply, sanitation, over-crowding, and of the use of homes for industrial occupations, multiplied, until we arrive at the appalling conditions revealed by the housing and sanitary enquiries of the 1840s. It is true that conditions in rural villages or weaving hamlets may have been quite as bad as conditions in Preston or Leeds. But the size of the problem was certainly worse in the great towns, and the multiplication of bad conditions facilitated the spread of epidemics.

Moreover, conditions in the great towns were—and were *felt* to be—more actively offensive and inconvenient. Water from the village well, rising next to the graveyard, might be impure: but at least the villagers did not have to rise in the night and queue for a turn at the only stand-pipe serving several streets, nor did they have to pay for it. The industrial town-dweller often could not escape the stench of industrial refuse and of open sewers, and his children played among the garbage and privy middens. Some of the evidence, after all, remains with us in the industrial landscape of the north and of the Midlands today.

This deterioration of the urban environment strikes us today, as it struck many contemporaries, as one of the most disastrous of the consequences of the Industrial Revolution, whether viewed in aesthetic terms, in terms of community amenities, or in terms of sanitation and density of population. Moreover, it took place most markedly in some of the "high-wage" areas where "optimistic" evidence as to improving standards is most well based. Common sense would suggest that we must take both kinds of evidence together; but in fact various arguments in mitigation have been offered. Examples have been found of improving mill-owners who attended to the housing conditions of their employees. These may well lead us to think better of human nature; but they do no more than touch the fringe of the general problem, just as the admirable charity hospitals probably affected mortality rates by only a decimal point. . . .

It is also suggested that worsening conditions may be somehow discounted because they were no one's fault—and least of all the fault of the "capitalist." No villain can be found who answers to the name of "Jerry." Some of the worst building was undertaken by small jobbers or speculative small tradesmen or even self-employed building workers. A Sheffield investigator allocated blame between the landowner, the petty capitalist (who offered loans at a high rate of interest), and petty building speculators "who could command only a few hundred pounds," and some of whom "actually cannot write their names."[1] Prices were kept high by duties on Baltic timber, bricks, tiles, slates; and Professor Ashton is able to give an absolute discharge to all the accused: "it was emphatically not the machine, not the Industrial

Revolution, not even the speculative bricklayer or carpenter that was at fault."[2] All this may be true: it is notorious that working-class housing provides illustrations of the proverb as to every flea having "lesser fleas to bite 'em." In the 1820s, when many Lancashire weavers went on rent-strike, it was said that some owners of cottage property were thrown on the poor-rate. In the slums of the great towns publicans and small shopkeepers were among those often quoted as owners of the worst "folds" or human warrens of crumbling mortar. But none of this mitigates the actual conditions by one jot; nor can debate as to the proper allocation of responsibility exonerate a process by which some men were enabled to prey upon others' necessities.

A more valuable qualification is that which stresses the degree to which, in some of the older towns, improvements in paving, lighting, sewering and slum clearance may be dated to the 18th century. But, in the often-cited example of London, it is by no means clear whether improvements in the centre of the City extended to the East End and dockside districts, or how far they were maintained during the [Napoleonic] Wars. . . .

Sheffield, an old and comparatively prosperous town with a high proportion of skilled artisans, almost certainly—despite the jerry-builders—saw an improvement in housing conditions in the first half of the 19th century, with an average, in 1840, of five persons per house, most artisans renting a family cottage on their own, with one day room and two sleeping rooms. It was in the textile districts, and in the towns most exposed to Irish immigrations—Liverpool, Manchester, Leeds, Preston, Bolton, Bradford—that the most atrocious evidence of deterioration—dense

---

[1] G. C. Holland, *The Vital Statistics of Sheffield* (1838), pp. 56–8.

[2] *Capitalism and the Historians*, pp. 43–51.

overcrowding, cellar-dwellings, unspeakable filth—is to be found.[3]

Finally, it is suggested, with tedious repetition, that the slums, the stinking rivers, the spoliation of nature, and the architectural horrors may all be forgiven because all happened so fast, so haphazardly, under intense population pressure, without premeditation and without prior experience. "It was ignorance rather than avarice that was often the cause of misery."[4] As a matter of fact, it was demonstrably both; and it is by no means evident that the one is a more amiable characteristic than the other. The argument is valid only up to a point—to the point in most great towns, in the 1830s or 1840s, when doctors and sanitary reformers, Benthamites and Chartists, fought repeated battles for improvement against the inertia of property-owners and the demagoguery of "cheap government" rate-payers. By this time the working people were virtually segregated in their stinking enclaves, and the middle-classes demonstrated their real opinions of the industrial towns by getting as far out of them as equestrian transport made convenient. . . .

Certainly, the unprecedented rate of population growth, and of concentration in industrial areas, would have created major problems in any known society, and most of all in a society whose *rationale* was to be found in profit-seeking and hostility to planning. We should see these as the problems of industrialism, aggravated by the predatory drives of *laissez faire* capitalism. But, however the problems are defined, the definitions are no more than different

ways of describing, or interpreting, the same events. And no survey of the industrial heartlands, between 1800 and 1840, can overlook the evidence of visual devastation and deprivation of amenities. The century which rebuilt Bath was not, after all, devoid of aesthetic sensibility nor ignorant of civic responsibility. The first stages of the Industrial Revolution witnessed a decline in both; or, at the very least, a drastic lesson that these values were not to be extended to working people. However appalling the conditions of the poor may have been in large towns before 1750, nevertheless the town in earlier centuries usually embodied some civic values and architectural graces, some balance between occupations, marketing and manufacture, some sense of variety. The "Coketowns" were perhaps the first towns of above 10,000 inhabitants ever to be dedicated so single-mindedly to work and to "fact." . . .

[Life]

If we accept that the national death-rate—and more particularly infant mortality rate—showed a slight decline over the first four decades of the 19th century, we must still ask of the statistics exactly the same questions as we have asked of wages and articles of consumption. There is no reason to suppose that dying children or disease were distributed more equitably than clothes or meat. In fact, we know that they were not. The moneyed man might—as Oastler noted—rarely wear two coats at once, but his family had tenfold the chances of diagnosis, medicine, nursing, diet, space, quiet. Attempts were made to assess the average age at death according to different social groups in various centres in 1842 [as shown in the table]. At Leeds, where the figures were estimated at 44, 27, 19 the *aggregate* average of the three groups was 21. In Halifax, a large dispersed par-

[3]G. C. Holland, *op. cit.*, p. 46 *et passim*. An excellent account of the working man's urban environment in mid-century Leeds is in J. F. C. Harrison, *Learning and Living* (1961), pp. 7–20.
[4]R. M. Hartwell, "The Rising Standards of Living in England, 1800–1850," *Economic History Review*, XIII (1961), 413. [Extended footnote.—Ed.]

	Gentry	Tradesmen	Labourers
Rutlandshire	52	41	38
Truro	40	33	28
Derby	49	38	21
Manchester	38	20	17
Bethnal Green	45	26	16
Liverpool	35	22	15

ish which compared favourably in its death-rate with more concentrated centres, a local doctor calculated the average age at death of "gentry, manufacturers and their families" at 55: shopkeepers, 24: operatives, 22.[5]

Demographers would be right to consider this as "literary" rather than statistical evidence. But it indicates that a substantial decline in infant mortality and increase in life expectation among several millions in the middle classes and aristocracy of labour would mask, in national averages, a worsening position in the working class generally. And in this view, Dr. Holland of Sheffield [1843] has anticipated us:

We have no hesitation in asserting, that the sufferings of the working classes, and consequently the rate of mortality, are greater now than in former times. Indeed, in most manufacturing districts the rate of mortality in these classes is appalling to contemplate, when it can be studied in reference to them alone, *and not in connexion with the entire population.* The supposed gain on the side of longevity, arises chiefly from ... a relatively much more numerous middle class than formerly existed. ...

"We may be deceived," he continued, by the "gross returns":

... into the belief, that society is gradually improving in its physical and social condition,

when indeed the most numerous class may be stationary, or in the process of deterioration.[6]

Childhood

We have touched already on child labour: but it deserves further examination. In one sense it is curious that the question can be admitted as controversial: there was a drastic increase in the intensity of exploitation of child labour between 1780 and 1840, and every historian acquainted with the sources knows that this is so. This was true in the mines, both in inefficient small-scale pits where the roadways were sometimes so narrow that children could most easily pass through them; and in several larger coalfields, where—as the coal face drew further away from the shaft— children were in demand as "hurryers"[7] and to operate the ventilation ports. In the mills, the child and juvenile labour force grew yearly; and in several of the outworker or "dishonourable" trades the hours of labour became longer and the work more intense. What, then, is left in dispute?

But "optimists" have, since the time of the Hammonds, surrounded the question with so many qualifications that one might almost suspect a conspiracy to explain child labour away. There was "nothing new" about it; conditions were as bad in the "old" industries as in the new: much of the evidence is partisan and exaggerated:

---

[5] *Report on the Sanitary Condition of the Labouring Classes* (1842), p. 153; G. C. Holland, *op. cit.*, p. 128; for Halifax, Dr. Alexander, cited in W. Ranger, *Report on ... Halifax* (1851), pp. 100 ff.; for later figures, see James Hole, *The Homes of the Working Classes* (1866), pp. 18 ff.

[6] G. C. Holland, *op. cit.*, p. 124.
[7] Coal cart pushers.—Ed.

things were already improving before the outcry of the 1830s was made: the operatives themselves were the worst offenders in the treatment of children: the outcry came from "interested" parties—landowners hostile to the manufacturers, or adult trade unionists wanting limitation of hours for themselves—or from middle-class intellectuals who knew nothing about it: or (paradoxically) the whole question reveals, not the hardship and insensitivity, but the growing humanity of the employing classes. Few questions have been so lost to history by a liberal admixture of special pleading and ideology.

Child labour was not new. The child was an intrinsic part of the agricultural and industrial economy before 1780, and remained so until rescued by the school. Certain occupations—climbing boys or ship's boys—were probably worse than all but the worst conditions in the early mills: an orphan "apprenticed" by the parish to a Peter Grimes or to a drunken collier at a small "day-hole" might be subject to cruelty in an isolation even more terrifying.[8] But it is wrong to generalise from such extreme examples as to prevalent attitudes before the Industrial Revolution; and, anyway, one of the points of the story of Peter Grimes is his ostracism by the women of the fishing community, and the guilt which drives him towards his grave.

The most prevalent form of child labour was in the home or within the family economy. Children who were scarcely toddlers might be set to work, fetching and carrying. . . . In all homes girls were occupied about the baking, brewing, cleaning and chores. In agriculture, children—often ill-clothed—would work in all weathers in the fields or about the farm. But, when compared with the factory system, there are important qualifications. There was

[8]See M. D. George, *London Life in the Eighteenth Century*, Ch. V.

some variety of employment (and monotony is peculiarly cruel to the child). In normal circumstances, work would be intermittent: it would follow a cycle of ta s, and even regular jobs like winding bobbin s would not be required all day unless in special circumstances (such as one or two children serving two weavers). No infant had to tread cotton in a tub for eight hours a day and for a six-day week. In short, we may suppose a graduated introduction to work, with some relation to the child's capacities and age, interspersed with running messages, blackberrying, fuel-gathering or play. Above all, the work was within the family economy and under parental care. It is true that parental attitudes to children were exceptionally severe in the 18th century. But no case has been made out for a general sadism or lack of love.

This interpretation is validated by two other circumstances: the persistence, in the 18th century, of games, dances and sports which would have been scarcely possible if children had been confined for factory hours: and the resistance of the hand workers to sending their children into the early mills, which was one cause for the employment in them of pauper apprentices. But it was not the factory only—nor, perhaps, mainly—which led to the intensification of child labour between 1780 and 1830. It was, first, the fact of specialisation itself, the increasing differentiation of economic roles, and the break-up of the family economy. And, second, the breakdown of late 18th-century humanitarianism; and the counter-revolutionary climate of the Wars, which nourished the arid dogmatisms of the employing class.

We shall return to the second point. As to the first, nearly all the vices known to the 18th century were perpetrated in the early decades of the 19th, but in an intensified form. As Dickens knew, Peter Grimes was as likely to be found in early

Victorian London as in Georgian Alde-burgh. The reports of the Children's Employment Commissions of 1842 showed new-model Boards of Guardians, in Staffordshire, Lancashire and Yorkshire, still getting rid of pauper boys of six, seven and eight, by apprenticing them to colliers, with a guinea thrown in "for clothes." The boys were "wholly in the power of the butties" and received not a penny of pay; one boy in Halifax who was beaten by his master and had coals thrown at him ran away, slept in disused workings, and ate "for a long time the candles that I found in the pits that the colliers left overnight."[9] The mixture of terror and of fatalism of the children comes through in the laconic reports. An eight-year-old girl, employed for thirteen hours a "day," to open and close traps: "I have to trap without a light, and I'm scared. . . . Sometimes I sing when I've light, but not in the dark; I dare not sing then." Or seventeen-year-old Patience Kershaw, who discussed the merits of different employments:

.. the bald place upon my head is made by thrusting the corves; my legs have never swelled, but sisters' did when they went to mill;
  hurry the corves a mile and more under ground and back; they weigh 3 cwt. . . . the getters that I work for are naked except their caps .. sometimes they beat me, if I am not quick nough. . . . I would rather work in mill than in coalpit.[10]

This is no more than the worst 18th-century conditions multiplied. But specialisation and economic differentiation led to children outside the factories being given special tasks, at piece-rates which demanded monotonous application for ten,

twelve or more hours. . . . The crime of the factory system was to inherit the worst features of the domestic system in a context which had none of the domestic compensations: "it systematized child labour, pauper and free, and exploited it with persistent brutality . . . ."[11] In the home, the child's conditions will have varied according to the temper of parents or of master; and to some degree his work will have been scaled according to his ability. In the mill, the machinery dictated environment, discipline, speed and regularity of work and working hours, for the delicate and the strong alike.

We do not have to rehearse the long and miserable chronicle of the child in the mill, from the early pauper apprentice mills to the factory agitation of the 1830s and 1840s. But, since comforting notions are now abroad as to the "exaggerated" stories of contemporaries and of historians, we should discuss some of the qualifications. . . .

It would be tedious to go over all the points. It is true that some of the worst atrocities were inflicted upon pauper apprentices at the end of the 18th century, and that the parish apprenticeship system gave way increasingly to "free" labour in the 19th. It is true—and it is heartening to know—that some employers . . . provided fairly decent conditions for their apprentices. It is true that some reformers dug up the worst cases, and quoted them many years after the event. But it is by no means true that this provides evidence as to the extinction of the same abuses in the 1830s. (The reformers often encountered the greatest difficulty in securing sworn evidence of contemporary abuses, for the simple reason that the workers were in fear of losing their employment.) It is true that Peel's two Acts, of 1802 and 1819, indicate

---

[9]*Children's Employment Commission. Mines* (1842), p. 43.
[10]*Ibid.,* pp. 71, 80. Butties were the mine operators, not owners. To trap was to open and close the ventilation ports in the mine so the coal carts could get through. To hurry or thrust the corves was to push the coal carts filled by the getters or diggers. —extended footnote.—Ed.

[11]H. L. Beales, *The Industrial Revolution* (1928), p. 60.

both a stirring of humanity and an attempt on the part of some of the larger masters to enforce regulation upon their smaller or most unscrupulous rivals. It is true also that there was a general improvement in conditions in Manchester, Stockport and environs by 1830. But this improvement did not extend to remoter areas or country districts nor outside the cotton industry. And since the first three decades of the 19th century see a great expansion in country mills, as well as the introduction of the full factory system to worsted-spinning, and its expansion in silk and flax, the gains of Manchester are offset by the abuses of Bradford, Halifax, Macclesfield, and the Lancashire uplands.

It is true—and a point which is frequently cited—that the evidence brought before Sadler's Committee of 1832 was partisan; and that historians such as the Hammonds ... may be criticised for drawing upon it too uncritically. With Oastler's help, Short-Time Committees of the workers organised the collection of evidence—notably from the West Riding—for presentation to this Committee; its Chairman, Michael Sadler, was the leading parliamentary champion of the 10 Hour Bill; and its evidence was published before any evidence had been taken from the employers. But it does not follow that the evidence before Sadler's Committee can therefore be assumed to be untrue. In fact, anyone who reads the bulk of the evidence will find that it has an authenticity which compels belief, although care must be taken to discriminate between witnesses, and to note the differences between some of the worst conditions in small mills in smaller centres (for example, Keighley and Dewsbury) as compared with conditions in the larger mills in the great cotton towns. There is no basis for Professor Hutt's assertions that the Factory Commission appointed—on the master's insistence—in

the following year provided "effective answers to nearly all the charges made before [Sadler's] committee"; nor that the charges of systematic cruelty to children were "shown to have been entirely without foundation"; nor that "such deliberate cruelties as did exist were practised on children by the operatives themselves, against the will and against the knowledge of the masters". Much of the evidence before the Commission tends towards different conclusions. Moreover, where the evidence conflicts, one is at a loss to follow the logic by which we are asked to give unhesitating preference to that adduced by the masters (and their overlookers) as against that of their employees.[12]

Those who, like Professors Hutt and Smelser, exalt the evidence of the Factory Commission (1833) as opposed to that of Sadler's Committee, are guilty of the same error as that of which the Hammonds are accused. . . .

"I was requested by one of my neighbours," declared one of Sadler's witnesses,

to recommend the Committee to come to Leeds Bridge at half past five o'clock in the morning, while the poor factory children are passing, and they would then get more evidence in one hour there than they will in seven years examination. I have seen some children running down to the mill crying, with a bit of bread in their hand, and that is all they may have till twelve o'clock at noon: crying for fear of being too late.

Even if we leave the stories of sadistic overlookers aside, there was then commenced a day, for multitudes of children, which did not end until seven or eight o'clock; and in the last hours of which children were

---

[12]*Capitalism and the Historians*, pp. 165–6. Professor Hutt even repeats the *canaille* of the masters and of Dr. Ure, such as the baseless charge that John Doherty had been convicted of a "gross assault" on a woman.

crying or falling asleep on their feet, their hands bleeding from the friction of the yarn in "piecing," even their parents cuffing them to keep them awake, while the overlookers patrolled with the strap. In the country mills dependent upon water-power, night work or days of fourteen and sixteen hours were common when they were "thronged."[13] If Professor Hutt does not regard this as "systematic cruelty," humane mill-owners like Fielden and Wood were in no doubt.

Nor are there any mysteries as to the attitude of the adult workers, many of whom were the parents or relatives of the children. As Professor Smelser has shown,[14] there is a sense in which the family economy of the domestic system was perpetuated in the factory. The child's earnings were an essential component of the family wage. In many cases, although probably not in the majority, the adult spinner or worker might be kin to the child working for him. The demand for the limitation of adult, as well as child, hours was necessitated by the fact that they worked at a common process; if children's hours only were limited, nothing could prevent evasion, or the working of children in double relays (thus lengthening the adult working-day). Only the actual stoppage of the mill machinery could guarantee limitation. If the adults also stood to benefit by shorter hours, this does not mean that they were indifferent to humane considerations nor does it justify the offensive suggestion that the great pilgrimages and demonstrations on behalf of the factory child in the 1830s were hypocritical.

It is perfectly true that the parents not only needed their children's earnings, but expected them to work. But while a few of the operatives were brutal even to their own children, the evidence suggests that the factory community expected certain standards of humanity to be observed. A spinner in the Dewsbury area, noted for his evil-temper and for striking children with the billy-roller, "could not get any one to work for him in the whole town, and he went to another place. . . ." Stories of parents who visited vengeance upon operatives who maltreated their children are not uncommon. . . .

This assorts ill with loose statements sometimes made as to the general indifference of the parents. The evidence of both Reports suggests that it was the discipline of the machinery itself, lavishly supplemented by the driving of overlookers or (in small mills) of the masters, which was the source of cruelty. To say that practices common to whole industries were continued "against the will and against the knowledge of the masters" does not require refutation. Many parents certainly connived at the employment of their own children under the legal age enacted in 1819 and 1833. It is to the credit of men like Doherty and of the Short-Time Committees that they campaigned imperiously amongst the operatives against such evils, encouraging dignity among the degraded and explaining the value of education to the uneducated. The Factory Movement also involved many thousands who were not factory operatives: the weavers who wished to "muzzle the monster steam": parents displaced from the mills by juveniles, and supported by their children's earnings. Gaskell saw (in 1833) that the workers' discontent arose less from simple wage issues than from—

the separation of families, breaking up of households, the disruption of all those ties which link man's heart to the better portion of his na-

---

[13]Piecing was the joining together of threads broken in the spinning machines. Thronged was when the factory was especially busy.—Ed.

[14]N. J. Smelser, *Social Change in the Industrial Revolution* (1959), esp. Chs. IX and X. Extended footnote.—Ed.

ture,—viz. his instincts and social affections. . . .[15]

The Factory Movement, in its early stages, represented less a growth of middle-class humanitarianism than an affirmation of human rights by the workers themselves.

In fact, few arguments are so specious as that which proposes that because unlimited child labour was tolerated in the 18th century but, in its new and more intense forms, became less tolerable by the 1830s, this is another sign of the growing humanitarianism of "the age.". . .

Blue Books in the early 19th century served many purposes, but reform comes low on the list. Parliamentary investigations took place as a routine response to petitions; as a means of "handling and channelling" discontent, procrastinating, or fobbing off ill-behaved M.P.s; or purely from an excess of utilitarian officiousness. Ireland's decline through misery after misery to the seemingly inevitable climax of the Great Famine was accompanied by the absence of any important measure of alleviation—and by an average of five parliamentary enquiries per year.[16] The hand-loom weavers and framework-knitters were duly enquired into as they starved. Eight enquiries in ten years preceded the establishment of the police. (The fact that action resulted in the latter, but not in the former, cases is instructive.) Mr. Gradgrind was most certainly out and about after 1815, but as Dickens knew perfectly well he stood not for an "awakening of social conscience" or "sensitiveness to distress" but for efficiency, cheap centralised government, *laissez faire,* and sound "political economy."

The Blue Books (at least until we came to the great sanitary enquiries) were not the product of "an age" or the fruit of "a generation," but a battle-ground in which reformers and obstructionists fought; and in which humanitarian causes, as often as not, were buried. As for the upper classes, what we see in the 1830s is not a new "awakening of conscience" but the almost volcanic irruption, in different places and people, of a social conscience quiescent throughout the Napoleonic Wars. This conscience is certainly evident in the second half of the 18th century. The campaign to protect the climbing-boys, in which Hanway took a part, reached the statute book, against little opposition, in 1788. Every abuse returned during the Wars, and attempts to secure new legislative protection in their aftermath met direct opposition, and were thrown out in the Lords—for, if boys had been dispensed with, their Lordships might have had to make alterations to their chimneys.[17] All Howard's honourable work on behalf of prisoners left little lasting impression, as conditions reverted after his death. We have noted already how the infection of class hatred and fear corrupted the humanitarian conscience. It is true that Peel's Act of 1802 stands out against this darkness; but its operation was confined to pauper apprentices, and it was less a precedent for new legislation than an attempt to extend customary apprenticeship safeguards in a new context. What is more important—and was more disastrous for the factory child—was the atrophy of the conscience of the country gentry, the only men who had the authority or the traditional duty to protect the poor.

Nothing more confirms this atrophy, and the profound moral alienation of

[15]P. Gaskell, *The Manufacturing Population of England,* p. 7.
[16]See E. Strauss, *Irish Nationalism and British Democracy* (1951), p. 80; and Mr. Strauss's comment—"Ignorance of the facts was not one of the causes of Irish misery during the nineteenth century."

[17]See J. L. and B. Hammond, *The Town Labourer,* pp. 176–93.

classes, than the manner of the real "awakening" when it came. Scores of gentlemen and professional men, who gave some support to humanitarian causes in the 1830s and 1840s, appear to have been living in the 1820s in the midst of populous manufacturing districts, oblivious to abuses a few hundred yards from their gates. Richard Oastler himself lived on the edge of Huddersfield, but it was not until the Bradford manufacturer, John Wood, *told* him about child labour that he noticed it. When girls were brought half-naked out of pits, the local luminaries seem to have been genuinely astonished:

Mr. Holroyd, solicitor, and Mr. Brook, surgeon, practising in Stainland, were present, who confessed that, although living within a few miles, they could not have believed that such a system of unchristian cruelty could have existed.[18]

We forget how long abuses can continue "unknown" until they are articulated: how people can look at misery and not notice it, until misery itself rebels. In the eyes of the rich between 1790 and 1830 factory children were "busy," "industrious," "useful"; they were kept out of their parks and orchards, and they were cheap. . . .

But the conscience of "the rich" in this period is full of complexity. The argument that the impassioned "Tory" attacks, in the 1830s, upon the abuses of industrialism, voiced by such men as Sadler, Shaftesbury, Oastler, Disraeli, were little more than the revenge of the landowning interest upon the manufacturers and their Anti-Corn Law League makes some sense in "party political" terms. It is true that they revealed deep sources of resentment and insecurity among traditionalists before the innovations and the growing power of the moneyed middle class. But even a hasty

reading of [Disraeli's] *Sybil,* of the Hammond's Life of Shaftesbury or of Cecil Driver's impressive life of Oastler will reveal the shallowness of any judgement limited to these terms. We seem to be witnesses to a cultural mutation: or, as in the case of 18th-century constitutionalism, to a seemingly hollow and conventional rhetoric which took fire, in individual minds, as a deliberate and passionate belief. . . .

We can scarcely attribute this eruption of compassion to an "age" which also jailed Stephens and vilified Oastler. Many of those who really exerted themselves on behalf of the factory children in the earlier years met with abuse, ostracism by their class, and sometimes personal loss. . . . The awakening was not, in any case, characteristic of Toryism as a whole: if we wished to anatomise the Tory conscience of 1800 or 1830, we should commence with the squire's attitude to his own labourers. The humanitarianism of the 1830s can certainly be found to have had a cultural ancestry, both in Tory paternalism and in the more subdued traditions, of service and "good works," of liberal Dissent. But, as an effective force, it crops up only here and there, in individual men and women. . . .

The claim, then, as to a general "awakening of conscience" is misleading. What it does is to belittle the veritable fury of compassion which moved the few score northern professional men who took up the cause of the children; the violence of the opposition to them, which drove them on occasions into near-revolutionary courses; and—as humanitarian historians have tended to do—it underestimates the part played in the agitation over twenty and more strenuous years, by such men as John Doherty and the workers' own Short-Time Committees. More recently, one writer has surveyed the issue with that air of boredom

---

[18]*Children's Employment Commission. Mines* (1842), p. 80.

appropriate to the capacious conscience of the Nuclear Age. The modern reader, he says, "well disciplined by familiarity with concentration camps" is left "comparatively unmoved" by the spectacle of child labour.[19] We may be allowed to reaffirm a more traditional view: that the exploitation of little children, on this scale and with this intensity, was one of the most shameful events in our history.

[19] R. M. Hartwell, "Interpretations of the Industrial Revolution in England," *Journal of Econ. Hist.*, XIX, 2, June 1959.

Suggested Additional Readings

The historical literature on the Industrial Revolution is enormous and is growing rapidly. An idea of its annual rate of growth can be gained, among other places, from the *Economic History Review's* annual list of journal articles and books on economic history, including those on the Industrial Revolution. It also reviews annually the more significant periodical literature, and every issue has reviews of the most important books. With such a vast literature, then, the suggested readings that follow must be selective.

A student interested in the Industrial Revolution should certainly start with the classic accounts. Two have already been introduced: Arnold Toynbee, *The Industrial Revolution* and J. H. Clapham, *An Economic History of Modern Britain.* Another is that of Paul J. Mantoux, *The Industrial Revolution in the Eighteenth Century.* Originally published in French in 1906 and translated into English in 1928, the book was reprinted in 1961 with an introduction by T. S. Ashton. The classics include also Ashton's brief essay, *The Industrial Revolution, 1760–1830* (London, 1948). One might add to this list Phyllis Deane, *The First Industrial Revolution* (London, 1964), excerpted in this book. The works of Toynbee, Mantoux, Ashton, and Deane appear in paperback as well as hard-cover editions.

A number of general works are useful either because they cast the Industrial Revolution into a broader framework of British or European social and economic history or because they show what happened just before or right after the initial period of the Industrial Revolution. General accounts of the course of British economic history include: W. H. B. Court, *A Concise Economic History of Britain from 1750 to Recent Times* (Cambridge, Eng., 1954); Pauline Gregg, *Modern Britain: A Social and Economic History Since 1760,* (5th rev. ed.; New York, 1967); and Arthur Redford, *The Economic History of Modern England, 1760–1860* (London, 1931 and 1961). Asa Briggs, *The Age of Improvement, 1780–1867* (London, 1959) and E. L. Woodward, *The Age of Reform, 1815–1870* (2d ed.; London, 1962) show the Industrial Revolution in its political and social context. J. D. Chambers, *The Workshop of the World: British Economic History from 1820–1880* (London, 1961) and S. G. Checkland, *The Rise of Industrial Society in England, 1815–1885* (London, 1964) are good surveys of the later stages of industrialization. A good introduction to the economic changes in the rest of Europe is W. O. Henderson, *The Industrial Revolution on the Continent: Germany, France, Russia, 1800–1914* (London, 1961). More detailed is the excellent volume VI, parts 1 and 2, of the *Cambridge Economic History,* "The Industrial Revolutions and After," edited by H. J. Habakkuk and M. Postan (New York, 1965). E. J. Hobsbawm's admirable *The Age of Revolution* (London and New York, 1962), excerpted in this book, surveys the political, economic, and social history of the critical sixty years that saw the French, Industrial, and 1848 revolutions. It and the Gregg book appear in inexpensive paperback editions. Recently Hobsbawm and Christopher Hill have done a two-volume social and economic history of Britain. The volume by Hill, *Reformation to Industrial Revolution* (London, 1968) is on the period 1530–1780 and Hobsbawm, *Industry and Empire* (London, 1968) refines some of his views, for the period after 1750.

The student should eventually consult some of the more technical accounts which make good use of statistics and the quantitative method. A good transition to these would be T. S. Ashton, *An Economic History of England: The Eighteenth Century* (London, 1955), since its style is less technical. More technical are: W. G. Hoffmann, *British Industry, 1700–1850,* translated by W. O. Henderson and W. G. Chaloner (New York, 1955); Arthur Gayer, W. W. Rostow, and A. J. Schwartz, *The Growth and Fluctuations of the British Economy, 1790–1850,* vol. 2 (London,1952); W. W. Rostow, *The British Economy in the Nineteenth Century* (London, 1948); and Phyllis Deane and W. A. Cole, *British Economic Growth, 1688–1959* (London, 1962 and 1967). Deane and Cole include an excellent and up-to-date bibliography on the Industrial Revolution.

Since economic growth theories play an increasing role in writings on the Industrial Revolution, the student of history should familiarize himself with some of the more important contributions in this field. Because this is not always easy for historians to do, perhaps the best place to start would be with the economics textbook of L. G. Reynolds, *Economics* (Homewood, Ill., 1966), which concludes with a long section on economic growth. From there one might advance to an economic growth textbook, such as that of Benjamin Higgins, *Economic Development: Problems, Principles, and Policies* (New York, 1968). Both books contain useful, up-to-date bibliographies of the literature on economic growth. A useful collection of articles relating economic growth theories to economic history is Barry E. Supple (ed.), *The Experience of Economic Growth: Case Studies in Economic History* (New York, 1963). It reprints articles by economic growth theorists such as Simon Kuznets and Ragnar Nurske as well as others by economic historians on the general problem and its application to Great Britain, the United States, France, Italy, Japan, and Russia. Another useful collection is W. W. Rostow (ed.), *The Economics of Take-Off into Sustained Growth* (New York, 1963), which reprints the papers and discussions of the Konstanz conference on the Rostow thesis. The views of Joseph A. Schumpeter, who has had perhaps the greatest influence on economic historians, are analyzed in R. V. Clemence and F. S. Doody, *The Schumpeterian System* (Cambridge, Mass., 1950). The student might also read D. C. Coleman's article, "Industrial Growth and the Industrial Revolution," *Economics,* new series, XXIII (1956), 1–22. Of course, no list on economic growth theory can omit the nineteenth-century classic *Capital* by Karl Marx.

Arnold Toynbee wrote of an agrarian, or agricultural, revolution that preceded and made possible the Industrial Revolution. According to Toynbee, the revolutionary rise in agricultural productivity—thanks to the enclosures, consolidation of small holdings into large ones, the end of open-field farming, and the new technology of crop rotation and improved implements, fertilizer, and selective breeding—freed large numbers of workers for factory employment. At the beginning of the twentieth century these views were expanded by R. E. Prothero (Lord Ernle), *English Farming, Past and Present,* edited by G. E. Fussell and O. R. McGregor (London, 1961) and Naomi Riches, *The Agricultural Revolution in Norfolk* (Chapel Hill, N. C., 1937). Recently these views have been challenged in much the same way that John U. Nef and J. H. Clapham contested the views of Toynbee on the Industrial Revolution. The major criticism has come from G. E. Mingay, "The 'Agricultural Revolution' in English History: A Reconsideration," *Agricultural History,* XXXVII (1963), 123–133, and J. D. Chambers and G. E. Mingay, *The Agricultural Revolution* (New York, 1966). On the impact of the enclosure movement, see J. D. Chambers, "Enclosure and Labour Supply in the Industrial Revolution," *Economic History Review,* 2d series, V (1953), 319–343, and H. C. Hunt, "Landownership and Enclosure, 1750–1830," *Economic History Review,* XI (1959), 497–505.

Interest in the Industrial Revolution has turned attention to the particular industries that made it possible. Some of the more important studies are Ephraim Lipson, *History of the Woollen and Worsted Industries* (London, 1921); G. W. Daniels, *The Early English Cotton Industry* (Manchester, 1920); T. S. Ashton, *Iron and Steel in the Industrial Revolution* (Manchester, 1924); Alan Birch, *The Economic History of the British Iron and Steel Industry, 1784–1879* (London, 1968); D. L. Burn, *The Economic History of Steelmaking 1867–1939* (Cambridge, Eng., 1940 and 1961); T. S. Ashton and Joseph Sykes, *The Coal Industry of the Eighteenth Century* (Manchester, 1929); Henry Hamilton, *The English Brass and Copper*

Industries to 1800 (London, 1926); E. C. R. Hadfield, *British Canals* (London, 1950); Peter Mathias, *The Brewing Industry in England, 1700–1830* (Cambridge, Eng., 1959); John L. Clapham, *The Bank of England,* (Cambridge, Eng., 1944); L. S. Pressnell, *Country Banking in the Industrial Revolution* (London, 1956); D. C. Coleman, *The British Paper Industry, 1495–1860* (London, 1958); L. F. Haber, *The Chemical Industry During the Nineteenth Century* (London, 1958); and Jack Simmons, *The Railways of Britain: An Historical Introduction* (London, 1961).

Another approach to a deeper understanding of the Industrial Revolution is through local or regional histories. Such studies not only point out the great variety in economic development as Clapham had suggested, but quite often relate local economic change to social conditions. Thus far, however, more attention has been paid to regional or local economic history than to local variations in the standard of living. Some of the more important local or regional economic studies include: A. H. Dodd, *The Industrial Revolution in North Wales* (Cardiff, 1933); Conrad Gill and Asa Briggs, *History of Birmingham* (London, 1952); J. D. Chambers, *Nottinghamshire in the Eighteenth Century* (London, 1932); W. H. B. Court, *The Rise of the Midland Industries, 1600–1838* (London, 1938); A. H. John, *The Industrial Development of South Wales, 1750–1850* (Cardiff, 1950); W. J. Rowe, *Cornwall in the Age of the Industrial Revolution* (Liverpool, 1953); T. C. Barker and J. R. Harris, *A Merseytide Town in the Industrial Revolution: St. Helens* (Liverpool, 1954); J. D. Chambers, "The Vale of Trent, 1670–1800," *Economic History Review,* supplement no. 3 (1957); J. D. Marshall, *Furness and the Industrial Revolution* (Barrow in Furness, Eng., 1958); W. L. Burn, "Newcastle in the Early Nineteenth Century," *Archaelogia Aeliana,* 4th Series, XXXIV (1954); E. R. R. Green, *The Lagan Valley, 1800–1850; A Local History of the Industrial Revolution* (London, 1949); Henry Hamilton, *The Industrial Revolution in Scotland* (New York, 1966); W. H. Chaloner, *The Social and Economic Development of Crewe* (Manchester, 1950); John Prest, *The Industrial Revolution in Coventry* (London, 1960); J. H. Morris and L. J. Williams, *The South Wales Coal Industry,*

1841–1875 (Cardiff, 1958); James E. Vance, Jr., "Housing the Worker: Determinative and Contingent Ties in Nineteenth Century Birmingham," *Economic Geography* (1967); S. D. Chapman, "The Transition to the Factory System in the Midlands Cotton-Spinning Industry," *Economic History Review,* 2nd series, XVIII (1965), 526–543; Herbert Heaton, *The Yorkshire Woolen and Worsted Industries from the Earliest Times, to the Industrial Revolution,* 2nd edition (New York, 1965); W. B. Crump, *The Leeds Woolen Industry, 1780–1820* (Leeds, 1931); A. P. Wadsworth and Julia de L. Mann, *The Cotton Trade and Industrial Lancashire, 1600–1780* (Manchester, 1931); Arthur Redford, *Manchester Merchants and Foreign Trade, 1794–1858* (Manchester, 1934); and H. B. Rodgers, "The Lancashire Cotton Industry in 1840," *Transactions of the Institute of British Geographers* (1960).

Another Toynbean criterion of the Industrial Revolution, that of population growth, has come in for its share of study. The causes of this growth and its relationship to the standard of living are summarized in the selection by A. J. Taylor. Early studies on the subject include G. T. Griffith, *Population Problems of the Age of Malthus* (Cambridge, Eng., 1926); M. C. Buer, *Health, Wealth, and Population in the Early Days of the Industrial Revolution* (London, 1926); and T. H. Marshall, "The Population Problem during the Industrial Revolution," originally published in *Economic History,* supplement to *The Economic Journal* (1929) and reprinted in E. Carus Wilson (ed.), *Essays in Economic History* (London, 1954). Contributions to the recent debate over whether population growth was due to declining mortality or rising birth rate include Thomas McKeown and R. G. Brown, "Medical Evidence Related to English Population Changes in the Eighteenth Century," *Population Studies* (1955); John T. Krause, "Changes in English Fertility and Mortality, 1781–1850," *Economic History Review,* 2d series, XI (1958), 52–70, and "Some Neglected Factors in the English Industrial Revolution," *Journal of Economic History,* XIX (1959), 528–540; and H. J. Habakkuk, "English Population in the Eighteenth Century," *The Economic History Review,* 2d series, VI (1953), 117–133, and "The

Economic History of Modern Britain," *Journal of Economic History*, XVIII (1958), 486–501. For a local study on population, see J. D. Chambers, "Population Change in Nottingham, 1700–1800" in L. S. Pressnell (ed.), *Studies in the Industrial Revolution* (London, 1960). For urbanization, see, for example, Asa Briggs, *Victorian Cities* (London, 1953).

Many of the works touching on social conditions and the standard of living have already been mentioned in this list and in the selection by A. J. Taylor. Some of these and others, however, might be singled out. For example, there are the price and wage studies about which so much was made in several of the selections: A. L. Bowley, *Wages in the United Kingdom in the Nineteenth Century* (Cambridge, Eng., 1900); G. H. Wood, "The Course of Average Wages between 1790 and 1860," *The Economic Journal*, IX (1899), 588–592; N. J. Silberling, "Business Prices and Business Cycles," *Review of Economic Statistics*, V, supplement 2 (1923); Elizabeth Gilboy, *Wages in Eighteenth Century England* (Cambridge, Eng., 1934); E. B. Schumpeter, "The Cost of Living and Real Wages in Eighteenth Century England," *Review of Economic Statistics*, XVIII (1936), 134–143; and R. S. Tucker, "Real Wages of Artisans in London, 1729–1935," *Journal of the American Statistical Association*, XXXI (1930), 73–84. To evaluate whether conditions improved or deteriorated during the Industrial Revolution, one should consult some of the studies on preindustrial social conditions, such as Dorothy George, *England in Transition: Life and Work in the Eighteenth Century* (London, 1931 and 1964); Dorothy Marshall, *English People of the Eighteenth Century* (New York, 1956); and Peter Laslett, *The World We Have Lost* (London, 1964). Surveys of working-class life, in addition to those found on the general list, are G. D. H. Cole, *A Short History of the British Working Class Movement, 1789–1947* (London, 1948) and G. D. H. Cole and Raymond Postgate, *The British Common People, 1744–1946* (London, 1961). More detailed studies for the period of the Industrial Revolution would include the works of the Hammonds, cited in the Introduction, E. P. Thompson, *The Making of the English Working Class* (New York, 1963), and Charles R. Fay, *Life and Labour in the 19th Century* (Cambridge, Eng., 1947). Discussion of working-class organization or movements for amelioration can be found in such works as P. H. S. H. Gosden, *The Friendly Societies in England, 1815–1875* (New York, 1961); Asa Briggs (ed.), *Chartist Studies* (London, 1959); G. D. H. Cole, *Attempts at General Union: A Study in British Trade Union History, 1818–1834* (London, 1953); Norman McCord, *The Anti-Corn Law League* (New York, 1958); Ivy Pinchbeck, *Women Workers in the Industrial Revolution, 1650–1850* (London, 1930); George Rudé, *The Crowd in History: A Study of Popular Disturbances in France and England, 1730–1848* (New York, 1964); and G. D. H. Cole, *A Century of Co-operation* (London, 1944). Sidney Pollard's significant contributions to the standard-of-living question are: *A History of Labour in Sheffield* (Liverpool, 1959); "Investment, Consumption and the Industrial Revolution," *Economic History Review*, 2d series, XI (1958), 215–226; and "Factory Discipline in the Industrial Revolution," *Economic History Review*, XVI (1963), 254–271. Chapter 5 of W. W. Rostow, *British Economy of the Nineteenth Century* (London, 1948) relates the business cycle to the standard of living and worker discontent. Other chapters in F. A. Hayek (ed.), *Capitalism and the Historians* (Chicago, 1954) criticize the Engels-Hammond school along the lines of the Ashton articles, as does W. Woodruff, "Capitalism and the Historians: A Contribution to the Discussion of the Industrial Revolution," *Journal of Economic History*, XVI (1956), 1–17. Particularly in his chapters on labor aristocracy and the tramping artisan in *Labouring Men* (New York, 1964), E. J. Hobsbawm develops ideas set forth in his article on the standard of living. R. M. Hartwell, "Interpretations of the Industrial Revolution," *Journal of Economic History*, XIX (1959), 229–249 complements his article excerpted in this book. Two local studies of wider significance are: Neil J. Smelzer, *Social Change in the Industrial Revolution: An Application of Theory to the Lancashire Cotton Industry, 1770–1840* (Chicago, 1959) and R. S. Neale, "The Standard of Living, 1780–1844: A Regional and Class Study," *The Economic History Review*, 2d series, XIX (1966), 590–606. Neale's study of Bath, "the eighteenth century Atlantic City," shows a decline in real wages

(1790–1812), a rise (1812–1832) to the 1790 level, a decline in the 1830s, and a rise after 1829–1840 with real wages in 1850 being 50 to 60 percent higher than they had been in 1790. One of the most recent additions to the controversy—J. E. Williams, "The British Standard of Living, 1750–1850," *The Economic History Review*, 2d series, XIX (1966), 581–589—argues that aggregate per capita consumption did not improve noticeably between 1751 and 1791, that it dropped thereafter, and that it surpassed the highest eighteenth-century mark only in 1821, but did not show any substantial improvement until after 1841.

A number of writers in this book touched on the willingness or unwillingness of the government to ameliorate social conditions through legislation. For an account of the principal government action in this regard, see M. W. Thomas, *The Early Factory Legislation* (Leigh-on-Sea, Essex, Eng., 1948). Much of the recent literature on this subject is reviewed by Jenifer Hart, "Nineteenth Century Social Reform: A Tory Interpretation of History," *Past and Present*, no. 31 (July, 1965), 39–61. She is especially critical of Oliver MacDonagh, "The Nineteenth Century Revolution in Government: A Reappraisal," *Historical Journal*, I (1958), 52–67; David Roberts, "Jeremy Bentham and the Victorian Administrative State," *Victorian Studies*, II (1959), 193–210, and *Victorian Origins of the British Welfare State* (New Haven, Conn., 1960); George S. R. Kitson Clark, *The Making of Victorian England* (London, 1962); Henry Parris, "The Nineteenth Century Revolution in Government: A Reappraisal Reappraised," *Historical Journal*, III (1960), 17–37; and W. L. Burn, *The Age of Equipoise* (London, 1964). Valerie Cromwell, "Interpretations of Nineteenth Century Administration: An Analysis," *Victorian Studies*, IX (1966), 245–255, is a reply to Hart, Parris, and MacDonagh. On the Poor Law of 1834, see David Roberts, "How Cruel Was the Victorian Poor Law?" *Historical Journal*, VI

(1963), 97–107, and Mark Blaug, "The Myth of the Old Poor Law and the Making of the New," *Journal of Economic History*, XXIII (1963), 151–184. For other aspects, see George S. R. Kitson Clark, "Hunger and Politics in 1842," *Journal of Modern History*, XXV (1953), 355–374; David Roberts, "Tory Paternalism and Social Reform in Early Victorian England," *American Historical Review*, LXIII (1957–1958), 323–337; and Asa Briggs, "1851," in Historical Association, *From Metternich to Hitler* (London, 1963), pp. 47–72.

A number of biographies and business histories illuminate the Industrial Revolution. On its economic aspects see, for example, Samuel Smiles, *Selections from the Lives of the Engineers*, edited by T. P. Hughes (Cambridge, Mass., 1966); George Unwin, Arthur Hulme, and George Taylor, *Samuel Oldknow and the Arkwrights* (Manchester, 1924); T. H. Marshall, *James Watt, 1736–1819* (London, 1925); H. W. Dickinson, *James Watt, Craftsman and Engineer* (Cambridge, Eng., 1935) and *Matthew Boulton* (Cambridge, Eng., 1937); T. S. Ashton, *An Eighteenth Century Industrialist: Peter Stubbs of Warrington, 1756–1806* (Manchester, 1939); Arthur Raistrick, *A Dynasty of Iron Founders: the Darbys and Coalbrookdale* (London, 1953); L. S. Sutherland, *A London Merchant 1695–1774* (London, 1933); R. S. Fitton and A. P. Wadsworth, *The Strutts and the Arkwrights* (Manchester, 1958); W. G. Rimmer, *Marshall of Leeds, Flax Spinners, 1788–1886* (Cambridge, Eng., 1960); and R. H. Campbell, *The Carron Company* (Edinburgh, 1961). On social conditions, see G. D. H. Cole, *Life of William Cobbett,* (3d ed.; London, 1947); Margaret Cole, *Robert Owen of New Lanark* (New York, 1953); S. E. Finer, *The Life and Times of Edwin Chadwick* (London, 1952); C. H. Driver, *Tory Radical: the Life of Richard Oastler* (New York, 1946); John L. and Barbara Hammond, *Lord Shaftesbury* (4th ed.; London, 1936); and Herman Ausubel, *John Bright, Victorian Reformer* (New York, 1966).